THE FRENCH NEW LEFT:
AN INTELLECTUAL HISTORY
FROM SARTRE TO GORZ

THE FRENCH NEW LEFT: AN INTELLECTUAL HISTORY FROM SARTRE TO GORZ

by Arthur Hirsh

SOUTH END PRESS   **BOSTON**

320. 530944
H669f

ℒW 210557

To Max who will be 21
and Cass who will be 30
in the year 2000.

Table of Contents

Preface

This study is not a history of the new left itself, but rather of its theoretical dimension as it evolved in its most developed form—i.e., in France. For it is in France that the intellectual origins of new left social theory are most obvious in the work of Jean-Paul Sartre and others. And it is also in France that the clearest political expression of the new left occurred—the May 1968 upheaval. Thus, an intellectual history of the French new left covers a rich field of experience. It surveys the efforts by radical social theorists both to confront the historically experienced limitations of marxism as a liberating social theory and to continue and extend the critical role of marxism by analyzing the new contradictions engendered in advanced industrial societies, as well as proposing strategies for liberating social change.

The study begins, in Part I, with a critical appraisal of the intellectual origins of French new left social theory as it emerged from the radical critiques of traditional marxism carried out by Sartre, Henri Lefebvre, and Cornelius Castoriadis in the period 1945 to 1968. Sartre's existentialist critique revolved around what he considered to be the lack of a marxist theory of subjectivity. Lefebvre's revisionist critique questioned the validity of the traditional marxist view of advanced industrial society. Castoriadis' *gauchiste* critique denied marxism revolutionary status, claiming it had been transformed into a bureaucratic ideology.

The existentialist, the revisionist, and the *gauchiste* critiques developed in the late 1940s and 1950s, and converged in the 1960s as a French new left social theory. Its main themes focused on the project of discovering egalitarian solutions to the problems of alienation and bureaucracy in advanced industrial society. The explosion of May 1968— which is discussed in Part II—appeared to confirm the relevance of this project and opened a new era of social contestation. In this sense May 1968 was an important turning point. It represented the culmination of new left social theory and opened the way for the incorporation of its assumptions and themes into the political and social movements of the 1970s.

In Part III I survey the legacy of the French new left in the aftermath of May 1968. On the one hand, we witness the resurgence of structuralism in the domain of theory, and the rise of Eurocommunism and left electoralism in the political arena. But more significantly, the social movements of self-management, feminism, and ecology emerge to continue the new left project and expand its meaning. It is toward these movements, I argue, that radical social theory must turn if it is to move beyond its present fragmentation and confusion to achieve a coherent vision capable of inspiring progressive social change.

As an essay in intellectual history, this work does not claim to be exhaustive of all the material which could conceivably be classified under the heading of the French new left. Rather, I have attempted to select what I think are the basic themes and to develop them in the context of a broad survey of recent French social theory. It is hoped that the result of such an approach is a work that may be of use for the general reader as well as for specialists in social theory and intellectual history.

At this point I would like to thank a number of people who helped me with this project. George Allan introduced me to social philosophy and the issues involved in this book when I was an undergraduate. My dissertation advisor, W. Warren Wagar, and Paul Breines both gave me the intellectual and moral support I needed in recent years to see this task through. Mary Lea, my editor at South End Press, was very supportive and helpful in preparing the final manuscript for publication.

I also benefitted from discussions with many others including: Michael Albert, Jim Alvino, Jean Agnew, Kathy Campbell, Jon Harris, Lowrie Hemphill, Bob Krim, John Liffman, Priscilla Offenhauer, Jon Schneer, and Jerome Wieler. Debbie Harris typed a portion of the manuscript.

Boston University and the Boston College history department both gave support to this study. But most of all I am indebted to my wife, Elizabeth, whose love, friendship, and personal example are the sources of inspiration out of which this book was created.

/PART I/

INTELLECTUAL ORIGINS
OF THE
FRENCH NEW LEFT

Introduction

Marxism arose as a social theory in the 1840s in the context of rapid industrialization accompanied by revolutionary social upheaval. Intellectually it represented a synthesis of German dialectical philosophy, British political economy, and French theories of socialism with the age-old moral eschatology of the oppressed. It was the first coherent social philosophy to convincingly unite a social morality with a social epistemology; i.e., to link the demands for social justice of the proletariat to a scientific class analysis of capitalist society. This synthesis of science and morality, of knowledge and values, is the basis of the strength and resilience of marxism as a social theory.

Historically, however, the political movements inspired by marxism have failed to maintain this synthesis. Through a one-sided emphasis on the scientific nature of marxism, twentieth century marxist movements have failed to develop the egalitarian and democratic kernel of the theory. On the other hand, many critics of marxism in the revolutionary movement have one-sidedly emphasized the moral aspect of

4 THE FRENCH NEW LEFT

the social problem to the point of denying the efficacy of a scientific approach *per se* to social theory. The practical results of such an orientation, however, have been equally disastrous. When the explosive force of moral outrage lacks a clear theoretical analysis and organizational strategy, this force quickly dissipates in disillusionment and despair. Thus the fundamental dilemma of revolutionary social theory: either the moral values of social justice and an egalitarian social order are sacrificed in the process of creating a scientifically organized social structure needed to defend them; or else they are sacrificed by not creating such structures to defend them for fear that such structures will become oppressive. Resignation or opting out has not proven a viable alternative to this dilemma since the crises of advanced industrial society remain unsolved and inescapable. Since 1945 a critical re-evaluation of marxism has taken place for the purpose of developing revolutionary social theory toward a new synthesis in which the scientific and moral aspects are united.

In postwar France this critical re-evaluation of marxism as a revolutionary social theory relevant to the crises of advanced industrial society was carried out in a somewhat unique situation.[1] The existence of a mass communist movement deeply rooted in the working class was a strong argument for the viability of traditional orthodox marxist theory. Nevertheless, a significant section of the leftist intelligentsia, who indeed were sympathetic to this movement, preferred to maintain a reserved posture of critical support. Jean-Paul Sartre, with his fellow existentialists grouped around the journal *Les Temps Modernes*, was the center of this important trend. In fact, in the immediate postwar period existentialism was the only real alternative to the marxism advanced by the communists. Instead of viewing Sartre merely as a hesitant ally, the communists considered him (and existentialism) a competitor cutting into their potential support. The communist criticism of his existentialism was quite extensive and often very bitter. The dialogue proved beneficial, however, in that it forced Sartre to develop a more rigorous critique of marxism as he simultaneously assimilated much of it.

Sartre's existentialist critique of traditional marxism revolved around what he considered to be the lack of a marxist theory of subjectivity, which in turn distorted its theory of consciousness *per se*. Sartre's evolution of an "existential" marxism was *the* fundamental development in the postwar re-evaluation of marxism in France.[2]

Within the communist movement itself a crisis of marxist theory emerged after the 1956 events.[3] Khruschev's revelations of Stalin's crimes, the Soviet invasion of Hungary, and the obvious lack of a real de-stalinization were too much for a number of French communist intellectuals to accept. Consequently, they quit (or were expelled from) the Party* and attempted to revise marxism in order to account for the changes occurring in advanced industrial society. They founded a journal, *Arguments*, in which they developed their criticism of marxism and its relevance to an analysis of modern society. Henri Lefebvre, the leading revisionist theorist, argued that the marxist methodology was still applicable to an analysis of advanced industrial society, but that the categories of analysis had to be revised to account for changes in social structure and structures of consciousness.

A third tendency on the postwar French left critical of marxist theory were the *gauchistes*.[4] These were the political activists who viewed the communist movement as a conservative, bureaucratic machine working toward integrating the working class into the status quo. They traced the origins of this bureaucratic conservatism to marxist theory itself— which they viewed as the theory of the bourgeois revolution! The journal *Socialisme ou Barbarie* was the focal point of this critique, and Cornelius Castoriadis was its leading spokesman.

The existentialist, the revisionist, and the *gauchiste* critiques of marxism developed in the late 1940s and 1950s, and more or less converged in the 1960s as a French new left

*The French communist party, or PCF, Parti communiste français.

social theory. This social theory rejects capitalist, reform socialist, and communist social systems as well as the social theories that justify them. Social inequality, elitist authoritarian hierarchy, and repressive manipulation are seen as the common coordinates of bureaucratic domination which lie behind the ideological mystifications buttressing each of these systems. In place of such structures, new left social theory posits the possibility of an egalitarian society free of the alienation characteristic of contemporary bureaucratic society.

The French social upheaval of May 1968 revealed the inability of the traditional marxist communist party leadership to understand, let alone deal in a creative fashion with, this unprecedented type of social crisis. For the themes of this crisis were the very ones examined by the Party's new left critics: the revolt against alienation in a bureaucratic society and the demand for control over one's own life (*autogestion*). However, the May 1968 explosion and its aftermath also revealed the limitations of new left social theory. Not only was no social transformation forthcoming, but even worse, the new leftists failed to formulate viable conceptions of how such a transformation could take place.[5] Nevertheless, new left social theory contains elements of a highly dynamic analysis of advanced industrial society. In Part I we will examine the intellectual origins of French new left social theory as it emerged from the leftist critique of traditional marxism and attempt to pinpoint its limitations.

/1/
The Leftist Critique of
Marxism in Postwar France

1. Traditional Marxism in Postwar France

The term "traditional marxism" refers to the general body of marxist literature. It consists of those works in which Marx's ideas have been propagated and popularized, from textbooks to political pamphlets to newspaper articles.[6] Thus, while few marxists have read all three volumes of *Capital*, many have read Engels' summaries of it, his *Socialism: Utopian and Scientific*, and his *Anti-Duhring*. These and other works by Engels set forth the basic insights and conclusions of Marx's thought in a simple, clear, and summary fashion. However, they leave out the intellectual ferment and the process by which these ideas developed. Marx's vision of the world was that of a dynamic dialectical totality which encompassed several of the latter-day academic disciplines: philosophy, history, politics, economics, and sociology. But the marxism which Engels taught the leaders of the Second International was primarily concerned with the economic analysis of capitalism and its scientific character. The He-

7

gelian origins of Marx's thought were quietly abandoned as well as their revolutionary consequences. Only the "scientific socialism" of the later Marx was emphasized.[7]

This marxism of the Second International (1889-1914) was a peculiar blend of positivism and evolutionism. It espoused a scientistic economic determinism rooted in a mechanistic materialism. Philosophical questions were not broached, for it was considered that Marx had long before disposed of philosophy by transcending it; overcoming it in the direction of science. In the revolution vs. reform debates of the Second International, basic philosophical agreement on a scientistic positivism was evident in the arguments of both Bernstein and Kautsky.[8] Even Lenin's reflection theory of consciousness (i.e., consciousness is nothing more than a reflection of being) was rooted in a mechanistic materialism.[9] Thus, the "scientistic" trend of traditional marxism goes back through Lenin, Kautsky, and Engels even to the last years of Marx himself.

In France marxism was conditioned by two further circumstances: its late introduction and its identification with stalinism. Marxism was assimilated in France very slowly, for it had to compete with all the rich varieties of French revolutionary and socialist thought: Jacobinism, Blanquism, Proudhon's theories, and syndicalism, etc.[10] Moreover, the initial French followers of Marx of the 1880s (Jules Guesde, Paul Lafargue, Charles Longuet, etc.) did not have a very good grasp of Marx's thought. In fact, it was in reference to some of these French marxists that Marx himself facetiously remarked, "I am not a Marxist."[11]

Intellectually, marxism was introduced to France under rather unlikely circumstances. The scholar, Lucien Herr, was able to bring marxism to France's intellectual elite in his capacity of librarian at the *Ecole Normale Supérieure*. It was under Herr's guidance that Jean Jaurès turned to socialism and marxism.[12] While Herr initiated the *normaliens* into marxist theory, it was Georges Sorel who, through his analysis of the Italians, Croce and Labriola, brought marxism to a larger audience in the 1890s.[13] Nevertheless, prior to World War I, marxist theory was still only partially assimilated, to the extent that Jaurès, its leading French advocate, could claim his socialist inspiration jointly from Marx, Michelet, and Plutarch![14] This lack of intellectual assimilation, however, did not immediately affect the political growth of the French socialist movement, but it may account for some of its problems.[15]

World War I and the Bolshevik Revolution unleashed a revolutionizing shock throughout Europe. In France the majority of socialists endorsed the October Revolution and formed a communist party in 1920. First Lenin's and then Stalin's political theories dominated French communist thought.

Of Marx's works, only *Capital, The Communist Manifesto*, and his political histories were translated into French before World War I. His early works (including the crucial *Paris Manuscripts of 1844*) were not translated until 1937[16] and then didn't have any real impact until after 1945.[17] It wasn't until 1929 that the first group of marxist intellectuals was constituted for the specific purpose of studying and propagating marxist theory.[18] The most significant philosophical work produced by a member of this group was Paul Nizan's *Les Chiens du Garde* (1932).[19] But this was not a treatise on marxist philosophy so much as a damning attack on non-marxist philosophy. For during the 1930s Nizan and the other French communist intellectuals viewed the communist movement as the only hope of human salvation in a capitalist world threatened by war, depression, and fascism. In such a Manichean political context, philosophy was viewed as an instrumental weapon to be used by one side or the other. This atmosphere hardly encouraged a critical examination of one's own philosophical assumptions. During the "heroic" years of the Popular Front and the Resistance, there was "no time" for philosophical analyses, for the immediate political tasks were all-consuming. Marxist theory, therefore, did not really begin to develop in France until after the Liberation.

Post-1945 French marxism was even more explicitly

scientistic and positivistic than that of the Second International. The leading marxist theoretical journal, *La Pensée, Revue du rationalisme moderne*, [20] was put out by prominent intellectuals and scientists associated with the Parti Communiste Francaise (PCF).[21] The leading scientists had an openly positivistic approach to marxism, a world-view which they considered to be the contemporary form of scientific rationalism. They viewed themselves as heirs of the materialism of Diderot and the French Encyclopedist tradition of the 18th century Enlightenment.

French marxism was further limited in the immediate postwar years by the political situation.[22] The Popular Front, the Resistance, and the defeat of fascism created an atmosphere pregnant with great hopes for socialist revolution. The communists and socialists won an electoral majority, social welfare legislation was passed, and major financial and industrial enterprises were nationalized. Even that last bastion of reaction—male chauvinism—was slightly jolted as French women finally won the right to vote. For a short time (1944-1947) it appeared that the French might finally fulfill their revolutionary tradition. But the outbreak of the Cold War in 1947 shattered the political unity of the left as the PCF was excluded from the government.

In 1947 the PCF was a political party claiming close to a million members and the electoral choice of over five million (mostly working class) French voters. Basking in the prestige of its Resistance record, its obvious working class support, and its marxist legacy, the PCF exercised a strong attraction on leftist and liberal intellectuals. It was a political party which confidently claimed to be in sole possession of a philosophically rigorous and scientific theory of history and society. It was a party that claimed to fight for social justice for the downtrodden and progress for all. And despite its many shortcomings, it was a party that compared quite favorably with the other political groupings of the postwar period.[23]

However, anti-communists emphasized the special relationship between the Soviet Union and the PCF and argued that the latter functioned as a vast fifth column doing the bidding of an aggressive and hostile foreign power. They also pointed to the dictatorial nature of the communist movement and claimed that the social justice ideology was merely a window-dressing to cover up the brutal machinations of a totalitarian police state seeking to conquer the entire world. The communists, for their part, replied in kind to such charges. It was the United States that was bent on world domination, and its supporters in France hid behind the facade of a democratic ideology to cover up their role as "agents of Wall Street" and world capitalism.

It is not surprising that a cultural and intellectual polarization accompanied this political polarization. French communists argued that since the Soviet Union was the first socialist state, it was the duty of socialists everywhere to protect it from attack by its capitalist enemies. Marxist intellectuals felt a deep moral commitment to defend the Soviet Union and demonstrate the superiority of its social system over that of the capitalist West. This doctrine of the two camps shackled marxist intellectuals in ideological constraints that virtually precluded a critical approach to marxist theory. Thus French marxism came to be identified completely with the Soviet Union and the "thought" of Joseph Stalin.[24]

The French stalinist version of marxism was that of a static, closed, finished philosophy known as diamat (dialectical materialism). Following Stalin's example, it was presented in the catechismic form of a sacred text consisting of seven theses, three principles, and four traits.[25] This dialectical materialism was a gross caricature of Marx's thought. Its dialectic affirmed the universality of contradiction, but the chief examples used to illustrate its operation were all mechanical (e.g., positive and negative numbers in mathematics, action and reaction in mechanics, the combination and dissociation of atoms in chemistry).[26] Its materialism consisted primarily of the undigested assertion that matter is primary and mind, a "reflection" of matter, only secondary. Its historical materalism was little more than an evolutionary economic determinist view of history and society. The economic base entirely determined the political-cultural superstructure of society. Any kind of autonomy of super-structure from base was denounced as illusory.

Stalinist diamat ignored most of the social and economic developments of the 20th century and reiterated Marx's analyses of mid-19th century Europe. Capitalist society was depicted as a battleground between two monolithic classes—bourgeoisie and proletariat—locked in mortal combat. Econo-mic crisis was considered endemic to capitalism, and the French working class was depicted as suffering increasing pauperization.[27] Armed with the "truth" of dialectical mater-ialism as rendered by Stalin, the PCF would lead the working class out of this land of the capitalist pharoahs and into the socialist promised land. The Party was the sole arbiter of this "truth." It always had the correct line on every subject. Those who chose to interpret marxism differently from the Party line were considered heretics and traitors to the working class. Thus, French marxism was frozen into the stalinist mold.

Many leftist intellectuals who were politically sym-pathetic to the working class and socialism found this mental machinery deeply disturbing. For, not only was stalinism intellectually constraining but the expression of any reserva-tions or disagreements with it was greeted with intense hostility and suspicion. The Party claimed for itself the exclusive right to determine the form and content of marxist theory. But the stalinist marxism which the PCF espoused was incapable of confronting the new situation of postwar France. For whatever the validity of the writings of Marx, Engels, or Lenin, the PCF refused to recognize the empirical changes taking place in French society right under its nose—such as the rise of a consumer society and the welfare state. The Party chose to repeat the old slogans and incantations without even infusing them with new content. Many leftist intellec-tuals, therefore, sought other sources to "thaw out" marxism so that it could be made relevant to the problems facing French society.

2. Sources of Renewal

What this task involved was a rethinking of the intellectual roots of marxism via a return to Hegel and the early works of Marx. The resulting rediscovery of the Hegelian dialectic and Marx's early concept of alienation demonstrated the inadequacies of stalinism as a valid philosophical interpretation of marxism.

a. Hegel's Phenomenology of Spirit

Prior to the 1930s Hegel was ignored for the most part by French intellectuals.[28] The narrow intellectual provincialism so prevalent in pre-1940 France partially accounts for this apparent lack of interest. However, the devastating defeat of 1940 shattered much of this long-standing smug, self-complacent cultural chauvinism. The collapse of the pre-war certainties, combined with the Resistance's promise of spiritual renewal, broke down much of the intellectual barriers to things foreign.[29] Thus, after the war an unprecedented revival of Hegel study burst forth upon the French intellectual scene.[30]

The groundwork for this "Hegel renaissance" was laid in the 1930s by Alexandre Kojève, a Russian emigré, and Jean Hyppolite. More than anyone else, these two philosophers molded the French perception of Hegel. From 1933 to 1939 Kojeve lectured regularly at the Ecole Pratique des Hautes Etudes on Hegel's *Phenomenology of Spirit*. Among those regularly attending were Raymond Aron, Maurice Merleau-Ponty, R. P. Fessard, Raymond Queneau, Jean Desanti, Georges Bataille, and Jacques Lacan—all prominent figures in postwar intellectual life. In 1947 Queneau collected and edited the notebooks of many who attended the lectures and published them with an article and notes from Kojève.[31]

Jean Hyppolite, a philosopher teaching at the Sorbonne and later at the College de France, wrote articles on Hegel in the late 1930s. But more significantly, he published the first complete and definitive French translation of Hegel's *Phenomenology* in 1941. After the war he published several important commentaries on Hegel as well.[32]

Kojève's lectures and notes and Hyppolite's translation and commentaries were the basic sources by which the French experienced Hegel. Their concentration on the *Phenomenology* (published originally 1807) made Hegel appear not as the dogmatic idealist associated with his later works (of the 1820s), but rather as a dynamic critical founder of a philosophical anthropology. By making the master-slave dialectic the focus of his analysis, Kojève laid the basis for a marxist reading of Hegel which emphasized class struggle.

Hyppolite, on the other hand, chose to emphasize the theme of the "unhappy consciousness," which experiences despair and anguish over its finitude and mortality. This theme was at the root of the existentialist reading of Hegel.

Both of these readings found a common ground in Hegel's historical concept of reason. Traditional French rationalism viewed reason and its categories as eternally valid. Hegel, on the other hand, argued that reason was not absolute in its structure but dialectical. That is, different forms of human consciousness emerged from the contradictions of preceding forms of consciousness. For example, the scientific and rationalist forms of consciousness in 17th and 18th century Europe, Hegel argued, grew out of the contradictions of medieval religious forms of consciousness. The forms of human consciousness throughout history reflected the development of human efforts to posit being-in-the-world and then comprehend the results of this action. Merleau-Ponty, one of Kojève's famous students, put it this way:

> Hegel's thought...views man not as being from the start a consciousness of its own clear thoughts but as a life which is its own responsibility and which tries to understand itself. All of the *Phenomenology* describes man's efforts to reappropriate himself.[33]

This notion of the historical conditioning of reason served as an antidote to the traditional tenets of French rationalism and French marxism. For the clear implication was that these reigning dogmas were not absolute in their validity (as each

claimed) but rather a specific stage in the totalizing movement of consciousness. Hyppolite himself put it this way:

> For the French, Hegel's vision of the world...is indispensible
> to know. According to Hegel, history and reason interpene-
> trate one another...it is with history that we must reconcile
> ourselves. Freedom is precisely this reconciliation. Our philo-
> sophers have thought about freedom in an entirely different
> way. From Descartes to Bergson, our philosophy is a refusal of
> history: rather it is dualist, looking for freedom in a reflection
> of the subject on himself.[34]

Hegel used the dialectic as a method of phenomenologically
describing the historical forms of reason as they *appeared*.
Truth, for Hegel, was the Whole, the unity of all the various
historical manifestations of reason and their simultaneous
comprehension by the individual (subject). This unity of substance (of reason) and subject he considered "Absolute
Knowledge." From this absolute standpoint the dialectical
development of specific modes of consciousness appears as
partial. And since the "truth is the whole," these partial truths
pale into insignificance. It is from this line of thought that the
dogmatic idealism associated with Hegel's later works derived.

The French reading of Hegel, however, discounted his
claim to Absolute Knowledge and the dogmatic dialectic
which accompanies it. Both Kojève and Hyppolite chose to
emphasize the *critical* dialectic of negativity, the process by
which the "partial truths" of consciousness superseded one
another. This inevitably lead to a similar attitude toward
traditional marxism: a rejection of the dogmatic results of
marxist inquiry and a return to Marx's critical method.

b. Marx's Paris Manuscripts of 1844

It is not surprising then that when French intellectuals
turned to a reading of Marx's early works they found that he
himself followed a similar intellectual journey. When Marx's
Paris Manuscripts of 1844 finally came to the attention of
French intellectuals a century later, they rediscovered how the
twenty-six-year-old Marx also rejected Hegel's Absolute

while retaining his dialectic of negativity. They also rediscovered a concretized concept of alienation:

> The outstanding achievement of Hegel's *Phenomenology*—
> the dialectic of negativity as the movement and creating prin-
> ciple—is, first, that Hegel grasps the self-creation of man as a
> process, objectification as loss of the object, as alienation and
> transcendence of this alienation, and that he therefore grasps
> the nature of *labor*, and conceives objective man...as the result
> of his *own labor*.[35]

Alienation is the central theme of both Hegel's *Phenomenology* and Marx's *Paris Manuscripts*. For Hegel objectification was the source of alienation. Estrangement from
oneself occurred because one's inner feelings were not recognized as one's own reality by others. Instead, individuals
objectify each other and thereby objectify themselves, view
themselves from the outside. Consequently, a struggle for
recognition ensues whereby individuals attempt to express
their inner selves by creating objects which can be recognized
by others. Even so, there is no guarantee that others will
recognize these objects as they were intended. In fact, they
almost certainly won't, laying the foundation for the next
stage of alienation. Thus alienation is rooted in the dilemma
of objectification. No objectification implies no recognition of
self. Yet, objectification, because it is *objectification*, implies a
distorted recognition of self.

In the *Paris Manuscripts* Marx develops this concept of
alienation one step further. For him it is not just the objectification of self in the products of one's labor that is central to
alienation. But also the *appropriation* of these objects by
another. Hegel's dialectic is a dialectic of alienation of self
experienced as "spirit." Marx concretizes this dialectic and
thus transforms it into a dialectic of the material alienation of
labor.

With the discovery of the *Paris Manuscripts*, alienation
was resurrected as a fundamental marxist concept. It served
as the focal point for the leftist critique of traditional
marxism. The existentialists, the revisionists, and the *gauch-*

istes all assimilated Marx's *Paris Manuscripts* and cited them as an authority for their various criticisms of stalinism. Stalinist intellectuals were caught unawares by this early Marx revival buttressed by the Hegel renaissance. Prior to this time, they had rebuffed all sorts of attacks on the orthodoxy of their marxism. In the writings of the young Marx himself they faced a formidable opponent.

One can say that the *Paris Manuscripts* revealed a Marx very different from the orthodox version. In post-1945 France the *Paris Manuscripts* had the impact of an intellectual bombshell. Leftist intellectuals felt they had discovered a telling critique of stalinism. For it appeared that Marx himself had envisioned the emergence of a dehumanizing "crude communism" (and, indeed, this is how the leftist critics viewed stalinism) in uncannily prophetic terms! Stalinist intellectuals for their part maintained an embarrassed silence or else dismissed Marx's youthful philosophical speculation as "immature" and claimed that he himself later rejected it as well.[36]

3. *The New Themes*

The theme of alienation thus became the rallying point for the critics of traditional marxism. What is wrong with captialism, they argued, is that it alienated the individual from one's authentic being. Instead of resolving this fundamental problem, stalinism only compounded it by creating further mystifications. The struggle against alienation in advanced industrial society gradually emerged as the focus of new left social theory. Alienation was seen as particularly characteristic of postwar society because of the increasing growth of bureaucratization. The lack of responsiveness of societal institutions to human needs was perceived as a function of a growing, impersonal, atomistic, and anonymous bureaucracy. In this context the Soviet Union and traditional marxism were increasingly perceived as a specific variation of the bureaucratic theme. For alienation was acutely apparent in the Soviet bloc as well as in the West.

From the late 1940s to the early 1960s, the leftist critics of marxism focused their analyses on the problems of alienation in modern bureaucratic society. As leftists they affirmed the need for a socialist solution. However, learning from the Soviet experience, they also emphasized the need for real political and economic democracy. Their egalitarian view of a free society surfaced in May 1968 in the slogan *autogestion*, or "self-management."

In the following chapters we will trace the development of the three major tendencies among the leftist critics of traditional marxism in France. In each case, we will first sketch an overview of the terrain and then analyze the critique of traditional marxism of the major theorist of each tendency. In this process we will see how each moved from a critique of traditional marxism to the themes of new left social theory: alienation, bureaucracy, and *autogestion*.

Notes

1. The leftist critique of traditional marxism is, of course, not unique to France. It is a European-wide phenomenon with worldwide impact. The Frankfurt School in Germany (with Marcuse in the U.S.), the *Praxis* group in Yugoslavia, marxist humanism in Poland and Czechoslavakia, and the Italian school of phenomenological marxism are all similar in inspiration with the French intellectual currents considered here.
2. For a cogent elaboration of this view see Mark Poster, *Existential Marxism in Postwar France: From Sartre to Althusser* (Princeton, 1975).
3. For the political and ideological aspects of this crisis see François Fejto, *The French Communist Party and the Crisis of International Communism* (Cambridge, 1967).
4. The political labels—"left," "right," etc.—have meaning only in specific contexts. When the term "left" or "leftist" is used in this study the implied context is the whole of French society. The term *"gauchiste"* is used in this study to refer to the left *within* the left.
5. In the post-May period the intense preoccupation with developing libertarian organizational forms was symptomatic of the fact that many

new leftists were themselves uncertain as to how a liberating social transformation could take place.

6. Thus it could be argued that the historical reality of traditional marxism is not to be found in Marx's works but rather in Engels' works or Bukharin's *ABC of Communism*, or even Edward Aveling's *The Student's Marx*.

7. George Lichtheim argues that Marx's life-work passed through a number of different phases. He distinguishes between a "pre-marxist" Marx and a Marx who develops (after 1860) towards economism. See his *Marxism* (New York, 1964).

8. See Eduard Bernstein's *Evolutionary Socialism* (1899) and Karl Kautsky's *The Road to Power* (1909).

9. See his *Materialism and Empirio-Criticism* (1907).

10. Cf. M. Dommanget, *L'Introduction du marxisme en France* (Paris, 1969); Alexandre Zevaès, *De l'Introduction du marxisme en France* (Paris, 1947); Maximilien Rubel, *Bibliographie des oeuvres de Karl Marx* (Paris, 1956); and George Lichtheim, *Marxism in Modern France* (New York, 1966).

11. See Pradeep Bandyopadhyay, "The Many Faces of French Marxism," *Science and Society*, 36:2 (Summer, 1972) p. 132. Also cf. Lichtheim *op. cit.* p. 9: "What passed for marxism before the 1880's...was a mere parody."

12. See Harvey Goldberg's, *The Life of Jean Jaurès* (Madison, 1962), pp. 62-63. Herr was the librarian at the Ecole Normale Supérieure from 1888-1924, and his influence spanned through at least three generations of marxist intellectuals. See Charles Andler, *La Vie de Lucien Herr* (Paris, 1932).

13. Benedetto Croce is not usually remembered for his marxism, yet in the 1890s his writings and those of his teacher, Antonio Labriola, were considered by Vilfredo Pareto as "indispensible for appreciating the present state of the question of *historical materialism*." (*Les Systèmes socialistes*, II, 402: quoted in H. Stuart Hughes, *Consciousness and Society* (New York, 1958), p. 82.) For the general significance of these two Italians and their influence in spreading marxism in France through George Sorel, see Hughes, pp. 82-96; and Neil McInnes, "Les débuts du marxisme théorique en France et en Italie (1880-1897)," *Cahiers de l'Institut de Science Economique Appliquée*, no. 102 (Paris, June 1960).

14. See the Introduction to his *Histoire Socialiste de la révolution française*, I (Paris, 1922).

15. The theoretical problems of the Second International are too complex and tangential to the present subject to be treated here. For an overview of these problems see James Joll, *The Second International, 1889-1914* (New York, 1966).

16. Marx's most important early writings—*The Paris Manuscripts of 1844* and *The German Ideology* (1846)—and the all-important *Grund-*

risse (1857-8) which shows the continuity between his early and later work, were all unpublished in any language and virtually unknown until the 1930s. German editions of the first two works appeared in 1932 and of the latter in 1939. A French edition of the *Grundrisse* did not appear until 1967!

17. Even the important philosophical works of Lenin and Engels were not translated into French until very late. Lenin's *Materialism and Empirio-Criticism* did not appear in French until 1928, and Engels' *Dialectic of Nature* appeared in 1957. Just on the basis of the availability of the texts it appears that a thorough evaluation of marxist theory was really impossible until the postwar period.

18. The *Philosophies* group of communist intellectuals functioned as a marxist study group between 1929 and 1934 although it had been constituted several years earlier. Its members were Georges Politzer, Henri Lefebvre, Norbert Guterman, Georges Friedmann, Pierre Morhange, and Paul Nizan. Lefebvre gives a history of the group in his *L'Existentialisme* (Paris, 1946) and W. F. Redfern discusses it in his *Paul Nizan* (Princeton, 1972), pp. 12-20.

19. Lefebvre's *Le Matérialisme dialectique* (Paris, 1939) did not appear until five years after the group dispersed.

20. Founded in 1939, its editors included such distinguished scientists as Frédéric Joliot-Curie, Paul Langevin, Marcel Prenant, and Henri Wallon.

21. The initials stand for "Parti communiste français."

22. For an excellent analysis of this political situation see Alexander Werth's *France 1940-1955* (New York, 1956).

23. By far the best studies on the PCF are by Annie Kriegel: *Aux origines du communisme français: 1914-1920* (Paris, 1964) and *Les communistes français* (Paris, 1969). A recent comprehensive study is Ronald Tiersky's, *French Communism 1920-1972* (New York, 1974).

24. Edgar Morin, an ex-communist intellectual who quit after 1956 and participated in the founding of *Arguments* describes this process as a "glaciation." See his *Autocritique* (Paris, 1959).

25. Cf. Joseph Stalin, "Dialectical and Historial Materialism," in his *Leninism: Selected Writings* (New York, 1942), pp. 406-433. For examples of French diamat see Roger Garaudy, *La Théorie matérialiste de la connaissance* (1953) or Guy Besse and Maurice Caveling, *Principes élémentaires de philosophie*. For a broad discussion of the relationship of French intellectuals to the PCF see David Caute, *Communism and the French Intellectuals* (New York, 1964); and on Stalin's impact in France see Alfred J. Rieber, *Stalin and the French Communist Party: 1941-1947* (New York, 1962).

26. Lenin used these examples in his essay, "On the Question of Dialectics" (1915). Stalin and his followers constantly repeated them.

27. This may well have been true comparing 1938 living standards with those of 1954, although a clear rise was evident from 1949 to 1954. On the standard of of living debate of the French working class see Werth *op. cit.*, pp. 631-637.

28. Apart from the surrealists and the *Philosophies* group there was little intellectual interest in Hegel and almost no academic interest. See Alexandre Koyré, "Rapports sur l'état des études hégéliennes en France," *Revue d'histoire de la philosophie*, 5:2 (April-June, 1931).

29. Cf. Lichtheim: After 1945, "Hegel, Kierkegaard, Marx, Freud, Weber, Husserl, and Heidegger, were assimilated almost simultaneously." *Op. cit.*, p. 82.

30. For the best account of the postwar Hegel revival see Poster *op. cit.*, Chapter One, "The Hegel Renaissance." Poster argues that the emergence of interest in Hegel was directly linked to the expectation of socialism among leftist intellectuals.

31. Kojève, *Introduction à la lecture de Hegel* (Paris, 1947).

32. See his *Genèse et structure de la phénoménologie de l'esprit de Hegel* (1947), *Introduction à la philosophie de l'histoire de Hegel* (1948), *Logique et existence: essai sur la Logique de Hegel* (1952), and *Etudes sur Marx et Hegel* (1955).

33. Merleau-Ponty, *Sense and Non-Sense* (Evanston, 1964), p. 65. Appeared originally as "L'Existentialisme chez Hegel," *Les Temps Modernes*, no. 7 (April 1946).

34. Jean Hyppolite, *Introduction à la philosophie de l'histoire de Hegel* (Paris, 1948), p. 123; translated by Poster, *op. cit.*, pp. 19-20.

35. This and the following quotations are from T. B. Bottomore's translation of the *Paris Manuscripts* in Erich Fromm's *Marx's Concept of Man* (New York, 1961), pp. 176-177. Incidentally, before undertaking the *Phenomenology* Hegel wrote an extended critique of Adam Smith and the concept of labor of classical political economy. See his *Jenenser Realphilosophie*, edited by Johann Hoffmeister (Hamburg, 1967).

36. See e.g., Roger Garaudy, "Les manuscripts de 1844 de Karl Marx," *Cahiers du Communisme*, p. 39 (March, 1963), Louis Althusser's *Pour Marx* (Paris, 1966), and Chapter 7 below.

/2/

Jean-Paul Sartre and Simone de Beauvoir: The Existentialist Challenge

1. *Introduction: Sartre's Rise to Prominence*

In the immediate postwar period existentialism struck a live nerve in the French public. The collapse of traditional values in the shame of defeat and collaboration, augmented by the death-fraught experience of the Resistance, created the circumstances whereby existentialism found a vast audience receptive to its anguished mood. In a world controlled by the vast forces of war, technology, and great power politics existentialism spoke of the crisis of the individual: the problems of guilt and responsibility, bad faith and authenticity, the individual's confrontation with one's own death and the very meaning of one's life. In short, existentialism spoke of the meaning of human freedom. It affirmed the irreducibility of the freedom of the individual to choose a course of action in every situation. When so much else seemed to indicate human reality was determined and unfree, the existentialists stubbornly and tenaciously advanced the view that to be human was to be free.

Any discussion of French existentialism inevitably leads to Jean-Paul Sartre (1905-1980).[1] For while existentialism was a broad intellectual movement with many different and often conflicting tendencies, Sartre towers above it as the leading and most representative figure of the existentialist left.[2] In fact, Sartre's move in the postwar period from existentialism toward marxism was the main event in the development of new left social theory.

Sartre came to marxism slowly and gradually. As a bohemian intellectual, he had an instinctive dislike for capitalist society, which he coupled with an honest sympathy for the poor and downtrodden—the working class. His experience in the Resistance viscerally convinced him that the working class was the only possible vehicle for progressive social change. Thus he became a supporter and advocate of the working class movement. However, while he supported marxist politics, he found marxist philosophy impossible to accept because of the dogmatic direction in which it was developed in the communist movement.

Nevertheless, by the 1950s, he came to the position that marxism indeed is the philosophy of our epoch, a philosophy which is unsurpassable for industrial society. The problem with marxism is that it has become "arrested" in the hands of stalinist ideologues. Under their tutelage, it has succumbed to a "sclerosis" and ceases temporarily to be a living philosophy. They have stifled the dialectical vitality of marxism with a reductionist, mechanistic determinism.

Compared to the philosophy of marxism, existentialism (Sartre was to claim by 1957) is a mere "ideology." However, it is an ideology which can serve an important service to marxism. With its emphasis on the individual, the particular, and the concrete, and its overriding concern for human freedom, existentialism could help to free marxism from the sterile abstractions of stalinism. It could help to unblock or revitalize marxism.

In this chapter we will trace Sartre's steps from existentialism toward marxism by examining his theoretical and political confrontation with the stalinism of the PCF during the period 1944-1956. In the next chapter we will look closely at his *Critique de la raison dialectique* (1960), the most ambitious and comprehensive philosophical effort to use existentialism to revitalize marxism.

* * *

Sartre always considered himself a man of the left, yet prior to 1940 he took no active part in politics. He went to the 14 July 1935 Popular Front demonstration in Paris more as an observer than as a participant. He never voted, not even for the Popular Front candidates of 1936. In 1972 he said:

> I was absolutely in favor of the Popular Front, but it would never have crossed my mind to vote, so as to give my opinion the value of a decision...I remained an individualist, drawn to the masses who *made* the Popular Front, but not realizing that I was one of them and that I must stand by them.[3]

While he found fascism repugnant, this did not deter him from living in Nazi Germany for a year to study under Heidegger, or from visiting Mussolini's fascist Exposition in Rome in exchange for a reduced rate trainfare that was being offered to guarantee large crowds.[4]

Nevertheless, his first literary works reveal his leftist sympathies. Antoine Roquetin's biting sarcasm toward the bourgeoisie and bourgeois morality in his first and most famous novel, *Nausea* (1938), reveal Sartre's anti-capitalist temperament. In the short story, *The Wall* (1939), which takes place in a prison cell in the Spanish Civil War, his sympathy for the Republicans is clear—just as his antipathy for anti-semitism and fascism is eloquently manifested in the short story, *Childhood of a Leader* (1939).

But it was the outbreak of the war and his experience as a prisoner of war that convinced him of the absolute necessity of political action:

> I remained inactive, doing nothing but writing, while in perfect sympathy with the Left. I lived through the whole

period from 1918 to 1939 as through the dawn of a lasting peace. It took the war to open my eyes. There I was seeing myself as a minute and gleaming atom, and then along came massive forces which took hold of me and flung me on to the battlefront without asking my opinion.[5]

Sartre was drafted into the French Army in late 1939. His entire unit was captured in June 1940 at the Maginot Line. As a POW he wrote, produced, and acted in his first Resistance play, *Bariona*, performed in Stalag XII at Trèves, Christmas 1940. Taking the biblical story of Bariona he was able to talk to his fellow prisoners about captivity, and through the use of allegory, suggest that all hope of resistance was not lost.[6]

Sartre was a POW from June 1940 to March 1941. By altering his military papers and demonstrating that he was nearly blind in his right eye, Sartre was able to convince the German authorities that he had never been in the army and had been captured by mistake. He returned to Paris and his teaching position at the Lycée Pasteur. Immediately following his release he sought out Maurice Merleau-Ponty and attempted to found a resistance group called *Socialisme et Liberté*. Together with Simone de Beauvoir they bicycled into and out of unoccupied France seeking the assistance of such prominent intellectuals as Gide and Malraux. No help was forthcoming and the group folded. It was, however, the first time that Sartre expressed what was to become his lifelong political goal.

At this time the communists were very suspicious about how Sartre obtained his release from the POW camp and branded him a German spy. They refused to have anything to do with him. By 1943, however, the climate had changed. It was pretty clear the Allies would eventually win the war. More and more people joined the various Resistance organizations. And the communists, who comprised a significant force in the Home Resistance, began to pursue a policy of coalition and reconciliation with other anti-fascists. Accordingly, they denied ever having made any accusations against Sartre and invited him to work on the *Comité National des Ecrivains*

(C.N.E.), which they dominated. Sartre accepted without hesitation.

In the same year Sartre's second and more famous Resistance play, *The Flies*, was produced in Paris. The tale of Orestes returning to avenge the murder of his father, Agamemnon, by killing Aegisthos the usurper and his own mother Clytemnestra was transformed by Sartre into a thinly veiled allegory of the circumstances of occupied France. He also took the opportunity in this play to dramatize his philosophical views on freedom, guilt, and responsibility. Because he accepts the responsibility for his own actions, Orestes is able to overcome the power of guilt and remorse which the flies exercize over the people of Argos. From this acceptance of responsibility, his freedom is born. The play was a great popular success and marked Sartre as the most significant literary *résistant*.

During the Occupation years 1943-1944, Sartre continued to teach and pursue his philosophical (*Being and Nothingness*), literary (*Roads to Freedom* trilogy), and dramatic (*No Exit*) interests. He continued his Resistance activity with the C.N.E. (under the direction of the Surrealist and PCF member, Paul Eluard), worked on the clandestine communist journal, *Les Lettres Françaises*, and wrote articles for Albert Camus' underground paper, *Combat*.

His stature as a major intellectual figure on the French scene dates from the Liberation period (1944-1946). In the first two years of peace in Paris, four of his plays were performed, two of his novels published, *Being and Nothingness* was widely circulated, *Les Temps Modernes* was launched, his services as a journalist were in demand by several major newspapers, and his popularity as a public speaker was increasing. Existentialism was all the vogue in Paris, and as its chief exponent, Sartre gained fame far and wide.

2. Sartre's Existentialist Social Theory

The sub-title of *Being and Nothingness—An Essay in Phenomenological Ontology*—indicates Sartre's intellectual debt to the German thinkers Husserl and Heidegger. From Husserl Sartre took the phenomenological method of analyzing the objects of consciousness as they appear for consciousness. From Heidegger, Sartre took the ontological concern for the individual's relationship to Being. Sartre interpreted Husserl and Heidegger through the Cartesian lenses of rationalism he acquired at the Ecole Normale. Thus his social theory remains situated in the individualist problematic.

The social theory that emerges from Sartre's early philosophical magnum opus, *Being and Nothingness* (1943), appears quite contradictory. For on the one hand, there is the optimistic assertion that one is unconditionally free.

> Human freedom precedes essence in man and makes it possible; the essence of human being is suspended in his freedom. What we call freedom is impossible to distinguish from the being of "human reality." Man does not exist *first* in order to be free *subsequently*; there is no difference between the being of man and his *being free*.[7]

On the other hand, we find the pessimistic assertion that the individual constantly flees from freedom into bad faith, that one's attempts to live and act authentically are doomed to failure. In short, "man is a useless passion."[8] The assertion of radical freedom in the first half of this dichotomy proved to be the basis of his eventual contribution to new left social theory. However, the individualist basis of this social theory and its ahistorical tragic sense of despair led French marxists to believe that existentialism represented a refurbishing of conservative idealist social theory under a leftist mask. They drew this conclusion because existentialist despair appeared to imply that social activism was futile.

In the debate that ensued between the existentialist Sartre and the traditional marxists an important theoretical transformation evolved. Sartre, without renouncing his conception of the fundamental irreducibility of individual freedom, came to accept step-by-step the historical and social dimensions conditioning it. This is evident in his *Critique de la raison dialectique* (1960). For their part, some of the marxists came to recognize the "existential" dimension of historical and social reality, and on this basis made their own contribution to the development of new left theory.[9]

The social theory of *Being and Nothingness* centers on the question: what is the subject's relationship to the world? In answering this question Sartre rejects classical metaphysics and idealism while retaining the primacy of consciousness. Still, the Cartesian *cogito* is accepted as the starting point,[10] but its implication is reversed. For consciousness is experienced as a *lack*. It is always consciousness of some *thing*—some thing other than consciousness. The very fact of consciousness implies otherness, implies the being of the world without the Cartesian resort to a divine cause. Therefore, the individual is not related *to* the world at all as classical metaphysics framed the question. Rather, consciousness reveals the being of the world because it is *in* the world. The subject/world relation, hence, is internal. Subject-*in*-the-world is a synthetic unity.

The existentialist view of the subject is thus a move away from traditional French idealism with its abstract view of the individual as a more or less spiritual essence divorced from concrete determinations. However, in *Being and Nothingness* Sartre stops short of materialism. For while human being-in-the-world is a synthetic unity, human reality is nevertheless fragmented and bi-polar. Its fundamental ontological structure is dyadic: *for-itself* and *in-itself*. For-itself is consciousness, in-itself is materiality. The fullness of Being is characteristic of the in-itself in its solidity and mass, while the for-itself, as a translucent negativity, is Nothingness.[11]

Existentialist freedom and authenticity consist of the effort of the for-itself (consciousness) to transcend (go beyond) the materiality of the in-itself. Bad faith, on the other hand, is the surrender of the for-itself to the inertness and opacity of the in-itself. It is the acceptance of object-status by a subject. It is from this distinction between freedom and bad faith that the political radicalism of existentialist social theory derives. For on the social level freedom (a positive existentialist value) means acting authentically and implies the necessity of *engagement*, commitment, and progressive social change. While bad faith (a negative existentialist value) implies acceptance of the status quo.

At the same time Sartre maintains such an overwhelming negative view of social relations as to cast doubt on the progressive character of his early social thought. For the Other is experienced primarily as a threat to my freedom. The existence of the Other, of a whole world of others, is a limitation on my absolute freedom. Sartre's view of social relations in *Being and Nothingness* is very close to the Hobbesian view of the war of each against all. The encounter with the Other is fraught with all sorts of danger. For through "the look"[12] the Other may attempt to reduce me to an object, reduce me to shame. Contact with the Other is strained and uncomfortable. S/he may attempt to steal my freedom from me, so I must be on my guard. Even friendship and love carry the threat of loss of freedom. Thus all social relations are essentially relations of *conflict*. This view denies the existence (or even the possibility) of healthy social relations characterized by trust and cooperation.[13] In short, "hell is other people."[14] This slogan from his play *No Exit* pithily summarizes Sartre's early view of social relations.

Here, then, are the main contradictions of Sartre's early existentialist social theory: Human being is unconditionally free *and* a useless passion. Existentialism exalts the dignity and humanity of the human spirit, and yet, hell is other people.

At the time of the Liberation, Sartre tried to play down the pessimistic and gloomy side of existentialism and portray it as an "optimism," "a humanist philosophy of action, of effort, of combat, of solidarity..."[15] He stressed the similarities between his thought and marxism, claiming both were compatible philosophies of freedom and action. Existentialism was not the product of defeat and despair; rather, it developed in the revolutionary climate of the Resistance. At first the communist intellectuals appeared receptive to this view. When Sartre claimed, "We were never more free than under the German Occupation," many of the communist intellectuals who had risked their lives by participating in the Resistance understood:

> The choice that each of us made of himself was authentic, because it was made in the presence of death...the question of freedom was posed, and we were brought to the edge of the deepest knowledge a man can have of himself.[16]

After the Liberation, however, the resistance aura gradually began to fade. The PCF was now close to power, a party pulsing with an overconfident, enthusiastic optimism.[17] Party leaders found something pernicious in the despair and anguish of Sartre's existentialism. They called it a bourgeois ideology of nihilism, decadence, and anti-humanism.[18] Also, the Party was wary of losing some of its mass following to existentialism, for the youth of France were flocking to it. Even many of the younger communist intellectuals were attracted to Sartre's thought, provoking a sharp split within the Party itself.[19] Thus, a strong marxist rebuttal became urgently needed.

Henri Lefebvre led the attack. In response to Sartre's *mise au point* in *Action*, Lefebvre claimed existentialism had nothing at all in common with marxism. The tone of the article was quite combative. For while he no longer charged Sartre "with having been a disciple of the Nazi Heidegger," he still considered him a subjective idealist and a "munitions-maker against marxism."[20]

Lefebvre also wrote the first book-length critique of *Being and Nothingness*. In his *l'Existentialisme* (1946) he claimed to uncover the social origins of existentialism in "the moral decomposition of the so-called higher classes."[21] Sartre was a spokesman for a decadent class bordering on neurosis and irrationalism: "In the queer existence described by Sartre, anxiety, vertigo, fascination, the need to destroy, etc., become sources of truth."[22] Philosophically, Sartre failed to overcome the dualism of idealism and materialism. For Lefebvre the basic difference between marxism and existentialism was revealed in Sartre's romantic-irrationalist attitude toward science:

> The essential difference between dialectical materalism and existentialism resides in the attitude toward science...Dialectical materialism saves reason because it makes it concrete without suppressing it...It integrates the irrational within Reason.[23]

Existentialism, on the contrary, attempts to interweave reason with the irrational. Its basic concepts are "magical," novelistic images lacking logical rigor or consistency. In fact, "there is morbidity, a neurotic element in it with infantile regression."[24]

Other marxist critiques of existentialism soon followed and were no less insulting.[25] Roger Garaudy, another leading communist philosopher claimed: "Every class has the literature it deserves. The upper bourgeoisie in decay delights in the erotic obsessions of a Henry Miller or the intellectual fornications of Jean-Paul Sartre."[26] And Jean Kanapa, a communist former student of Sartre's, wrote a personal attack decrying the "degeneracy" and "perversion" of the existentialist "cafe revolutionaries."[27]

Amid all this rancor some solid points were raised. Sartre had not escaped the individualist problematic. His critique of idealism was a step in the right direction (as far as the marxists were concerned), but because he failed to embrace materialism, Sartre became hopelessly mired in a murky nether-world between idealism and materialism. The fact that he could not adequately account for the intersubjectivity of social relations (except through the "magic of the look") stemmed from these weaknesses.[28]

Sartre responded to these polemics with a lecture in 1945 called "Existentialism is a Humanism," and an article in *Les Temps Modernes* in 1946, "Materialism and Revolution." In the lecture he gave in October 1945, he denied the charges against him. Existentialism, he said, is not "an invitation to people to dwell in the quietism of despair."[29] It is not "gloomy." Rather, it is a philosophy of action. It is an attempt to look reality in the face, accept the tragic character of human existence, and forge ahead into *engagement* and social commitment. In response to charges that his existentialism fosters amoral nihilism Sartre denied that the maxim, "Everyone can do what he likes,"[30] follows from his thought. Instead he argued that existentialism is a humanism that demands a Kantianesque universalization of one's values. Thus, "in committing myself, I also commit the whole of humanity."[31] On the other hand, the individual alone is free to create one's essence by the actions one performs. Existential humanism requires action that is both universal and free. It is the only philosophy, Sartre claimed, that is suitable for revolutionary politics.

This defense of existentialism was unconvincing to the marxists because it was still rooted in the individualist problematic. Sartre would not join a revolutionary group where he would have to "count on men whom I do not know."[32] His individual freedom could be preserved only "in the unity of a party or group which I can more or less control."[33] This was justified in Sartre's eyes because Cartesian subjectivity was his point of departure. Yet he could not demonstrate any rational connection between his concept of individual freedom and collective action. It appeared that a mystical leap of faith was the only connection between his existential philosophy and his leftist politics.

In his essay, "Materialism and Revolution," Sartre turned this charge around and attacked the stalinists for making such a leap of faith themselves—into materialism. To Sartre materialism was "a doctrine that destroys thought," that attempts to "reduce the action of mind to that of matter...to eliminate subjectivity by reducing the world, and the individual to a system of objects linked together by universal relationships."[34] It was such a monstrous doctrine that it could only be accepted on faith as a useful myth of furthering revolutionary politics. Yet the marxists demanded that it be accepted not as myth but as truth. In one very clear passage Sartre went to the heart of the practical difference between his existentialism and marxist materialism:

> I know that man has no salvation other than the liberation of the working class; I know this before being a materialist and from a plain inspection of the facts. I know that our intellectual interest lies with the proletariat. Is that a reason for me to demand of my thinking, which has led me to this point, that it destroy itself? Is that a reason for me to force it henceforth to abandon its criteria, to think in contradictions, to be torn between incompatible theses, to lose even the clear consciousness of itself, to launch forth blindly in a giddy flight that leads to faith?[35]

Sartre also presented a telling critique of the materialist view of subjectivity. Stalinism, Sartre claimed, did not have a valid theory of subjectivity and consequently was inadequate as a social theory. For objective conditions of hunger and exploitation do not create revolutions in the same manner that heat makes water boil. Revolutions are not passively experienced as the result of objective factors. Rather, they are actively initiated by individuals of free minds and free wills. Since stalinist materialism denies the importance of such individual freedom, it blocks the path to revolution. This last charge infuriated the communists and yet they could not refute it. For they could not explain in individual cases why some people became revolutionaries and others did not. Nor could they explain, except in the most general sense, why revolutionary consciousness developed in certain historical situations and not in other similar situations. Sartre had uncovered a serious weakness in marxism. This lack of a concrete theory of consciousness and of the individual was the

weak point in marxism at which Sartre hammered away again
and again.

In this 1946 article he presented many arguments which
the materialists couldn't answer, while qualifying the more
unguarded claims about human freedom he made in *Being and
Nothingness* and "Existentialism is a Humanism" (1945).
Limitations on the absolute freedom of the individual were
now recognized in the "plurality of freedoms."

> A revolutionary philosophy ought to account for the plurality
> of freedoms and show how each one can be an object for the
> other while being, at the same time, a freedom for itself. Only
> this double character of freedom and objectivity can explain
> the complex notions of oppression, conflict, failure, and
> violence.[36]

For the first time Sartre had begun to grapple with marxism
on a serious level. The issues and themes raised in "Materialism and Revolution" proved to be the kernel of the social
theory he eventually elaborated in his *Critique*. Thus, the
debate of existentialism with marxism in post-1945 France
required Sartre to assimilate marxism and led him to attempt
to transform it by incorporating his existentialism within it.
While this effort was rejected by orthodox marxists, it proved
to be essential to the new left social theory that emerged in the
1960s.

3. Simone de Beauvoir: Existentialism and Feminism

In *Being and Nothingness* Sartre is concerned with the
existential relation man-in-the-world, while in *The Second
Sex* Simone de Beauvoir is concerned with that of woman-in-
the-world.[37] Indeed, her encyclopedic, ground-breaking study
of the oppression of women is firmly rooted in existentialist
social theory. This is reflected in the two main theses of the
book: (1) that man, in pursuit of recognition of himself as
subject, has transformed woman into the Other, a dependent

and inessential being; and (2) that such a status for woman is not inherent in her nature but is a product of historical development and thus subject to change.

The concept of woman as the Other is the central thesis of de Beauvoir's study. In fact, she considered calling the book *The Other* or *The Other Sex* before finally settling on her title.[38] "The category of the *Other*," she tells us, "is as primordial as consciousness itself...It is a fundamental category of human thought."[39] As we saw with Sartre the world is revealed to consciousness as otherness, and the Other is always a threat to the subject. This threat derives from the fact that the Other may deny recognition of my subjectivity and view me as an object, may attempt to deny my freedom while acting out his own. Following Hegel's analysis of the master-slave relationship, de Beauvoir claims,

> We find in consciousness itself a fundamental hostility toward every other consciousness; the subject can be posed only in being opposed—he sets himself up as the essential, as opposed to the other, the inessential, the object.[40]

Thus far de Beauvoir's view of social relations accords with Sartre's. Unlike Sartre, however, de Beauvoir recognizes historical and social constraints on the freedom of the subject to pursue self-realization. In particular, she points out the constraints on women: "Men compel her to assume the status of the Other."[41] He is the Subject, he is the Absolute—she is the Other.[42] *The Second Sex* examines from an existentialist perspective why and how man forced this role on woman and explains how she can escape it and assert her freedom as subject.

Throughout the ages the commonly accepted view was that the inequality of the sexes was not man-made but rather a fact of nature, of biology. The elemental realities of human reproduction and the general disparity of muscular strength between men and women created what appeared in pre-literate and traditional societies to be a natural division of labor between the sexes. Menstruation, pregnancy, and childbirth were involuntary, natural functions which woman could not escape or control. Thus, the limitations on woman's freedom appeared to be created by nature, not by man.

De Beauvoir takes seriously the impact of biology on woman's condition. Yet she argues that biology alone is not sufficient to explain woman's lot. It is not the biological and anatomical differences themselves that give rise to inequality. Rather, it is the social meaning—the values—assigned to such differences that are the sources of inequality. The question, then, is where do such values come from?

Freud claimed they come from within the human psyche, from within the unconscious, and that sexuality alone is the basis for understanding human conduct. Consequently, woman's condition is comprehensible from the psychoanalytic concept of the Electra complex: as a conflict between her masculine and feminine tendencies, expressed in the differences between clitoral and vaginal eroticism.

Although de Beauvoir gives Freud credit for establishing certain basic sexual phenomena, she rejects the psychoanalytic view of woman as monocausal and deterministic. It is monocausal in that it reduces woman to her sexuality, which de Beauvoir sees as only one—though obviously a significant—aspect of woman's being. And it is deterministic in that it explains woman's adult behavior as a result of early childhood experience, thereby denying the reality of choice, the basis of the existentialist concept of freedom.

Finally, de Beauvoir sees in psychoanalysis a denial of woman's humanity. "Among psychoanalysts," she claims, "man is defined as a human being and woman as a female—whenever she behaves as a human being she is said to imitate the male."[43] In opposition to the psychoanalytic view of woman as torn between masculine and feminine tendencies, Beauvoir offers the existentialist view of woman: torn between accepting the role of object (the Other), or asserting her freedom as subject. In order to achieve the latter, she must establish her own values in the world.

Traditional marxism also provides an explanation for

the origins of inequality between the sexes. In *The Origin of the Family, Private Property, and the State*, Engels laid the foundation for the marxist view of the oppression of woman in terms of changes in the mode of production. Based on an evaluation of 19th century knowledge of anthropology, archeology, and ancient history, Engels speculated on the nature of prehistoric society. He hypothesized the existence of a primitive communist society with a subsistence economy. While there was a division of labor between the sexes, equality nevertheless prevailed because woman performed important agricultural activities. But the invention of the bronze tool, which was too heavy for woman to wield, allowed primitive man to increase his productivity and create a surplus beyond subsistence needs. This technological revolution simultaneously displaced woman in production and laid the foundation for the institution of private property. It resulted in change in the mode of production from primitive communism—where land was owned in common by all members of the clan—to slavery, where man appropriated the surplus produced by his fellow man as his own private property. Woman lost her role in production and became a dependent and inessential being. Engels concluded that woman's oppression was caused by the creation of private property. Woman could be emancipated, he argued, only by the abolition of private property and her return to social production alongside man.

De Beauvoir agrees with much of Engel's speculations as well as his conviction that woman could be emancipated in a socialist society. Nevertheless, she also had serious reservations about his analysis. He doesn't really explain why the appearance of a social surplus should lead to the institution of private property; nor why the latter must inevitably lead to the oppression of woman. Further, she objects to his "economic monism" and claims that "to reduce the antagonism of the sexes to class conflict...is simply untenable... Woman cannot in good faith be regarded simply as a worker."[44] Finally, she notes that while the ideal of a truly socialist society is consistent with the emancipation of woman, the practice of the Soviet Union has been to revive the "ancient patriarchal restraints" on woman as well as "paternalistic concepts of marriage."[45]

Thus, in seeking to account for the oppression of woman and the inequality of the sexes, de Beauvoir finds the biological, psychoanalytic, and marxist explanations inadequate. What is missing in each of them is a view of woman "as a human being in quest of values in a world of values."[46] Only the existentialist perspective speaks to this fundamental point. For it views the individual as free to create oneself by creating values in the world. Like Sartre, de Beauvoir affirms the plasticity of human nature. Both claim there is no fixed human essence because human existence precedes essence. Thus, de Beauvoir argues there is no such thing as a feminine nature as the biological and psychoanalytic perspectives maintain. What is assumed to be feminine nature is actually a social construction, not a fixed essence. Hence her famous claim:

> One is not born, but rather becomes, a woman. No biological, psychological or economic fate determines the figure that the human female presents in society; it is civilization as a whole that produces the creature.[47]

Woman as the Other is a product of society. More specifically, she is the product of male-dominated society. With the invention of the bronze tool, man was able to use his superior physical strength to clear forests, cultivate fields. He acted independently to transform nature, to transcend the givens of the world as he found it, often risking his life in the process. In pursuing such projects man achieved a certain self-realization. He was the subject of his projects. His actions were essential to their success. Woman, however, did not participate in his efforts of transcendence. She was not essential to them. She was not active in them. She was dependent on him. Instead of pursuing projects of transcendence, she was caught up in the immanence of her biological functions of pregnancy and childbirth. She was caught up in the doing of monotonous, repetitive household tasks. Thus, man became the Subject and she his Other.

> A woman keeps busy, but she doesn't *do* anything. She is not recognized as an individual through her functions as a wife, mother, housekeeper. The reality of man is in the houses he builds, the forests he clears, the sick people he cures. But a woman, unable to fulfill herself through projects and goals, is forced to find her reality in the immanence of her person.[48]

To liberate herself, then, woman must pursue her own projects of transcendence. She must seek economic independence. Further, such independence is possible only if woman's biological functions are consciously regulated via birth control methods.

Such is the existentialist foundation of de Beauvoir's view of the oppression of woman.

From this perspective she conducts an exhaustive analysis of women's experience ranging over the fields of history, sociology, anthropology, literary criticism, and comparative anatomy. She examines the life cycle and life changes of woman in intimate detail, as well as the history of women's efforts to change their lot. From housework and childcare to substandard wages, to frigidity and lesbianism, she describes the innumerable ways in which women are victims of sexist attitudes and practices.

When it was published in 1949, *The Second Sex* was received with shock and outrage and provoked a backlash of sexist vulgarity against the author. François Mauriac, the conservative critic, simultaneously condemned the work as pornography and exclaimed in private that "[de Beauvoir's] vagina has no secrets for me."[49] Her friend Camus accused de Beauvoir of "making the French male look ridiculous."[50] The Catholic Church predictably put the book on its index of forbidden reading, while Communist critics considered it a misleading diversion from the class struggle and argued that the advent of socialism would eliminate the "woman problem." In 1949 Beauvoir agreed that woman's hope for equality ultimately lay with the socialist cause, but the Soviet model was not encouraging, and what was one to do until the Revolution?

Feminism, of course, was not a new perspective in postwar Europe. Advocates of women's equality and women's rights have existed through the ages. Indeed, a modern tradition of feminism emerged in Europe in the late 18th century and developed in the 19th century in both liberal and socialist directions.[51] The victory of the women's suffrage movements for formal political equality in the early 20th century culminated this first great wave of feminism. With the publication of *The Second Sex* in 1949, de Beauvoir both anticipated and helped to lay the foundation for a new wave of feminism that followed in the wake of May 1968 (see Chapter 9) and radically questioned not just political inequality but every aspect of women's oppression. Her book is widely recognized, even by critics, as "the most important, the most forceful vindication of women's rights to have appeared in the 20th century."[52]

4. *Les Temps Modernes and Existentialist Politics*

In October 1945 Sartre, Simone de Beauvoir, Maurice Merleau-Ponty and several others founded the review, *Les Temps Modernes*. Throughout the postwar period it was a beacon of independent, critical, leftist, social thought. Under Sartre's direction this journal served as the essential point of reference for non-communist intellectuals of the existentialist left. Almost all of Sartre's important work appeared initially between its covers. During the first eight years of its existence, Merleau-Ponty was its political editor, and Camus and de Beauvoir regularly wrote articles on a broad range of subjects. *Les Temps Modernes* thus proved to be the unofficial theoretical organ of the existentialist "party."[53]

In the first issue Sartre attempted to define the theoretical orientation of the review and consequently the social responsibility of intellectuals: "To sum it up, our intention is to participate in bringing forth certain changes in our society...Without being materialist...we want to side with those who want to change both the social condition of a man and his conception of himself."[54] To achieve this goal intellectuals needed a different conception of their own role than the commonly accepted ones. Traditionally, intellectuals regarded abstention from social concerns as the only way of maintaining their intellectual purity. But, Sartre argues, intellectuals are not above the affairs of society nor are they members of a quasi-monastic order divorced from temporal considerations. "For us, the writer is neither a Vestal nor an Ariel. He is 'in the thick of it'; whatever he does has far-reaching consequences."[55] The intellectual must accept this social responsibility not just as any other private citizen, but as one with greater opportunity to affect public opinion:

> The writer is *situated* in his time. Every word has consequences. Every silence, too. I hold Flaubert and Goncourt responsible for the repression which followed the Commune because they did not write one line to prevent it. One might say that it was not their business. But was the Calas trial Voltaire's business? Dreyfus' condemnation Zola's? the administration of the Congo, Gide's? Each of these authors, in a special circumstance of his life, measured his responsibility as a writer. The Occupation taught us ours.[56]

Thus the intellectual must be *engagé*, a committed advocate of a certain conception of the individual. The conception to which *Les Temps Modernes* commits itself is, of course, the existentialist view that "the person is nothing else but his freedom."[57]

The general political orientation of the journal emerged as a leftist critique of the "Resistance betrayed." For many of the *résistentialistes* expected an apocalyptic socialist revolution to follow the Liberation of 1944. When their hopes were shattered by *tripartisme*, they blamed the PCF for disarming the F.F.I. (Resistance guerrilla units) and pursuing the parliamentary, legalistic road to power instead of armed revolution.[58] Thus the journal pursued a double thrust reminiscent of *Socialisme et Liberté*. As Sartre put it, "We must militate in our writings in favor of the freedom of the person *and* the socialist revolution. It has often been claimed that they are not reconcilable. It is our job to show tirelessly that they imply each other."[59]

It was in accordance with this conception of *engagement* that Sartre participated in 1948 in the founding of the *Rassemblement Démocratique Révolutionnaire* (RDR). Sartre conceived of the RDR as a movement (as opposed to a heirarchical political party) which would be revolutionary in opposition to the reformism of the mainline socialists[60] and democratic in opposition to the dictatorial thrust of the communists. Its goal was "to rediscover the great democratic tradition of revolutionary socialism."[61] Sartre envisioned a united, democratic, and socialist Europe as an intermediary force or "third way" between the Cold War superpowers. He also hoped the RDR would provide a practical solution to the theoretical "third way" he sought between idealism and materialism, between individual freedom and social responsibility: "the old conflict between individualism and society is one that RDR members take as transcended...our aim is the integration of the free individual in a society conceived as the unity of the free activities of individuals."[62]

The RDR was launched in the early part of 1948 by a group of left-wing journalists from various Resistance-inspired newspapers and reviews. Sartre and David Rousset, a former trotskyist, were its top leaders. In February 1948, a manifesto proclaiming the founding of the RDR was distributed in Paris and published by *Combat* and *France-Tireur*. It read in part, "Between the rottenness of capitalist democracy and the weaknesses and flaws of a certain kind of social democracy and the limitations of communism in its Stalinist form, we think that a party of free men is capable of giving new life to the principles of freedom and human dignity by relating them to the struggle for social revolution."[63] In

March, Sartre and Rousset held a press conference and organized a public meeting (attended by one thousand people) at which Sartre spoke. An organization newspaper, *La Gauche*, was also launched that month. Sartre and Merleau-Ponty opened the columns of *Les Temps Modernes* to the RDR as did the editors of *Combat* (Claude Bourdet and Albert Camus) and *France-Tireur* (George Altman and Bernard Lefort).

After having rejected the stalinist version of marxism (in "Materialism and Revolution") Sartre now set out in RDR to synthesize his existentialism and the marxism of *The Paris Manuscripts* with its concept of alienation.

> ...Man, as Marx said, is in a state of alienation; that is he does not possess his own destiny, his own life, his own work; the ideas he has are not formed directly by him...We desire concurrently to deliver him on the ideological level of his mystifications that prejudice the democratic exercise of his freedom and on the social level, of all forms of exploitation that make him an alienated man.[64]

But a politics devoted to rooting out alienation proved to be premature in the late 1940s. It wasn't until the 1960s that a social base for such a new left politics emerged.

Because the RDR was conceived of as a loose "gathering" instead of a disciplined political party, hope for success depended on a mass appeal which never materialized. In practice the RDR appealed primarily to a few dissident members and factions of other leftist organizations. Aside from the journalists, some left-wing members of the Section Française Internationale d'Ouvrière (S.F.I.O) joined as well as some members of Jeune Republique (a Christian leftist organization), and Rousset's former trotskyist followers. Instead of a mass movement, another splinter sect was appended to the French left.

However, the RDR was not completely ineffectual. Five thousand people attended an RDR sponsored "day of studies" in which Sartre, Camus, de Beauvoir, André Breton, Richard

Wright, and Carlo Levi participated. In January 1949 the RDR's Indochina peace petition was successful in gathering thousands of signatures, showing for the first time that a significant portion of French public opinion opposed the Indochina War.

Sartre's relations with the PCF reached an all time low during his association with the RDR. Not only was Sartre trying to recruit the party membership to another organization, but this occurred at the same time as the first run in Paris of his play, *Dirty Hands*, which the French right adored. The murder in the play of Hoederer, the party leader, by a member of a dissident party faction was interpreted as similar to the crimes imputed to Stalin. In fact, this is not what Sartre intended. Nevertheless, the communists took it as anti-Soviet propaganda. "For thirty pieces of silver and a mess of American pottage, Jean-Paul Sartre has sold out what remained of his honor and probity," was the opinion of one communist review of the play.[65] The PCF sent militants to picket the theaters when a film version was released. They continually repeated the refrain that Sartre was an intellectual *flic* (cop) and an agent of Wall Street and world capitalism. The successful RDR "day of studies" they attacked as "an anti-Soviet meeting organized by a clique of intellectuals whose showy generalities and literary slogans scarcely dissimulate a deliberate acceptance of the capitalist regime."[66]

In fact, there was a legitimate basis for the PCF hostility to the RDR. Rousset was moving further and further to the right and taking the organization with him. His pro-Americanism became so pronounced that the U.S. Embassy and the communist-purged U.S. labor federation (C.I.O.) supported and participated in an RDR "International Day for Resistance to Dictatorship and War," on 30 April 1949. Essentially this was an attempt to upstage and embarrass the annual communist May Day celebrations scheduled for the next day. Sartre opposed this move and for several months he fought to reverse this trend and preserve RDR's neutralism. But his efforts came to no avail. In October 1949 he officially resigned from the organization and soon after, it collapsed. Sartre later wrote on the RDR's failures, "Circumstances merely seemed to be favorable to the association. It answered an abstract need defined by the objective situation but not any real need among the people. Consequently they did not support it."[67]

For Sartre and his fellow existentialists at *Les Temps Modernes* a period of political confusion followed the collapse of the RDR. The revelations concerning the existence of a widespread system of forced labor camps in the Soviet Union, followed by the outbreak of the Korean War, pushed Sartre toward political fellow-traveling with the PCF. (Simone de Beauvoir in her novel *The Mandarins* presents a moving fictional account of how the Soviet labor camp issue affected the personal lives and political convictions of those in her milieu.) In January 1950, Sartre and Merleau-Ponty jointly signed an editorial in *Les Temps Modernes* on the Soviet labor camp issue admitting that it "placed the whole meaning of the Russian system in doubt."[68] After much soul-searching, however, they decided that the circumstances of the Cold War required support for the Soviet Union:

> The USSR is on the whole, situated, in the balance of powers, on the side of those who are struggling against the forms of exploitation known to us. The decadence of Russian Communism does not make the class struggle a myth, "free enterprise" possible or desirable, or the Marxist criticism in general null and void.[69]

But even more than the camps, the Korean War pushed Sartre politically closer to the PCF. It was true that North Koreans attacked first. The communists only discredited themselves by lying about this. But in Sartre's view the attack was a trap set by MacArthur into which the North Korean Army fell after being taunted by a series of border provocations. Further, Sartre argued, the American troops were ruthlessly murdering Korean peasants and burning their villages and crops. Thus, he saw the Korean War in the same way that many people viewed the Vietnam War a generation later: an overwhelming case of racist, almost genocidal, aggression by the U.S. government. By 1952 he was ready to ally with the PCF.

This alliance was cemented in the aftermath of the Ridgeway "riots."[70] The PCF organized a militantly provocative demonstration against the U.S. general, Ridgeway, who had come to Paris on 28 May 1952 fresh from the Korean War zone. The French government brutally repressed the demonstration, seized the communist newspapers, and raided PCF offices throughout the country. French police arrested every party leader they could find, including Jacques Duclos, who as a senator supposedly had parliamentary immunity. Duclos had two dinner squab in his car at the time of his arrest and was ludicrously accused of intending to use them as carrier pigeons to send secret communiques to Stalin! The PCF called on the workers to protest in the form of a one day general strike, which did not materialize. Ignoring the implications of the government's repressive measures, a number of leftist dissidents, hoping to find a following of their own in the working class, expressed pleasure in the fact that the workers did not heed the call of the Party.

Sartre was in Italy at the time, but he quickly returned to Paris and worked night and day on a series of articles in defense of the PCF. He later wrote: "These sordid childish tricks turned my stomach. There may have been more ignoble ones but none more revealing. An anti-communist is a rat. I couldn't see any way past that and I never will...After ten years of ruminating, I had come to the breaking point, and only needed that one straw. In the language of the Church, this was my conversion."[71]

In the series of articles, *The Communists and Peace*, Sartre allied himself unconditionally with the PCF.[72] He argued that the Party is the necessary and exact expression of the working class: "The working class still recognizes itself in the forced trials which the Party institutes in its name."[73] To the non-communist left he warned that destruction of the

Party would be a blow against the working class and humanity in general. "We cannot go against the working class without becoming the enemy of mankind and of oneself...and at all costs we must not count on the liquidation of the Communist Party."[74]

Thus Sartre's conversion was unequivocal. For all intents and purposes he had joined the Party without taking out a membership card. Although he embraced the Party on his own terms, he could not do so on its terms. Isolated as it was, the PCF was not in a position to quibble. The Party accepted Sartre's support without asking him to endorse stalinism, even though some of his now former friends (Camus, Merleau-Ponty) believed this was exactly what he was doing, Sartre averred. In was a question of laying idealism to rest: "to cease saying no to everything, to cease dreaming of a proletariat in absolute conformity with one's own wishes, to cease hoping for an ideal communism born of a few proclamations to the working class and cleansed of Stalinism." For all its evils the defeat of stalinism would be "primarily a defeat of the workers and only secondarily of Stalinism."[75]

In addition to the political consequences of *The Communists and Peace*, Sartre began to develop in this series of articles the historical and social categories of theory which he eventually set forth in the *Critique*. The ahistorical framework of *Being and Nothingness* is discarded in favor of the historical conditioning of individual action: "The historical whole determines our powers at any given moment, it prescribes their limits in our field of action and our *real* future; it conditions our attitude toward the possible and the impossible, the real and the imaginary, what is and what should be."[76] History is granted its full weight, but within its limitations the freedom of the individual to create oneself is preserved. This concept is given full elaboration in the *Critique*.

Sartre also begins to develop his social categories. In analyzing the working class, he argues that the individual worker cannot achieve authentic freedom without the situation of his entire class being transformed. Yet serious social obstacles block the path of such a transformation, chief among them being the atomization of the working class itself. In the *Critique* Sartre develops this insight into his later concept of serialization.

Fellow-traveling with the PCF cost Sartre the friendship of Albert Camus and Maurice Merleau-Ponty. Sartre interpreted Camus' *The Rebel* (1951) as denying any meaning to history and social commitment. He felt that Camus, philosopher of the absurd and former Resistance activist, was advocating a retreat into art as an individual solution to the absurdity of human existence. In a review published in *Les Temps Modernes*, Sartre's protégé, Francis Jeanson, sharply attacked these assertions.[77] Sartre himself rebuked Camus:

> The problem is not to ask whether history makes sense or not, and whether we should deign to take part in it or not; we are in it up to our necks one way or the other. The problem is to try to give it the meaning which seems to us most right...it is idle to debate whether there are values which transcend history: if there are, they are those which manifest themselves in what men do, in human actions.[78]

Sartre distorted Camus' position, for Camus did not give up his social commitment. Even so, Sartre was able to reaffirm in a somewhat different context his principle that the meaning of human freedom is found *in* history and through social commitment.

In 1945 Merleau-Ponty was much closer to the marxism of the communists than Sartre. He even wrote a book in 1947, *Humanism and Terror*, defending the Soviet Union to the point of justifying Stalin's purge trials. As political editor of *Les Temps Modernes* he tried to win Sartre closer to marxism. Ironically, as Sartre's political thought came closer to marxism his own drifted away. Sartre's "conversion" came just when Merleau-Ponty was having his most serious doubts. By the summer of 1953, it was obvious they were moving in opposite political directions so Merleau-Ponty found a pretext and resigned from *Les Temps Modernes*. In *The Adventures of the Dialectic* (1955) he subjected Sartre's "ultra-bolshevism" to a thorough critique. In an intricate fashion he took apart *The Communists and Peace* showing that at bottom it was built on the shaky foundations of an existentialist ontology sagging under the weight of stalinist politics. Although there were several polemical rebuttals forthcoming, Sartre took the criticism seriously and incorporated much of it into his later *Critique*.[79]

From 1952 to 1956 Sartre marched side-by-side with the PCF. Occasional disagreements did not mar the real friendship that developed. Sartre and Jacques Duclos shared the speaker's platform at public meetings. *L'Humanité*, the PCF newspaper, reported favorably on Sartre's activities and writings. Sartre, on his part, joined the Soviet-led World Peace Movement, spoke at the Vienna World Congress for Peace (November 1952), reported favorably on his visit to the Soviet Union, became an officer of the Franco-Soviet Friendship Association, and forbade a revival of his play *Dirty Hands* because of the bad memories it recalled.

This honeymoon lasted until the 1956 Soviet invasion of Hungary. In an article published in *L'Express* Sartre condemned the invasion: "From every point of view the intervention was a crime. It is an abject lie to pretend that the workers are fighting side by side with Soviet troops. The Red Army opened fire on an entire nation."[80]

5. Sartre and the Origins of the French New Left

The Hungarian invasion brought about an important change for Sartre. He broke completely with his communist friends and the stalinist view which assumed the Soviet Union was the only hope in the world for progressive change. In *The Ghost of Stalin* (1956), Sartre sought to uncover the reasons for the invasion in a socio-historical analysis of Soviet and East European socialism. But more importantly he sought to analyze the political potential in France of the PCF.

Consider this monstrous Party which blocks and freezes five million voices, demobilizes the working class, abandons the interests of the masses for parliamentary maneuvers, lightly denounces Algeria in order to threaten the socialists, quite in vain, but at the same time does not hesitate to rationalize its contempt with stupid declarations about the situation in Hungary...Alliance with the Communist Party as it is and intends to remain can have no other effect that compromising our last chances for a common front.[81]

With the socialists condoning torture and massacre in Algeria and the communists applauding this Soviet intervention, Sartre could only conclude that the plight of the established left in France was hopeless.[82] While this was no cause for joy, it nevertheless freed Sartre to take the political and theoretical initiative to revitalize marxism. His effective protests against the Algerian War in the late 1950s and early 1960s earned him the respect of the disrespectful youth (and almost got him killed by the O.A.S.!).[83] Thus the emerging new left student movement began to look to *Les Temps Modernes* and Sartre for political and theoretical direction.

The break with the old left also freed Sartre to pursue an independent approach to marxism. The theoretical advances toward marxism he made over the years had been very uneven and undeveloped. Freed from his pro-stalinist political practice and PCF frame of reference, he was able to develop his systematic synthesis of marxism and existentialism that was so crucial to new left social theory: the *Critique de la raison dialectique.*

Notes

1. The essential starting point in secondary Sartre bibliography is François and Clair Lapointe's, *Jean-Paul Sartre and His Critics: An International Bibliography (1938-1975),* (Bowling Green, 1975). This work lists literally over 5000 titles of books, articles, dissertations, etc., on Sartre and his works! Sartre's more than 75 volumes of writings have yet to be collected in a single edition. The best primary bibliographic source on

Sartre's writings is *Les Ecrits de Sartre* (Paris, 1970). In year-by-year order (1923-1969) this work gives an annotated list of over 500 separate publications by Sartre.

2. French Existentialism is, of course, a broad intellectual movement representing all sorts of political and cultural views. While Sartre is an atheistic leftist, Gabriel Marcel, for example, is a religious rightist. Due to the nature of this study we will only be concerned with the existentialist left.

3. *On a raison de se révolter* (Paris, 1974), p. 27. In the conversations presented in this volume with two French new leftists, Phillippe Gavi and Pierre Victor, Sartre gives us his self-interpretation of his political development. See also Michel-Antoine Burnier's *Choice of Action*, trans. by B. Murchland (New York, 1968), and Rossana Rossanda's, "Sartre's Political Practice," *Socialist Register* (London, 1975), pp. 48-74 for sympathetic accounts of his political activity.

4. Simone de Beauvoir, Sartre's lifelong companion, recounts these and other events in Sartre's life during the 1930s in *The Prime of Life*, trans. by R. Howard (New York, 1960). This is the second volume of her four volumes of autobiographical memoirs. It covers the period 1929-1944, and is one of the best available sources for biographical material on Sartre for this period. The best actual biography is Francis Jeanson's *Sartre dans sa vie* (Paris, 1974).

5. Sartre, *On a raison... op. cit.*, p. 28. See also de Beauvoir *op. cit.*, pp. 396-397.

6. Sartre's performance as Balthasar was so "sincere, ardent, and burning with faith" that it supposedly converted an atheist doctor to religious belief. *Le Figaro Litteraire*, 26 March 1960.

7. Sartre, *Being and Nothingness: An Essay in Phenomenological Ontology*, trans. by Hazel Barnes (New York, 1966), p. 30.

8. *Ibid.*, p. 784.

9. In this respect I agree with Mark Poster's thesis in his excellent study, *Existential Marxism in Post-War France* (Princeton, 1975).

10. "Any study of human reality must begin with the Cogito." Sartre, *op. cit.*, p. 84.

11. Here is where the influence of Husserl and Heidegger is evident. An excellent study of the impact of these two on Sartre is Ronald Aronson's, "Interpreting Husserl and Heidegger: The Root of Sartre's Thought," *Telos*, no. 13 (Fall, 1972), pp. 47-67.

12. Sartre, *op. cit.*, pp. 340-399.

13. Many of his examples of social relations are drawn from disquieting and disturbing or even deviant situations—e.g., a man is caught peeping through a keyhole and feels shame when confronted with "the look of the Other." *Ibid.*, pp. 347-354. On the other hand, marxists tend to view social

relations as rooted in relations of production and class conflict—allowing for positive social relations *within* the working class. Thus, they tend to be more optimistic than the early Sartre, who perceived individual conflict as the essence of all social relations.

14. Sartre, *No Exit and Three Other Plays*, trans. by Lionel Abel (New York, 1949), p. 47.

15. Sartre, "A Propos de l'existentialisme, mise au point," *Action*, 17 (29 December 1944), p. 11. Sartre wrote this article in response to a request from the editors of *Action* (a communist Resistance journal) who asked him to clarify his views and their relation to marxism.

16. Sartre, *Situations III* (Paris, 1949), pp. 11-13. Trans. and edited by Robert Cumming in *The Philosophy of Jean-Paul Sartre* (New York, 1966), pp. 233-234.

17. See Werth, *op. cit.*, and Tiersky, *op. cit.*

18. See, for example, Roger Garaudy's *Literature of the Graveyeard*, trans. by J. Berstein (New York, 1948).

19. On the internal debate within the PCF on Sartre's existentialism see Edgar Morin, *Autocritique* (Paris, 1959), pp. 83-86; and Dominique Desanti, *Les Staliniens: une expérience politique* (Paris, 1975), pp. 5, 22.

20. Henri Lefebvre, "Existentialisme et Marxisme: réponse à une mise au point," *Action*, 40 (8 June 1945), p. 8. Heidegger's brief membership (in 1933) in the Nazi Party hurt his intellectual reputation for many years after the war.

21. Lefebvre, *L'Existentialisme* (Paris, 1946), p. 113. In an interesting section on the history of the *Philosophies* group, of which he was a member, Lefebvre claimed that he had discovered existentialism in the 1920s long before Sartre! In 1946 he considered it an immature stage of adolescent rebellion on his way toward the "mature" thought of marxism.

22. *Ibid.*, p. 227.

23. *Ibid.*, p. 249.

24. *Ibid.*, p. 82.

25. See, for example, Henri Mougin, *La Sainte famille existentialiste* (1947); Jean Kanapa, *L'Existentialisme n'est pas un humanisme* (1947); G. Mounin, "Position de l'existentialisme," *Les Cahiers d'action*, 2 (May, 1946); Pierre Hervé, "Conscience et connaissance," *Les Cahiers d'action*, 2 (May 1946); V. Leduc, *Le Marxisme, est-il dépassé?* (Paris, 1946); R. Garaudy, *Le Communisme et la morale* (Paris, 1947). Georg Lukacs' *Existentialisme ou Marxisme* (1948) was also important in the French debate because of his international stature as the world's most distinguished communist intellectual.

26. Garaudy, *op. cit.*, p. 61.

27. See Kanapa, *op. cit.* Lefebvre, for his part, characterized Sartre's thought as "the magic and metaphysics of shit," and called his novel,

Nausea, the manifesto of the pederast! *Op. cit.*, pp. 82, 221.

28. Even Merleau-Ponty, a friend and fellow existentialist, criticized Sartre for concentrating too much on extreme situations and not taking into account the "inter-world" of relations. See his *Phenomenology of Perception* (1945), trans. by C. Smith (London, 1962).

29. Sartre, "Existentialism is a Humanism," in *Existentialism: From Dostoevsky to Sartre*, ed. by W. Kaufmann (New York, 1956), pp. 287-312. This is the lecture in which Sartre gave the now classic definition of existentialism as the philosophy for which "existence precedes essence," p. 289.

30. *Ibid.*, p. 288.

31. *Ibid.*, p. 305.

32. *Ibid.*, p. 299.

33. *Idem.*

34. Sartre, "Materialism and Revolution," in his *Literary and Philosophical Essays* (New York, 1967), p. 214.

35. *Ibid.*, p. 221.

36. *Ibid.*, p. 251.

37. While Sartre did not consciously limit his study to the male sex, de Beauvoir was one of the first theorists to note that the use of masculine terms to refer to all human beings reflected a deeply ingrained unconscious assumption that "humanity is male" and that women are somehow less as human beings. In this book I have generally attempted to avoid such usage except where necessary for a faithful rendering of a particular theorist's work.

38. See de Beauvoir, *The Prime of Life, Volume I.*

39. Simone de Beauvoir, *The Second Sex*, (New York, 1953), pp. xvi-xvii.

40. *Ibid.*, p. xvii.

41. *Ibid.*, p. xxviii.

42. *Ibid.*, p. xvi.

43. *Ibid.*, p. 47.

44 *Ibid.*, p. 52.

45. *Ibid.*, p. 53.

46. *Ibid.*, p. 47.

47. *Ibid.*, p. 249.

48. *Ibid.*, p. 353.

49. De Beauvoir, *The Prime of Life, op. cit.* See pp. 185-193 for a discussion of the reaction to *The Second Sex*.

50. *Ibid.*, p. 190.

51. For a history of feminism see Sheila Rowbotham, *Women, Resistance, and Revolution* (London, 1972).

52. R. Cottrel, *Simone de Beauvoir* (New York, 1975).

53. Initially the committee of directors also included Raymond Aron, Michel Leiris, Albert Ollivier, and Jean Paulhon. Malraux was asked but refused to participate. Camus declined because of his responsibilities as editor of *Combat*. As the initial basis of unity was the Resistance and anti-fascism, splits developed very quickly with Aron and Ollivier going over to Gaullism. See Burnier, *op. cit.*, pp. 19-20.

54. "Introduction," *Les Temps Modernes* 1 (October 1945), trans. by Françoise Ehrmann and reprinted in *Paths to the Present*, edited by Eugen Weber (New York, 1962), p. 435.

55. *Ibid.*, p. 433.

56. *Ibid.*, p. 434.

57. *Ibid.*, p. 441.

58. The sub-title of Albert Camus' Resistance newspaper *Combat* captured this expectation: *De la Résistance à la Révolution*.

59. "Introduction," *op. cit.*, p. 435.

60. Sartre, *What is Literature?*, trans. by B. Frechtman (New York, 1952), p. 191. Appeared originally in 1947 in *Les Temps Modernes*.

61. After the Popular Front the socialists of the SFIO (Section Française Internationale Ouvrière) were seriously compromised. One commentator claims, "the SFIO had no appeal for a radical intellectual." Rossanda, *op. cit.*, p. 55.

62. Sartre, *Entretiens sur la politique* (Paris, 1949). These discussions originally appeared in 1948 in *Les Temps Modernes*.

63. *Ibid.*, p. 133.

64. *Combat*, 27 February 1948.

65. *Entretiens*, *op. cit.*, p. 39.

66. De Beauvoir, *Force of Circumstance*, trans. by R. Howard (New York, 1964), p. 151 ff. gives details of this episode.

67. *L'Humanité*, 15 December 1948.

68. Unpublished notes of Sartre, cited by de Beauvoir, *op. cit.*, p. 177.

69. Sartre and Merleau-Ponty, "Les Jours de notre vie," *Les Temps Modernes* 51 (January 1950), pp. 1153-1168; in Merleau-Ponty's *Signs*, trans. by R. McCleary (Evanston, 1964) as "The USSR and the Camps," p. 264.

70. *Ibid.*, p. 269.

71. Sartre got this information from the battlefield reporting of I. F. Stone.

72. Sartre, *L'Affaire Henri Martin* (Paris, 1953).

73. On the communist demonstrations against General Ridgeway, see Werth, *op. cit.*, pp. 575-586.

74. Sartre, "Merleau-Ponty," in *Situations*, trans. by Benita Eisler (New York, 1965), p. 287.

75. Sartre, *The Communists and Peace*, trans. by M. Fletcher and P. Beak (New York, 1968). These articles originally appeared in the following issues of *Les Temps Modernes*: 81 (July 1952), 84-86 (October-November 1952), and 101 (April 1954).

76. *Ibid.*, p. 49.

77. *Ibid.*, p. 6.

78. *Ibid.*, p. 134.

79. *Ibid.*, p. 80.

80. Jeanson, "A. Camus, ou l'âme révoltée," *Les Temps Modernes* 79 (June 1952). Note the date of this article is simultaneous with the Ridgeway affair.

81. Sartre, "Reponse à Albert Camus," *Les Temps Modernes* 82 (August 1952), pp. 334-353, trans. by Eisler in *Situations*, pp. 54-78; 77.

82. See de Beauvoir's "Merleau-Ponty et le pseudo-Sartrisme," *Les Temps Modernes* 114-115 (June-July 1955). Also the communist intellectuals defended Sartre against Merleau-Ponty. See Garaudy, *et al.*, *Mésaventures de l'anti-marxisme* (Paris, 1956).

83. *L'Express*, 9 November 1956.

84. Sartre, *The Ghost of Stalin*, trans. by M. Fletcher (New York, 1968), p. 29. This work originally appeared as "Le Fantôme de Staline," *Les Temps Modernes*, 129, 130, 131 (November, December 1956 and January 1957).

85. As Francis Jeanson put it, "Our point of reference is the impotence of the Left," in "Lettre à Jean-Paul Sartre," *Les Temps Modernes* 169-170 (April-May, 1960), p. 1537.

86. *Les Temps Modernes* was seized by the government four times during the Algerian War for exposing the widespread use of torture and urging French Army draftees to insubordination and desertion. Sartre and de Beauvoir were threatened with prison for protecting and aiding the "Jeanson network" of anti-war agitators. See Burnier, *op. cit.*, pp. 113-135. During the Algerian War Sartre held up Paul Nizan to the youth of France as embodying the spirit of revolt. "His life was exemplary because it was an outrage." *Situations*, p. 172.

/3/
Sartre's Critique of Marxism

1. Introduction: Marxism and Existentialism

While Sartre's entire life work may be considered a critique of marxism, his *Critique of Dialectical Reason* (and its prefatory volume, *Search for a Method*) represents a rigorous systematic effort on his part to revitalize marxism by pinpointing the sources of its problems and providing it with an ontological foundation.[1] Many critics have scoffed at the possibility of such a project, claiming that the subjective, individualistic orientation of Sartre's existentialism is incompatible with the objectivist, societal orientation of marxism.[2] However, Sartre does not attempt a reconciliation of immutable contraries as these critics suggest. Rather, he tries to establish a common grid for interpreting mutually complementary levels of human experience.[3] For him, marxism is a way of understanding the objective dimension of human history from the perspective of the results of human action; existentialism is a way of understanding the subjective individual lived experience *within* the general framework that marxism provides. "We were convinced," says Sartre, "*at one and the same time* that historical materialism furnished the only valid interpretation of history and that existentialism remained the only concrete approach to reality." (*Search*, 21)[4] The apparent contradiction in this position stemmed from the unwillingness of orthodox marxism to account for the experience of the individual in other than a superficial manner. For Sartre, this weakness meant that marxism had stopped short of fulfilling its role of developing into a total living philosophy.

Sartre's primary intellectual interest in marxism is, indeed, that of the philosopher: the philosopher rooted in the historical tradition of Descartes, Hume, Kant, Hegel, and Marx. In many respects, Sartre can be considered one of the last of a breed, the breed of great traditional philosophers.[5] For Sartre clearly believes that philosophy is the fundamental domain of Truth, Reality, and Knowledge. From this point of view, philosophy is the primary intellectual discipline, the "Queen" of the sciences from which the foundations of the natural and social sciences have been derived.

Sartre, however, does not believe there is such a thing as "philosophy-in-general." Rather there are particular philosophies which give expression to the general movement of society. As such, a philosophy is simultaneously a totalization of contemporary knowledge *and* a particular method by which the "rising class" becomes conscious of itself as the dynamic force in society. Thus philosophy is not just an abstract exercise for ivory tower recluses. It is practical. It is a political and social weapon which remains effective so long as the social dynamism with which it is associated remains active. A philosophy, then, is a particular vision of the world that is "simultaneously a totalization of knowledge, a method, a regulative Idea, an offensive weapon, and a community of language...an instrument which ferments rotten society... [and] becomes the culture and sometimes the nature of a whole class." (*Search*, 6)

Given this conception of the nature of philosophy, Sartre's overriding concern with marxism becomes evident. For Marx was the last of the great philosophical system builders. Prior to Marx, Sartre claims, there were two other great "moments" in modern philosophy: the one of Descartes and Locke (which he associates with the rising 17th century commercial bourgeoisie), the other of Kant and Hegel (associated with the rising industrial bourgeoisie). Marxism, of course, is associated with the rise of the proletariat, and since Sartre more or less takes as a first principle that the proletariat is the rising class of our epoch, it follows for him that marxism is the "philosophy of our time" ("I consider Marxism the one philosophy of our time which we cannot go beyond..." (*Search*, xxxiv) From this point of view, contemporary non-marxist and anti-marxist trends of thought do not represent new philosophies, but rather the refurbishing of pre-marxist philosophies.[6]

But marxism—the philosophy of our time, the philosophy which we cannot go beyond—is stopped. It is arrested. It is undergoing a crisis. Such a philosophical crisis represents for Sartre a social crisis, a crisis of the society which engenders the philosophy. In this case, marxism stopped developing as a philosophy because it had been subordinated to the political needs of the stalinist party leaders. Thus marxism was transformed from a living dynamic philosophy of the concrete into a static absolute *idealism*: a fixed doctrine with universal categories in which the real events of lived experience were dissolved. Thus,

> Stalinized Marxism assumes an air of immobility; a worker is not a real being who changes with the world; he is a Platonic Idea. Indeed, in Plato, the Ideas are the Eternal, the Universal, the True. Motion and the event, as confused reflections of these static forms, are outside the Truth. Plato seeks to approach them through myths. In the Stalinist world the [actual] event is an edifying myth. (*Search*, 125)

Events thus have no meaning in themselves since the stalinist mythology predetermines the meaning of all events as well as the content of all thought. Everything is determined in advance. Human reality is divided into two static spheres, good and evil. All that which is in accord with stalinist policy objectives is good (revolutionary, proletarian, progressive) while all that which is contrary to such objectives is evil (counterrevolutionary, petit-bourgeois, anti-Soviet). Thus a strike by French workers against harsh living conditions is viewed as an authentic expression of working class discontent with capitalism. But a similar strike by Polish or Hungarian workers against even harsher living conditions is interpreted as a counterrevolutionary, anti-Soviet plot against socialism. In either case the real lived experience of the workers is dissolved into the abstract universality of pre-ordained categories.

When philosophy—any philosophy—is subordinated to the level of an instrument of state policy, it degenerates into a crude systematic distortion of reality. It becomes frozen, sterile, and narrow, a scholasticism devoid of intellectual vitality. Or, as Sartre says, "the open concepts of Marxism have closed in." (*Search*, 27)

In spite of this grim fate Sartre asserts that marxism is "still young" and can recover from its "sclerosis." For the conditions which gave rise to it in the first place still prevail. "We cannot go beyond it because we have not gone beyond the circumstances which engendered it." (*Search*, 30) For so long as human beings are tied to the "yoke of scarcity," the circumstances which generate class society and class conflict will prevail. Only in some presently inconceivable future when scarcity will have been overcome for *everyone*, then "marxism will have lived out its span." (*Search*, 34)

In the meantime, existentialism seeks to "reconquer Man within Marxism." (*Search*, 83) Existentialism—which Sartre now calls an ideology, "a parasitical system living on the margin of Knowledge" (*Search*, 8)—seeks to restore the particularity of lived experience to marxism. In order to do this, Sartre finds it necessary to develop what he calls the progressive-regressive method to interpret the mediations between the particularity of lived experience and the "skeleton of universality" of the general marxist framework.

2. Mediations and the Progressive-Regressive Method

We reproach contemporary Marxism for throwing over to the side of chance all the concrete determinations of human life and for not preserving anything of historical totalization except its abstract skeleton of universality. The result is that it has entirely lost the meaning of what it is to be human. *(Search*, 82-83).

In this scathing judgment, Sartre pinpoints the problem of vulgar marxism. For him marxism is a set of guiding principles or regulative ideas and not concrete truths or ready-made knowledge. Thus he accepts, even "support(s) unreservedly" (*Search*, 33), the general framework of marxism. But as a general framework this is only the beginning of analysis, not the final product as it is for vulgar marxism. For the latter, marxism is an *a priori* method of analysis which does not derive its concepts from experience (or at least not from the experience it seeks to interpret). In fact it is a form of *idealism.* The specific form this idealism takes is that of economism or economic determinism. The significance of all historical events is reduced to the economic interests of the various social classes, while the individual participants are viewed simply as the historical agents of these classes. Sartre in no way opposes the concepts of class, class analysis, and class struggle. What he objects to is the lazy use of them. He objects to allowing them to become a brittle and stale formalism which suppresses and eliminates concrete facts and thereby distorts the lived reality. Sartre criticizes two specific examples of this approach in French marxist scholarship: Daniel Guérin's analysis of the Gironde's war policy during the French Revolution, and Roger Garaudy's analysis of the writer Valéry.[7]

Guérin claims that beneath all the republican rhetoric, the war policy of Brissot and the Girondists was actually an attempt by the French commercial bourgeoisie to move in on the markets of the British commercial bourgeoisie. Sartre objects to this analysis because it eliminates all the real human factors which conditioned the events. The individuals (e.g., Brissot, Guadet, Gensonne, Vergniaud) who carry out the action disappear in this analysis or else become nothing but the passive instruments of their class. The clearly defined political group (the Gironde) loses its reality as a political group since consciously stated political aims are discounted as mere masks to hide economic motives. What is left of the Gironde and its spokesmen? Not much.

Even more graphically, in Garaudy's analysis of Valéry, the writer and his work disappear in the very analysis which claims to illuminate them! Valéry is "situated" by an analysis of his historical period, his class and its relation to other classes, and the general state of the conflict of materialism and idealism. What emerges is a petit-bourgeoisie of the late 19th century that is threatened from above by the concentration of capital and from below by the popular movement. This accounts for the fluctuations in its social attitudes. Valéry is then considered as a particular example of the general vacillations in petit bourgeois attitudes of the time. "Valéry is a petit bourgeois intellectual, no doubt about it. But not every petit bourgeois intellectual is Valéry. The heuristic inadequacy of contemporary Marxism is contained in these two sentences." (*Search*, 56)

Again it is not the general framework of marxism to which Sartre objects. In fact, he agrees that the framework could be of valuable assistance in the two examples just given, but not as used here. The point is that vulgar marxism tends to jump immediately to the universal, reducing the dynamic process of lived totalizations to static, inert, totalities. This sort of reductionism disregards the mediating levels of human experience (e.g., in the family) between the pre-categorized individual action and the universal categories of class. "Marxism lacks any hierarchy of mediations which would permit it to grasp the process which produces the person and his product inside a class and within a given society at a given historical moment." (*Search*, 56)

This reductionist tendency deeply imbedded in marxism goes back to Engels.[8] Sartre considers it "an arbitrary limitation of the dialectical movement, an arresting of thought, a refusal to understand." (*Search*, 57) He thinks this problem can be overcome by finding *mediations*, by examining those processes and institutions which allow the individual to emerge within the general matrix of a class society conditioned by the productive forces and class conflict.

As an example of how this analysis could be achieved, Sartre gives us the first hints in his emerging study of Gustave Flaubert.[9] Vulgar marxism situates Flaubert's realism as a function of the political and social evolution of the petit-bourgeoisie of the Second Empire but discovers nothing about the author. As a landowner who lived on a *rentier* income, Flaubert is situated in the rural bourgeoisie, and the bourgeois character of his work is thereby "explained." But this fact does not explain why he became a writer, why he wrote what he did, or why his audience read him. In short, it does not deal with the real content of Flaubert's existence. Certainly Flaubert was a bourgeois, because he was born into and raised in a bourgeois family. It was in this particular family that his bourgeois class attitudes, instincts, and feelings were formed, that his particular bourgeois character was formed. Furthermore, it was as a child in this family that his project—to write—was formed, in relation to the members of his family: his mother, father, and his older brother.

Vulgar marxism claims that consciousness is formed almost exclusively in the relations of production, that is, through work experience. But such an approach ignores the fact that the young worker's character is formed first in the family during childhood. Because vulgar marxism is unwilling to investigate this dimension of consciousness-formation, psychoanalysis (i.e., Sartrean *existential* psychoanalysis) alone provides us with a framework for studying the process by which the child is socialized into a class, a society, and an historical moment through the institution of the family. Sartre argues that the traditional marxist scepticism of psychoanalysis is unwarranted. ("one would be entirely wrong in supposing that his discipline is opposed to dialectical materialism." *Search*, 60) As a method which focuses on the way the child experiences family relations in a given class, in a given society, psychoanalysis does not threaten the primacy of productive forces and productive relations as sectors of social determinants. Rather, it acts to "flesh out" the marxian "skeleton of universality." Thus, even though it has been used as an explicitly anti-marxist methodology, it is not necessary that the two be in conflict. "Existentialism believes that it can integrate the psychoanalytic method which discovers the point of insertion for man and his class—i.e., the particular family—as a mediation between the universal class and the individual." (*Search*, 62)[10]

There are other mediations as well. Human relations are not limited to economic relations and family relations. There is a multiplicity of other types of social relations. Individuals participate in groups other than work groups and family groups, for instance, residential groups, religious organizations, cultural and educational groups, social clubs. These are all areas where ideas and attitudes are developed and reinforced, where consciousness is formed. Vulgar marxism is supposed to be concerned with the formation of class consciousness. Yet it looks upon such social relations with disdain and refrains from studying their impact on class consciousness, abandoning this field of analysis to the sociologists.

Sociology, like psychoanalysis, is looked upon with suspicion by marxists. It is seen as an instrument of capitalist integration, a method of destroying class consciousness and defusing class confict, thereby maintaining bourgeois hegemony within society. Sartre agrees with some of this criticism. He claims that much sociological research is based on three sorts of false "autonomies"—an ontological autonomy, a methodological autonomy, and a reciprocal autonomy. Ontologically, many sociologists attribute a substantive thinghood to the group which they study. Thus the group takes on an existence of its own apart from the individuals who compose it. Sartre, on the other hand, denies that a group can have ontological status as an entity in and of itself.[11] It consists solely of the individuals who compose it, the relations among them, and the manifold relations of the group with other groups and individuals. Here Sartre endorses Marx's theory of "fetishism," in which collectives are shown to be not objects at all but reified relations among individuals. Methodologically, Sartre objects to the structural-functional, hyper-empiricist, and ahistorical approaches which deny the fundamental reality of dialectic and dialectical method. Finally, Sartre objects to what he considers to be the false objectivity of sociology, which either denies or fails to account for the subjectivity of the researcher.[12]

Given all these reservations Sartre maintains that sociology still provides significant mediations which are lacking in marxist analysis. He asks marxists to avail themselves of the empirical data sociologists provide and apply the dialectical method of analysis to it. Further, he admonishes them to "take into account *at the same time* the circularity of the material conditions and the mutual conditioning of the human relations established on that basis" (*Search*, 75). For marxists fail to grant relative autonomy to the different levels of social life.[13] Collectives are not mere appearances. They have a reality of their own as lived experience and follow certain genuinely autonomous dynamics within the general class framework.

This discussion of mediations essentially demonstrates for Sartre that at its heart dialectical materialism lacks a theory of subjectivity, a theory of the individual. That is why it is unable to integrate the givens of psychoanalysis and sociology. Sartre thus sets for himself the task of providing such a theory, which he calls a "concrete, structural anthropology."[14] In order to do this he finds it necessary to develop his own method: the progressive-regressive method.

The progressive-regressive method is an analytic-synthetic approach for understanding the simultaneous backward and forward movement of the temporal dimension of human action. In the regressive moment we begin with the individual—one's past, present and futural projection—and move toward an understanding of the social whole. The temporal dimension is key to this regressive understanding. For the present exists as a dynamic moment conditioned by the past and projected toward the future. The individual does not experience life as a series of ready-made discrete events. Rather, the objectification of an individual life is experienced as a process of motion across a field of instrumental possibilities, conditioned by a project.[15] The project itself is conditioned by the individual's past: one's childhood within the family and all the experiences which are involved in the process of character formation.

In a study of Flaubert, for example, we begin with a study of his childhood and his family relations. Sartre claims that one's life project is formed during childhood.[16] He further claims that in Flaubert's case, the project to write was directly a product of young Gustave's relations with his parents and older brother. "As a child, Flaubert feels that he is deprived of parental affection because of his older brother" (*Search*, 106). Sartre claims to show that Flaubert resented the success of his older brother Achille and the praise bestowed on him by the father. He eventually chose a commitment to literature as a way of rejecting his father's rejections and affirming his mother's compensations of affection. Through such a regressive analysis Sartre hopes to show *why* Flaubert became a writer and why he wrote the books he wrote. The analysis is an effort more or less to re-experience the individual lived experience. It is also a method of moving from the individual experience to the social whole, for the family opens out toward society. It is related to other families and situated in a class. Its members are also the conditioned products of their projects. The school as a socializing institution where Flaubert acts out the rejection of his father (by purposely being only an average student) also opens out toward society. The intellectual influences, the social and political attitudes of his teachers and fellow students, the political influence of the Church and the regime on education: all serve to show the unity of the social whole and the individual development.

The progressive moment starts with this social whole and works back to the individual. The marxist method in this sense is a progressive method. But it lacks the mediations which emerge through regressive analysis and it lacks the cross-references which a simultaneously progressive-regressive method can provide.

Sartre claims this method is applicable not only to the study of individual lives and events, but also to the entirety of human experience and human history. It is in essence a dialectical method and as such is capable of establishing the intelligibility of dialectical reason itself. In short, the pro-gressive-regressive method is the method of Sartre's *Critique of Dialectical Reason*. With the search for a method now completed, we can turn to the main body of the *Critique*.

3. The Dialectic

The crucial issue of Sartre's *Critique* is the validity of the dialectic—as a concept of reality and as a method for comprehending that reality. Dialectical thought is as old as Western civilization itself. From Heraclitus to Hegel this world view of human reality as a contradiction-ridden process of conflict and change has had many able proponents. Marx's materialist refashioning of this tradition had the most profound consequences. It laid the foundation for the marxian synthesis of knowledge, society, and human action. The materialist dialectic (i.e., dialectical materialism) provides the philosophical foundation for the marxist view of political, social, and economic reality. However, the dogmatization of dialectical materialism into very undialectical, fixed, static categories has revealed the fact that dialectical materialism itself does not have a rational foundation, that its criteria of intelligibility have not been clearly established.

Sartre is not questioning the validity of social scientific knowledge derived from marxist analyses, just as Kant in his *Critique of Pure Reason* did not question the validity of natural scientific knowledge.[17] Rather, he is asking (as Kant asked), how is this knowledge possible? What are the necessary and sufficient conditions for any knowledge whatsoever of human *praxis*? What is the basis of this knowledge, what is its character, and what are its limits? Sartre's entire *Critique* is concerned with answering these questions. The overall structure of the work is presented as dealing with three distinct moments of the Dialectic: 1) constituting dialectic, in which the fundamental structures constituting individual praxis are analyzed and demonstrated as carrying within them the germs of 2) anti-dialectic, the field of matter, of the practico-inert wherein praxis is reified, thwarted in its very realization giving rise to alienation, (3) the constituted dialectic, in which individual alienation is overcome in social commitment and social action, only to re-assert itself again and again.[18]

Before examining each of these moments of the Dialectic some further comments on its overall intelligibility are in order. First of all, as Sartre uses it the term "dialectic" is no mystical shibboleth enshrouded in mystery and obfuscation. It refers simply to human history, individual action, and a dynamic process of comprehending them as concretely inter-related. The term "praxis" as Sartre uses it refers to purposeful, rational human activity directed toward a goal of realization. It involves a felt need, a posited solution, and a transformation of the given situation in order to satisfy that need. The activity of praxis is a distinctly human activity as opposed to the various processes of change and transition characteristic of the world of matter. The dialectic that Sartre seeks to render intelligible is the dialectic of praxis. Thus he *limits* the scope of the dialectic in a very significant manner, which undermines the traditional marxist conception of the dialectic of nature.

Sartre denies outright the applicability of dialectic to nature.[19] Dialectic is the content of *human* experience, *human* reality, and as such we have no way of knowing whether it applies to the non-human domain of physical-chemical processes. Further, the idea of a dialectic in nature distorts our understanding of human experience. For those who advocate this idea substitute Newtonian mechanics and a mechanical materialism for a dialectical materialism. This is a chief source of the undialectical "sclerosis" of materialism characteristic of traditional marxism. In fact, it is not a valid materialism at all but a subjective dogmatic idealism since those who advocate it seek to regard *their* ideas about nature as an absolute truth.

Further, it threatens to foreclose the domain of human freedom. First, certain ideas about nature are claimed to have a superhuman validity. Then, these ideas are imposed on human reality and claimed to have originated in nature. Human reality is made dependent upon the laws of a reality outside of itself. Human history thus becomes no more than a special branch of natural history. Its *meaning* becomes dependent on a dialectic outside itself. "This external materialism imposes the dialectic as exteriority. Man's nature is found outside him in an *a priori* principle of extra-human Nature." (*CRD*, 124)[20] This is an implication which Sartre wishes to avoid, for he wants to affirm the irreducibility of human freedom. Traditional marxism, on the other hand, uses the dialectic of nature to justify a view of human beings as essentially determined by objective reality. It relegates the truth claims of human subjectivity to the status of mere phenomenal appearance. Marx once remarked, Men make history but they do so on the basis of prior conditions. Sartre's view of freedom in *Being and Nothingness* accepted the first half of this thesis while rejecting the latter half, which traditional marxism focuses on. In the *Critique* Sartre attempts to put Marx's statement back together and elucidate it. He puts forward a view of human freedom as conditioned, but nevertheless irreducible. It is a view which *must* deny the efficacy of a dialectic of nature in order to be consistent with its own dialectical logic. Of course this doesn't mean that Sartre denies any role at all to nature. The individual has a dialectical interrelationship with nature *within* its domain. It is a relationship which Sartre explores in his discussion of anti-dialectic.

If the dialectic is not operative in nature and its foundation cannot be found there, then where can it be found? For Sartre the foundation must be within the individual;[21] that is, dialectic must be self-grounded or else it is unprovable. It must be both discoverable in everyday human experience, and it must also be universal in its truth and applicability. Thus it must be *a priori*. Furthermore, since dialectical reason is its own foundation, it can only be demonstrated dialectically. That is, it must be assumed in order to be proven; its evidence must be self-evidence. But how can we show it deserves such a privileged status? It can be its own justification only if it is not just one more fact among the facts of human experience. To be its own justification, its own foundation, it must be the unifying principle for any human experience of the world whatsoever. Thus the issue becomes whether or not there is a sector of being which consists of such unifying activity.

At this point it is necessary to explain what Sartre means by the term "totalization." This is a synthesizing process by which a multiplicity is formed into a whole. It is a unity-in-the-making process. As a unifying activity dialectical reason is the general movement of totalization. It is a totalizing process which includes as an essential moment the awareness of that process. The sector of being to which it applies, then, is the ontological intelligibility of human history. Such totalization can be grasped only by dialectical reason. Analytic reason which has its own domain of intelligibility—totalities, the finished products of totalizations—is unable to grasp the living inter-relatedness of the totalizing process since its knowledge is derived from fragmenting and dissecting its object of inquiry.

What further evidence and proofs are needed to establish the intelligibility of dialectical reason? For Sartre evidence and proof cannot be established externally. The investigator him/herself is implicated in this movement of knowledge. For the subject of inquiry is the entirety of human history considered as a single, unified totalization, a process which the investigator and his/her knowledge are part of. Thus, "only a man living inside a sector of totalization can grasp the ties of interiority that unite him with the totalizing movement." (*CRD*, 142) Just as he earlier criticized certain sociologists for not taking into account the subjectivity of the investigator, Sartre now makes this subjectivity the starting point of his own analysis.[22]

> The epistemological point of departure must always be *consciousness* as apodictic certainty of itself, and as consciousness *of* some object... the object it must set itself is precisely *life*, i.e., the subjective being of the investigator in a world of Others, insofar as this being has totalized itself from birth, and will totalize itself until death... Starting from this, his own life, his understanding of his own life must lead to the denial of its singular determination in favor of a search for its dialectical intelligibility in the whole human experience. (*CRD*, 142)

The individual and individual praxis is the starting point for his study of the intelligibility of the ontological structures underlying human history. We see the importance of the progressive-regressive method. For it is a method that can be applied to the study not only of particular individuals (such as Flaubert) or complex social events (the French Revolution), but also to the whole of human history. Sartre conceives of the entire first volume of the *Critique* as a regressive investigation of the fundamental structures which allow us to grasp the intelligibility of history. As such it is *not* concerned with history proper at all: "The experiment attempted here...is not intended to be a study of the movement of history... Its goal is simply to discover and to establish dialectical rationality, that is to say, the complex play of praxis and totalization." (*CRD*, 134) Only when this task is completed will it be possible to reconstruct by use of the progressive method the actual movement of history in its full intelligibility.[24]

To sum up, the purpose of Sartre's *Critique* is to demonstrate the validity of dialectical reason by regressively analyzing the ontological structures of individual action, human history, and their inter-relatedness in a totalizing whole. It is an attempt to provide a philosophical foundation for marxist historical research which has already been completed. He argues that there is a sector or region of being (ontology) which can be made intelligible only through dialectical reason. Dialectical reason can illuminate the dynamic of individual action within the historical movement of society as the inter-related unity of praxis and totalization. This work is a critique of dialectical reason in that it attempts to specify the limits of its intelligibility. In this sense, Sartre is performing something of a mopping-up operation for Marx. Marx, the great visionary system-builder, left a lot of loose ends in the wake of his somewhat untidy, but nevertheless creative, intellectual frenzy. Sartre presents himself as sort of an intellectual janitor, tidying up the loose ends and lubricating the equipment which has become rusted and outworn under shoddy stalinist maintenance. However, we should not be misled by the self-effacing, almost Socratic humility with which Sartre approaches his task. For while it is true that he frees marxism from stalinist caricature, the end result is highly ambiguous.

4. A Social Ontology of Alienation

The ambiguity with which Sartre leaves us is immediately evident in the very categories he lays out in the *Critique*. For while they vaguely remind us of traditional marxist categories, they distinctly resemble those of *Being and*

Nothingness. In fact they represent a socialization of those categories. Man-in-the-world* of the earlier work was fundamentally characterized by a desire to fill a *lack*, an insufficiency in his being. Now he is characterized as a man of *need* confronted by a world of *scarcity*. In this context, praxis is the totalizing effort by man to overcome need, to negate it, by negating scarcity and thereby reaching fulfillment or satisfaction. This "negation of the negation" is dialectical in that it is a totalizing movement of a praxis directed toward a specific goal. Confronted with a given situation, man attempts to overcome it by reaching beyond it, by transforming it in accordance with his goal. Thus, temporality or the futural projection of human action is an essential component of praxis situated in the structures of need and scarcity.

These structures, however, are different in status. Need is an ontological structure but scarcity is not. Need is basic in the sense that in order for there to be any praxis or dialectic of praxis, man must exist, man must survive. Man is a being who carries within himself the possibility of not being. The continued existence of man depends on his ability to act upon his environment in such a way as to insure his survival. The praxis by which need is satisfied is thus fundamental to human existence.

But scarcity is not. Scarcity is universal, but it is a contingent universal. That is, it does not *have* to be. It is not necessary. It just *is*. The absurdity of human existence that was rooted in contingency in *Being and Nothingness* is now found to be rooted in the arbitrary all-pervasiveness of scarcity.

The man of need in this world of scarcity attempts to satisfy his need by transforming his given situation toward his goal, to shape his environment for his own purposes. He attempts to organize his situation around himself, unify it instrumentally as a practical field and move through it on his way to a determinate end. In this way individual praxis reveals itself as a *totalization*, as a negation of the given toward a futurally-anticipated outcome. Totalization, this unifying process, thus corresponds to what was called the project in

*See footnote 37, Chapter 2.

Being and Nothingness. (Totalities are finished projects, the outcome as separated from the process of its accomplishment.) Individual praxis as a totalization can be shown to be dialectical for it involves the double negation of need and scarcity in a unifying synthesis. (History itself then is also dialectical since it consists of the totalization of all totalizations.) But man is not alone in his confrontation with the world of materialities. Individual praxis faces not only matter but other individual praxes seeking to totalize other given situations. The *other* of *Being and Nothingness* reappears, not just as a specific other but rather as a general anonymous Other whose praxis appears in the form of counter-finality. The Other is a given as well as matter. The Other cannot be ignored. The existence of the Other is as basic as the existence of subject. The relation of individual praxis to the Other is as fundamental an ontological structure as need. This relation is that of reciprocity. It is a relation mediated by scarcity. Scarcity, that arbitrary universal insufficiency of materiality, is at the root of the individual's relation to matter (nature) and to others.

This relationship is fraught with the possibility of conflict: conflicting praxes, conflicting totalizations, and conflicting goals. It contains the threat that the other may totalize me within his praxis, or vice-versa. But this self-other dyad (of *Being and Nothingness*) is now replaced by a triad. For the self-other relation Sartre now claims is always mediated by a third person.

The example of this basic triadic relationship which Sartre gives us is very telling.[25] Sartre, the petit bourgeois writer, takes a vacation. Outside his hotel window he sees two laborers separated by a high wall. On the one side, a gardener is caring for the grounds; on the other side, a workman is repairing the street. They are engaged in their proximate, yet disconnected labors. Each of them can see Sartre but not each other. They are not aware of each other's existence. Their reciprocity is negative, purely mechanical and external. Sartre, the third, takes in the whole scene and unifies it. Their mutual ignorance presupposes a third person who knows them as so related. Not that he really "knows" them in any significant sense. His relation to each of them also is purely negative. Thus, even in the act of unifying the field of relations, the third does not establish a positive reciprocity. Rather, what is established is that reciprocity, the basic relationship between individuals, is fundamentally dispersed into a multiplicity by the actions of individuals upon matter (nature).[26]

In another example, Sartre shows us how this dispersed multiplicity thwarts the goals of individual praxis *even as they are successfully achieved*. The Chinese peasant, in struggling against scarcity, decides to expand his/her acreage by cutting down trees and clearing more land. The goal is to increase the size of the crop. In the short term this may actually happen. But other peasants decide to do likewise. Thousands of individual praxes, in fulfilling their individual goals, result in general calamity: deforestation and erosion. Instead of increasing his/her crop, the Chinese peasant finds that the praxis of other individuals returns to him/her as a counter-finality. The dispersed multiplicity of individual actions produces what Sartre calls *alterity*—that is, the meaning of the individual's action is stolen and returns misshapen and distorted. The goal is thwarted in its very realization.[27]

Thus we begin to see the ontological basis of human alienation. Man of need struggles to overcome scarcity only to have his labors turn against him because others are engaged in the same project. The arbitrary and contingent fact of scarcity is at the root of his alienation. For scarcity mediated his relation to matter and to other men. It turns worked matter, processed matter, matter which he has transformed with his own labor, into an alien force—the *practico-inert*. In the practico-inert, the objects of human labor reign over the individual who is merely a servant of one's own creations. The subject becomes the machine of the machine, and the relations among individuals become reified, dominated by the objects of their creation.

The significance of this concept of alienation is crucial to new left social theory. It implies that alienation is prior to and more fundamental than exploitation as a source of human suffering. Under capitalism, the two are bound together since the objectification of human labor in the form of goods and machines is directly appropriated by the capitalist Other. However, the abolition of exploitation does not necessarily imply the disappearance of alienation. Alienation is rooted in scarcity. Therefore, only when scarcity is overcome will alienation disappear. As we have seen, scarcity is all-pervasive, but it is not *necessary*. It is contingent. It is possible to overcome scarcity, but it will continue to shape human destiny for the forseeable future. Nevertheless, this concept of alienation and the distinction between it and exploitation is one of the major building blocks of new left social theory.

Even though it does not have ontological status, scarcity looms large in Sartre's social ontology. In addition to being the root of alienation, it creates the very *possibility* of history. Sartre claims that it was only with the collective project of transcending scarcity that history becomes possible. The substance of history consists of the deliberate social efforts to overcome scarcity. Further, the *rationality* of history (as with individual praxis) emerges as a process of totalization negating scarcity and the negative reciprocities that are constituted among individuals within its domain. It is this latter process to which we will now turn to see how individuals struggle against alienation through social commitment, only to reproduce that alienation in a different context. For as long as scarcity remains, so does alienation... *and* the struggle against it.

5. Social Being: Series and Groups

Individual praxis in the context of scarcity creates the practico-inert. In this field, social relations are atomized and fragmented. Individuals are isolated and separated. Their reciprocity is negative and external as with the gardener and the road-mender who share a common field of activity but no awareness of each other. The collectives of which society is composed are similarly built on such atomized and external reciprocity. The primary structure of such collectives is *seriality*, a structure in which individuals organize themselves negatively as an expression of the practico-intert.

For example, a group of individuals is waiting for a bus on a Parisian street corner. As bus riders they have certain common interests and goals both immediate (they use the same bus route to get to their destination) and more general (bus fares, the quality of the mass transit system, etc.). Yet, even if they wait at the same street corner for the same bus every working day, year in and year out, they nevertheless remain isolated, separated, and anonymous. If they talk to each other it is usually superficial, impersonal, idle chatter. There is almost nothing personal about such serial relations. Yet these relations are structured. When the bus arrives, those waiting queue up in the order by which each arrived at the stop. The structure of the series is thus an ordinal structure, impersonal, and quantitative. It disregards the real being of the individual and reduces him/her to just "one more," one who may, in fact, be expendable.[28]

The series is a field in which praxis is dominated by the practico-inert, a field in which the individual is dominated by the objects of one's own creation, which thereby reduce the individual to an object. It manifests itself everywhere in social activity. It is a field of powerlessness and impotence for the individual. In short, it is a field of alienation.

Even if this alienation is all-pervasive, it nevertheless is not absolute. Alienation in seriality rooted in the practico-inert is the domain of the anti-dialectic. As such, it is the second "moment" in the overall dialectical movement of reason. The constituting dialectic of individual praxis creates the anti-dialectic of the practico-inert. This latter moment is surpassed by the constituted dialectic, in which group action negates and overcomes the alienation of seriality. In the group, the negative, external reciprocity of the series is transformed into a positive, internal reciprocity, a free cooperative association of mutual recognition. The atomistic dispersal into multiplicity characteristic of the series yields to the organic solidarity of the spontaneous group-in-fusion.

Throughout his discussion of group dynamics, Sartre uses the French Revolution as his explicit model. Groups may emerge spontaneously from the series when a multiplicity of dispersed individual praxes become conscious of a vital common danger—e.g., the encirclement of Paris by the king's troops in July 1789. Each member of the crowd experienced the threat to him/herself as a threat to all others as well. An absolute reciprocity of praxis emerged as the series dissolved into the group-in-fusion. Sartre compared this group-in-the-making to what Malraux called the Apocalypse in *Man's Hope*.[29] Each saw in the other one's own project, one's own being. This reciprocity of recognition is rooted in the "third-to-third" structure of human relations (described earlier) which is now internalized. The atomization, isolation, and impersonalization characteristic of the series dissolves and is replaced by intensely personal and direct relations of free praxes. "Each individual reacts in a new fashion: not as individual or as Other, but as singular incarnation of the common person." (Cumming, 470, *Critique de la Raison Dialectique*, 391) Alienation is thereby surpassed and the freedom of the common praxis is realized. "The essential characteristic of the group-in-fusion is the sudden restoration of freedom." (Cumming, 472, *CRD*, 425) Because the reciprocity of recognition is absolute, there is no hierarchy in this structure. Absolute equality reigns. Spokespersons emerge and fade quickly for they directly express the common will. They articulate what everyone else already feels. In short, this is the most democratic structure possible and the most definitive expression of human freedom.[30]

Even in this discussion of groups and social action, the parallels of the marxian Sartre and the early Sartre are striking. The "extreme situation" of existentialism in which the truth of the human condition is revealed becomes the revolutionary upheaval in the *Critique*. The overcoming of alienation and the realization of freedom in the early Sartre was a fleeting experience of the unity of the for-itself and the in-itself. Now it is the unity of praxis and the practico-inert, and it is just as fleeting.

In order to preserve the freedom realized in the spontaneous group, it must be organized and structured. A commitment or an "oath" must be given by the members to preserve the group.[31] Also, in order to function effectively, the group needs a degree of formal organization and job specification. At this stage, some spontaneity of action is lost, but the division of labor within the group does not affect its cohesiveness. The common goal continues to outweigh the separation that emerges with the division of labor. However, the group's very efforts to realize the common goal require more and more specialization and differentiation and it is slowly transformed toward the very condition it was created to overcome—seriality.

When the organization becomes an institution, praxis shows more and more signs of being overtaken by the practico-inert. Terror arises as an instrument to prevent the dissolution of the group back into the series. It arises thus, not out of opposition to freedom, but out of opposition to seriality.

The group, as institution, undergoes a bureaucratization process as it becomes dominated by the practico-inert. A petrification of functions sets in as the group's common purpose becomes subordinated for each individual to one's own differentiated and narrow tasks. Praxis becomes exteriorized. Members become identified with their particular roles and experience their tasks as alien obligations. Group participation thereby slacks off, and a hierarchical authority emerges to insure that members perform their tasks. Alienation re-emerges as the group gradually slides back toward the series.

Human collectives traverse a dialectical path from series to groups to series and so on. But this is not to imply that the series is chronologically or historically prior to groups. They appear simultaneously in all societies. In fact such units are the basic structures of all social interaction. Society is composed of groups and series, or rather groups of groups and series of series. The larger social units—social classes, the state, etc.—are the matrices of groups or moving ensembles of groups and series.

Social classes are not monolithic substances. Rather they are historically conditioned collections of social relations. As such they are differentiated and fragmented, composed of series and groups engaged in the struggle against scarcity. On the societal level this struggle takes the form of class struggle. Groups within social classes tend to organize themselves in modern society as political parties. Because such parties are caught up in the dialectic of institutionalization and bureaucratization, they tend to distort the intentions of their members. The membership no longer has a real active participation and is reduced to the status of a constituency. The membership is serialized while the leadership acting as a group adopts an internal cohesiveness directed against the constituency experienced as Other.

A similar process occurs within state institutions. The state functions as a group dominating all the other groups and series. Its pretentions to sovereign unity over the whole of society are contradicted by its reliance on a "class apparatus." It maintains its power by manipulating the serialized mass of society through a process of "extereo-conditioning," i.e., through the use of advertising methods and new techniques of propaganda. Thus the constitutive elements of all the basic social units (classes, etc.) are the series and the group in their manifold relations of dialectical movement.

6. The Critique and New Left Social Theory

The overall vision of Sartre's *Critique* emerges as an ontologically intelligible view of history as totalization without a totalizer or a final totalization. The dialectic appears intelligible as a dialectic of praxis *in* history, but not as a dialectic *of* history. Negation remains ever-present. The structures in human existence which give rise to alienation have been analyzed and their essentiality demonstrated. The significance of individual praxis for the intelligibility of history has been preserved. The open-endedness of the dialectic and history has been rendered explicit. "Man is not a useless passion, but rather an unending passion."[32]

The significance of the *Critique* for new left social theory is evident. Sartre has provided a compelling philosophical foundation for each of the new left themes. His earlier existential view of alienation is now grounded in the socio-historical framework, and he has taken society and history into account without abandoning the primacy of individual praxis. For, the individual he considers is now the social individual, whose alienation is surpassed in social action and social commitment.

With the group-in-fusion Sartre provides new left theory with an archetype of egalitarian democracy, a philosophical foundation to the apocalyptic vision. His analysis of group formation and decomposition provides new left theory with a tool for understanding both the general phenomena of bureaucracy and the reasons why past revolutions have failed to fulfill their promise. As we shall see, Sartre's critique of marxism was to prove quite fruitful as a philosophical foundation for the emerging new left social theory.

Notes

1. *Critique de la raison dialectique (précédé de Questions de Méthode)*: *Tome I, Théorie des ensembles pratiques* (Paris, 1960). For a translation of *Questions de Méthode*, see *Search for a Method*, trans. by Hazel Barnes (New York, 1963). Translated selections from the main body of the *Critique* appear in *The Philosophy of J. P. Sartre*, ed. by R. D. Cumming (New York, 1965), pp. 415-483. Two important commentaries on the *Critique* are: Wilfred Desan, *The Marxism of J. P. Sartre* (New York, 1965) and R. D. Laing and D. G. Cooper, *Reason and Violence: A Decade*

of Sartre's Philosophy: 1950-1960 (London, 1964). A full English translation of the *Critique* has been done by Alan Sheridan-Smith, *Critique of Dialectical Reason: Theory of Practical Ensembles* (London, 1976).

2. Both conservative thinkers and orthodox marxists arrived at this conclusion in their reviews of the *Critique*. For the conservatives, see Raymond Aron, "La Lecture existentialiste de Marx," reprinted in *D'Une Sainte famille à l'autre* (Paris, 1969), pp. 29-67 and Julien Freund, "Note de la Critique de la raison dialectique de J. P. Sartre," *Archives de philosophie du droit*, 46 (July 1961), pp 219-236; for the orthodox marxists, see Lucien Sève "L'Existentialisme, peut-il être l'anthropologie du marxisme," *La Pensée*, 92 (July-August 1960), pp. 34-68, and Roger Garaudy, *Lettre ouverte à J. P. Sartre* (Paris, 1960). Aron, of course, made something of a lifework of criticizing Sartre's philosophy. In the course of this work he has demonstrated many of the problems with Sartre's thought. See his *Marxism and the Existentialists* (New York, 1969) and *History and the Dialectic of Violence* (New York, 1973).

3. An American commentator, Frederic Jameson, answers these critics in a very convincing fashion. See his *Marxism and Form: Twentieth Century Dialectical Theories of Literature* (Princeton, 1971), Chapter 4, "Sartre and History," pp. 206-305.

4. References for this and all subsequent quotations from *Search for a Method* will be included in the text.

5. In one of his later interviews, Sartre draws a distinction between the traditional intellectual and the intellectuals of "a new type." He reluctantly, but nevertheless clearly, sees himself in the former category. See "Interview with Jean Paul Sartre," by Michel Contat and Michel Rybalka, *Le Monde Weekly*, 17-23 June 1971.

6. This implies that Anglo-American political philosophy is "pre-marxist" in that it is rooted in Locke's concepts of constitutionalism, private property, and individualism. Also, given this assessment of Kant and Hegel, it seems very strange that Sartre should rely so obviously on them for his refurbishing of marxism.

7. For Sartre's analysis of Guérin's *La Lutte des classes sous la première République* and Garaudy's essay on Valéry, see *Search*, pp. 35-56.

8. Sartre appears to hold Engels responsible for much of the reductionist and deterministic tendencies within marxism. As we will see later he is particularly opposed to the concept of a dialectic of nature which Engels introduced into marxism.

9. For Sartre's Flaubert study see his *L'Idiot de la famille* (Paris, 1971-), of which three volumes have already been published and a fourth is in preparation.

10. The debate on psychoanalysis among independent German marxists (Reich, Fromm, Marcuse, and the entire Frankfurt School movement) developed much earlier and in much more depth than in France where the reigning stalinist orthodoxy among marxist intellectuals smothered the

possibility of such a debate until Sartre opened it up with these volleys in *Search*.

11. This denial of ontological status is crucial to Sartre's concept of the group which he develops in the main body of the *Critique*. For it is from the conflict of the necessity and the simultaneous impossibility of thinghood that the dialectic of the group unfolds.

12. For a broadly similar critique of sociology by an early American new left theorist, see C. Wright Mills, *The Sociological Imagination* (New York, 1959).

13. Considering the eventual convergence of their views it is interesting that Sartre cites Henri Lefebvre and his study of rural sociology ("Perspectives de sociologie rurale," *Cahiers internationaux de sociologie*, 14 (1953), pp. 122-140) as an exceptional example of marxist research which does not fall into this trap. See *Search*, 51n-52n.

14. Sartre uses the term "anthropology" in the classical, humanistic, European sense as a "study of Man." The structures he intends to analyze are the concrete ontological structures underlying human history and as such have nothing at all in common with the structural anthropology of Lévi-Strauss.

15. The "project"—one of the basic concepts of *Being and Nothingness*— reappears in the *Critique* in the concept of totalization.

16. In the one autobiographical volume he has written, *The Words* (New York, 1964), Sartre claims that his own project to write was formed between the ages of eight and ten as a result of his interaction with his family.

17. Sartre consciously models his *Critique* along the lines of Kant. In fact at one point he calls it a "Prolegomena to any Future Anthropology," parodying Kant's *Prolegomena to any Future Metaphysics. (CRD*, p. 153). See note 6 above.

18. This structure is consciously modeled on Hegel's *Phenomenology of Mind*. Also see note 6 above.

19. See note 8 above. The following debate on the scope of the dialectic may appear obscure to some American readers. It is interesting to note, however, that when Sartre and Hyppolite (the French Hegel scholar) faced Garaudy and Jean Vigier (the French marxist scientist) in a public debate on this question in December 1961, 6000 people filled La Mutualité to hear it. A transcript of the debate was published as *Marxisme et existentialisme: controversie sur la dialectique* (Paris, 1962).

20. *CRD* stands for *Critique de la raison dialectique*. References to all subsequent quotations will appear in the text.

21. The continuity between the early Marx and the later Sartre is evident here as Sartre re-expounds the theme of Marx's *1844 Manuscripts*—i.e., that "man is his own origin."

22. Or, as the sympathetic commentator André Gorz quipped, "everyone

is explicable to the sociologist, except he himself who does the explaining," Gorz, "Sartre and Marx" *New Left Review* 137 (May-June 1966), p. 35.

23. This striking passage could also be taken as autobiographical, as a recognition by Sartre of the limitations of his earlier existential ontology and the need for social relevance in his own life.

24. He never completed the second volume. In a June, 1973 interview with Francis Jeanson, Sartre claimed he didn't know enough history to do it! ("Je ne sais pas assez d'histoire pour entreprendre ça."), Jeanson, *Sartre dans sa vie* (Paris, 1974), p. 298. The fact that he never completed this projected second volume may be a telling sign of the weaknesses of his approach.

25. This example speaks volumes on Sartre's view of social relations. His outlook on life is still that of the little boy he describes in *The Words* looking out on the world from a sixth floor Parisian apartment window. In-the-world and yet profoundly separated from it, this boy seeks to render the world intelligible by objectifying it in words.

26. *CRD*, pp. 182-188.

27. *Ibid.*, pp. 232-234.

28. *Ibid.*, pp. 308-317.

29. *Ibid.*, pp. 391-394.

30. Some commentators see a similarity here with Rousseau's concept of the general will. See, e.g., G. Lapassade's "Sartre et Rousseau," *Etudes philosophiques*, 17:4 (Winter, 1962).

31. Sartre gave the storming of the Bastille as his example of the apocalyptic group-in-fusion. He now gives us the Tennis Court Oath as one example of such "oaths" (434-437), and the Terror of the Convention (567-580) as an example of that general phenomenon.

32. For an elaboration of this interpretation of the *Critique* see George Allan, "Sartre's Constriction of the Dialectic," *Review of Metaphysics* (September 1979).

/4/

Lefebvre and French Revisionism: Marxists Question Marxism

1. Introduction

a. 1956: Year of Transition

1956 was a year of political and ideological crisis for the international communist movement and the PCF.[1] In January 1956, a leading PCF journalist published a book that publicly attacked stalinism. Pierre Hervé's *La Révolution et les Fétiches* was motivated by a desire to promote reform and de-stalinization within the Party. As a Resistance leader, a former deputy, Jacques Duclos' private secretary, and journalist for *Action* and *L'Humanité*, Hervé was a well-known, prominent party leader. In his book he attacked the PCF's intellectual dogmatism and theoretical degeneration, in particular mentioning party chairman Maurice Thorez's theory of the absolute pauperization of the working class. He pleaded for more intellectual openness and responsiveness to criticism. In addition, citing the threat of nuclear war in the event of an armed revolution in France, he argued for a peaceful transition to socialism through a program of reforms "that would be provisionally inapplicable in the political situation, but could, in view of their attraction for the masses, push the struggle forward."[2] Citing the fallacy of the traditional marxist immiseration theory and the possibility of socialism through reforms, Hervé's critique agreed in its essential features with the classical revisionism of Eduard Bernstein's *Evolutionary Socialism* (1899).

The effect of this critique could have been devastating for the Party's stalinist leadership. Hervé was publicly announcing what many knew but would not admit—that the emperor had no clothes. The surge of PCF growth in the 1940s was directly linked to widespread hopes of imminent socialist revolution. Through 1948 such a national renovation under PCF leadership appeared to be a possibility. But the Cold War drove the Party into prolonged isolation, and the likelihood of revolution grew more and more remote. Further, the growth of the French economy in the 1950s and the rise of working class living standards contradicted the Party's view of economic reality.[3] Hervé argued that the PCF should admit to itself the changes taking place underneath its nose and revise its program and strategy accordingly.

For his effort Hervé was sharply attacked by his fellow communists. "Mr. Dulles could not dream of a more docile commentator," wrote Guy Besse.[4] Even Sartre called him to task for falling into a simple reformism.[5] On 14 February 1956 he was expelled from the Party.

Ironically, this was the day on which the Twentieth Congress of the CPSU (Communist Party of the Soviet Union) began. At this Congress the new Soviet chief, Nikita Khruschev, denounced the long venerated communist deity, Joseph Stalin, and laid all the crimes and errors of Soviet rule at his feet. All sorts of people whom Stalin had executed (from the 1930s purge trials, the Doctor's Plot, the Slansky Trial, etc.) were now politically rehabilitated. In addition, Khruschev began to speak of "peaceful coexistence" and a "peaceful road to socialism," whereas stalinists traditionally foresaw world war, civil war, and armed revolution as the path to socialism.

The Twentieth Congress of the Communist Party of the Soviet Union had a profoundly unsettling effect upon PCF intellectuals. Their absolute faith in the Stalin personality cult was severely shaken. Many of them had personally defended the campaigns against Stalin's enemies who, now it seemed, were unjustly accused. PCF intellectuals were further shaken by the social upheavals that de-stalinization unleashed in Eastern Europe. The unrest in Poland resulted in some reforms and a change of leadership, but the veritable revolution that broke out *against* communist dictatorship in Hungary was brutally suppressed by Soviet tanks. These political events of 1956 caused a number of PCF intellectuals to break with the Party and reconsider the relevance of marxist theory to modern society.[6]

b. Sources of Theoretical Revision

The theoretical revision that emerged from this reassessment of marxism was different in a significant respect from the earlier Bernsteinian version. For it was not merely a political-economic revision (although this was included) but a philosophic revision as well. As mentioned in Chapter I, Bernstein's revision of marxism was limited to questioning the validity of marxist economic analysis of capitalism and the political consequences of that analysis. He did not question the scientific and positivistic philosophical assumptions of traditional marxism and its built-in bias toward economic determinism. He did not question the *homo economus* conception of human being.

Many of the French revisionists of the 1950s were academic philosophers. For their philosophical revision of traditional marxism they turned to the early Marx with his concept of alienation and to the existentialists Sartre and

Heidegger. As former communists they sought some vindication for their views within the history of communist thought itself. This they found in the "Western marxism" of Lukacs, Korsch, and Gramsci.

Before stalinization was consolidated among the communist intellectuals of Europe, thinkers like the Hungarian Georg Lukacs, the German Karl Korsch, and the Italian Antonio Gramsci wrote some very interesting works of marxist philosophy centering on the problems of subjectivity and consciousness.[7] In the intervening years these works were suppressed in one way or another (Lukacs was pressured into a public recantation, Korsch was driven out of the communist movement into a kind of libertarian opposition, and Gramsci languished and finally died in a fascist prison). Yet Lukacs' discussion of the concept of alienation in *History and Class Consciousness* (1923), Korsch's early marxist critique of the communist movement in *Marxism and Philosophy* (1923), and Gramsci's emphasis on the importance of the superstructure of culture and ideas in the class struggle all proved to be important sources for the French revisionists of the 1950s.[8]

Georg Lukacs was by far the most influential. As a student he studied in the German universities of Berlin and Heidelberg under Simmel and Max Weber. In addition he read and was deeply influenced by the writings of Hegel and Kierkegaard. Radicalized during the WWI years, he was attracted to the syndicalism of Georges Sorel and the marxism of Rosa Luxemburg. After the outbreak of the Russian Revolution, he joined the Hungarian Communist Party and participated as Commissar of Education and culture in Bela Kun's abortive Hungarian Soviet Republic of 1919. Exiled in Vienna he wrote the essays that were collected and published as *Geschichte and Klassenbewusstsein* (History and Class Consciousness) in 1923. Its emphasis on the significance of alienation and the importance of revolutionary culture as the decisive factor necessary for a successful revolution was a sharp rebuke to the economic determinism of bolshevik strategy. Soviet leaders sensed a threat to their political leadership of the communist movement and attacked Lukacs (along with Korsch) relentlessly. At the 1924 Comintern Congress, as prominent a political figure as Zinoviev warned:

> Theoretical revisionism cannot be allowed to pass with impunity. Neither will we tolerate our Hungarian comrade Lukacs, doing the same in the domain of philosophy and sociology...We have a similar tendency in the German party. Comrade Korsch is a professor (Interruption: "Lukacs is also a professor!") If we get a few more of these professors spinning out their Marxist theories, we shall be lost. We cannot tolerate...theoretical revisionism of this kind in our Communist International.[9]

In light of Korsch's expulsion from the Party, Lukacs wrote a perfunctory self-criticism, since "to be expelled from the Party meant that it would no longer be possible to participate actively in the struggle against Fascism. I wrote my self-criticism as an 'entry ticket' to such activity."[10] Lukacs, therefore, recanted and personally participated in the suppression of his book. For the next thirty years his display of public stalinism was continually belied by his sensitive and profound scholarly research. Thus during the 1956 Hungarian uprising it was not surprising that he identified with it by accepting the post of Minister of Education in the short-lived Imre Nagy government.[11]

In *History and Class-Consciousness* Lukacs rejects the positivist bias of the traditional marxism of Engels, Bernstein, and Kautsky for its mechanical separation of matter and consciousness. For him matter and consciousness form a dialectical totality: "We find the subject and object of the social process co-existing in a state of dialectical interaction."[12] Traditional or vulgar marxism denies the role of the subject and thus provides an "external" and one-sided distortion of social reality. It is on the basis of this distortion that the view of the social superstructure as a mere reflection of the economic base of society arises. Base and superstructure, Lukacs argues, are dialectically interrelated. Thus, the necessary condition for socialist revolution is not just a crisis in the economic base of society (contradiction between the forces and relations of production) but the proletariat's *class-consciousness* of the nature and causes of this crisis. The proletariat, however, is not directly aware of the dynamics of capitalist crisis. It experiences the contradictions of capitalism only through its own alienation. The decisive factor then becomes alienation and the process of transforming it into class-consciousness. In this light the superstructure takes on a new importance. As the arena of consciousness and aliena-tion, the superstructure becomes the battleground of revolu-tionary struggle. The goal of this struggle is now conceived as the abolition of alienation and the realization of "authentic humanity," of the individual's "total personality."[13]

This revalorization of subjectivity within marxism, while officially suppressed, was introduced to the French by one of Lukacs' students, Lucien Goldmann. Goldmann em-phasized the libertarian and existential elements of his thought and claimed that Lukacs' book *The Soul and Its Forms* (1910) was "an important stage in the birth of modern existential philosophy."[14] Thus Lukacs' early work became an important point of reference for those French ex-communists who attempted a theoretical revison of marxism in the 1950s.

2. *Arguments: Marxism in Question*

In December 1956 several former PCF intellectuals founded a journal, *Arguments*, which became the focal point of marxist self-questioning in France in the late 1950s and early 1960s.[15] Its editors, Edgar Morin, Jean Duvigneaud, Henri Lefebvre, Kostas Axelos, and Pierre Fougeyrollas, were for the most part Paris-based academics and ex-communists. Disillusioned through bitter personal experience with the communist version of socialism, they wrenched themselves free from their stalinist bearings without abandoning a radical critique of capitalist society.

Edgar Morin in his autobiographical *Autocritique* (1959)

gives us an illuminating personal reflection of this experience. Born in 1921 Morin was twenty years old when he joined the PCF after the Nazi invasion of the Soviet Union. His view of marxism and Russian socialism was heavily tinged with a romanticism born of the Resistance. To him and many of his generation the war was an apocalyptic struggle between the forces of good and evil. On one side were the forces of life, truth, justice, and freedom; on the other side death, falsehood, oppression, and slavery. The PCF, the Resistance, the Soviet Union, and the Red Army were on the side of the Good, while the Vichyites, the collabos, the Germans, and the Nazis represented Evil. After the war, the Americans and the Gaullists replaced the Nazis in his world-view. It was from this perspective, conditioned by the Resistance experience, that Morin's continued support of the communist movement derived.

Morin learned an Hegelianized version of marxism from Georg Szekeres, an Hungarian communist and disciple of Lukacs. He was one of the chief instigators of the existential opposition within the Party, arguing along Lukacsian lines that the PCF should pay more attention to the role of culture and the superstructure.[16] His romantic vision of marxism was jolted when his arguments were rejected by the Party leadership. His perception of the Soviet Union as the idyllic "fatherland of socialism" did not correspond with Soviet postwar policy (e.g., Zhdanovism, the Rajk trial, the labor camps, the anti-Tito campaign, etc.). Under the pressure of such new realities his commitment to the communist movement foundered. The Party finally expelled him in 1951 for "breaking discipline" by publishing an article without permission in a non-Party periodical.

Morin gradually reoriented his thought away from the rigid certainties of stalinist orthodoxy toward an open, critical marxism. A reading of the *gauchiste* critique of the Soviet bureaucracy in *Socialisme ou Barbarie* gave him the theoretical tools he needed to reject stalinism without abandoning marxism. During the 1956 upheavals he visited the Polish workers councils with Claude Lefort of *Socialisme ou Barbarie* and experienced at first-hand their demands for worker self-management. On his return Morin met with several other ex-communist intellectuals whose life experiences were broadly similar and initiated the founding of *Arguments*.

Freed from stalinist discipline, the ex-communist intellectuals subjected marxism and Soviet socialism to scrutiny and criticism. All the questions that they were inhibited from pursuing by the Party were now explored with impunity. Was Russian socialism an authentic expression of marxism?[17] Was the marxist theory of knowledge valid?[18] What was the role of the superstructure and its relation to the base? Was the marxist concept of social classes applicable to advanced capitalist societies? And what of the apparent failure of the working class movement in the West? What, indeed, was the nature of Western society? Post-industrial? Technological? Consumer?

In addition to a common political experience the theme that united the work of such divergent thinkers as Kostas Axelos, Pierre Fougeyrollas, François Chatelet, and Henri Lefebvre was the theme of alienation. These men experienced bourgeois society as fundamentally alienated politically, economically, culturally, and personally. They had viewed the communist movement as a vehicle for overcoming alienation only to find new and more elaborate forms of it. Outside the Party they returned to philosophy as the vehicle for expressing this experience.

Philosophically, they sought to return to Marx's original thought, particularly the *1844 Manuscripts*. Influenced by the existentialism of Sartre and Heidegger, they attempted to resolve the problems in Marx's view of alienation and the transcendence of philosophy. Following Heidegger's critique of Marx,[19] Kostas Axelos, for example, claimed that ultimately the dilemmas of marxism stem from the fact that Marx failed to transcend philosophy. His thought remained mired in the metaphysical tradition of Western philosophy since Plato.[20] Pierre Fougeyrollas also pursued this Heideggerian critique of the "metaphysical residues" in marxism.[21] Francois Chatelet and Henri Lefebvre looked to Sartre rather than Heidegger for their revision of marxism. They took Sartre's notion of authenticity (see p. 28) as a basis for developing concepts of satisfaction, play, and the festival as viable channels for resolving alienation.[22] By pursuing such questions freely, the *Arguments* revisions contributed dramatically to the revitalization of French marxist thought. By the time the journal ceased publication in 1962, a critical, independent, and interrogative spirit had been established within French marxism. In 1962 the editors of *Arguments* replaced the journal with a publications series by the same name in which they published French translations of the major works of Western marxism (Lukacs, Korsch, etc.) as well as book-length works of their own in which they elaborated ideas first presented in the journal articles.

3. Henri Lefebvre: Communist Philosopher

Henri Lefebvre is the most interesting and significant thinker of the *Arguments* group. A generation older than the rest, his leftist intellectual activity spans from the 1920s through the 1970s. Born in 1901, he received his philosophy degree from the Sorbonne at the age of eighteen. Lefebvre studied philosophy under the Cartesian luminaries of the time, Maurice Blondel and Leon Brunschvicg, whose work he and other young avant-garde intellectuals rejected as dry, arid formalism.[23] Disenchanted with establishment philosophy (both Cartesian and Bergsonian) and its concern for abstract, eternal, and absolute categories of thought, Lefebvre joined with several of his peers to form the *Philosophies* group in 1924.[24]

Initially this was a group of bohemian philosophers akin in spirit to the surrealists (with whom they allied themselves).[25] Proust and Gide were their heroes. In their cerebral fictional depictions of lived human experience, Proust and

Gide captured the spiritual revolt of such young intellectuals trained to think abstractly, yet longing for experiential content in their thought. "Our thought," Lefebvre wrote in 1926, "is earthbound and concrete. It is no longer thought with a capital T."[26]

From 1924 to 1929 the group moved gradually from a romantic rebellion against bourgeois culture and society to a serious consideration of marxist philosophy. Accordingly they joined the PCF en masse in 1928 and began publishing *La Revue Marxiste* the following year. As previously mentioned, this was the first real marxist theoretical journal to appear in France. Articles on Lenin, socialist state planning and political economy dominated the pages of the review, although selections from Marx's *1844 Manuscripts* (translated by Lefebvre) also appeared. In the early 1930s Lefebvre was interested in pursuing Marx's newly published early works and the theme of alienation but was discouraged by the atmosphere within the Party.[27]

Lefebvre's first major study of marxist philosophy, *Le Matérialisme Dialectique* was not published until 1939. It immediately established him as the Party's leading philosopher. In this work he examined the differences between formal logic and dialectical logic, arguing in favor of the Hegelian dialectic. Following in Marx's footsteps he then criticized the idealist ediface of Hegel's system, while retaining his dialectical method as developed in the *Phenomenology*. Feurbachian materialism was given its due as an important stage of transition from Hegel's idealism to Marx's dialectical materialism. The latter was presented as a philosophical method for analyzing the totality of knowledge and reality. Even while advocating the orthodox assertion of the dialectic of nature, Lefebvre laid stress on praxis as the core of Marx's thought. He also carefully avoided the dogmatic constriction of marxism to nothing more than a positivist theory of political economy. He presented dialectical materialism as a *totality*, and, quoting freely from Marx's *1844 Manuscripts*, he introduced the concepts of alienation and "total man." Through revolutionary praxis, the alienated individual could overcome self-fragmentation and emerge as a total human being, completely reconciled with self and the totality of Nature and human being.[28]

This work was very influential in broadening the PCF's appeal among intellectuals. It was not polemical in tone. In fact, it presented a rather sophisticated analysis of the philosophical developments from Hegel to Marx. Today such works are legion. But this was the first such study to appear in France, and it quickly became a minor orthodox classic. Yet even in his orthodoxy, he ran against the current. For the concepts of alienation, praxis, and "total man" were not to be found in Stalin's catechism. In fact, his pursuit of such topics eventually earned him the disapproval of the Party hierarchy even though he assiduously carried out the Party's line on culture.[29]

After the war Lefebvre wrote and edited several books on Marx: *Marx et la liberté* (1947); *La Pensée de Karl Marx* (1947); *Le Marxisme* (1948); and *Pour connaître la pensée de Karl Marx* (1948). His earlier translation of selections from the *1844 Manuscripts—Introduction aux morceaux choisis de Karl Marx* (1934) was now widely read. Lefebvre was clearly the most prominent marxist philosopher in postwar France. Many of the philosophers who joined the PCF were influenced at least to some extent by his prestige.[30] As he became more prominent, the Party's leadership sensed a political threat from him and maneuvered him into a public self-criticism. In 1949 he retracted his "neo-Hegelianism." Regretting that his formulations tended to present marxism merely as a theory of knowledge, he apologized for overestimating the importance of Hegel and the young Marx.[31] In the early 1950s he moved away from philosophy altogether and took up sociological research. Lefebvre's studies of the horizontal and vertical complexities of rural communities broke new ground in the development of marxist historical sociology.[32] Yet, none of his Party colleagues chose to pursue his imaginative methodology.

Lefebvre found the intellectual constraints within the Party increasingly confining. Even before the 1956 events, he publicly criticized this atmosphere. However, his unwillingness to break with the Party caused him to moderate his tone.[33] After the 1956 events Lefebvre worked covertly within the PCF for reform and real de-stalinization. Clandestinely he collaborated with other dissidents in and out of the Party in publishing such opposition journals as *Voies Nouvelles* and *La Voie Communiste* subtitled *Bulletin de l'opposition communiste continuant l'Etincelle—Tribune de Discussion*. Dissatisfied with the lack of progress of such covert activity, he brought matters to a head in the spring of 1958 by publishing a book, *Problèmes Actuels du Marxisme* in which Lefebvre sharply criticized Stalin personally and condemned the refusal of the PCF leadership to de-stalinize. In his remarkable autobiography *La Somme et le Reste* (1959) Lefebvre recounts how he was interrogated by the Central Committee about his "lack of discipline" in publishing his critical remarks. After 30 years of membership he was expelled for his "factional activities" in June 1958.[34]

4. The Re-thinking of Marx

Outside the Party Lefebvre returned to his study of Marx and posed new questions in the manner of the *Arguments* group. By attempting to "reconstruct Marx's original thought," he raised the question of the theoretical status of marxism, beginning with the question of whether marxism is a philosophy or some other form of thought.[35] Modern philosophy, according to Lefebvre, arose as a critique of religion and religious alienation. Philosophy (particularly Hegel's), in turn, became a justification for the state. Marx's achievement, Lefebvre contended, was to show that the state is not a neutral unifying principle above society but rather an expression of the social relations which constitute its core. Social relations serve as an intermediary between the base and superstructure of society. As the realm of alienation and praxis they are the focal point of Marx's thought. But just as marxism is not merely a form of political economy or a view of history, marxism is also not merely a philosophy, a politics, or a sociology. Marx's originality was "to conceive as a totality, the production of man by his own efforts, his own labor...the genesis of mankind as a totality, object of every science of human reality and goal of action."[36] This theme of totality continued at the center of Lefebvre's own thought. On this account he continued to draw on Marx:

> Marx asserts the unity of knowledge and reality, of man and nature...He explores a totality in process of becoming and in its present stage of development, a totality comprising levels and aspects which are now complementary, now distinct, now *contradictory*.[37]

In his *Métaphilosophie* (1965) Lefebvre tried to develop a form of thought capable of continuing this project. He claimed that traditional philosophy was actually a form of alienation since it attempted to interpret the world but not to change it. Consequently, this philosophy had become an exercise of thought turned in on itself, devouring its own vitals, so to speak. Marx had attempted the transcendence of philosophy toward total thought but was only partially successful. His followers failed to complete this task and wavered between the realization and the abolition of philosophy without achieving the proper synthesis. Such a systhesis, Lefebvre claims, is possible only in a classless society in which alienation has been eliminated.[38] In the meantime it is necessary to develop a new mode of thought that will anticipate and contribute to this process of transforming the world. Such a mode of thought must be anti-systematic because social reality itself lacks a systematic unity. It would begin with Marx's concept of alienation and develop it further, based on the new forms of alienation manifested in 20th century advanced capitalist society.

Lefebvre also recognized the limitations involved in basing himself on Marx. He argued that alienation is more elaborate and complex than Marx indicated. Also, Lefebvre found Marx's concept of praxis too instrumental and limited. He added to it the concept of *poésis* (to account for the creative—imaginative impulse) and *mimesis* (to indicate the weight of routine and repetitive activity within praxis). Further, he mentioned certain "residues" of human activity which are essential in understanding the totality but do not fit neatly into any particular category or schematization.[39] Thus, only when we comprehend these limitations of Marx's thought will we understand why "capitalism has displayed a vitality and elasticity Marx could not foresee."[40] Nevertheless, Lefebvre retained his commitment to a marxian interpretation: "Marx predicted the end of competitive capitalism under the double pressure of the proletariat and the monopolies, and on this score his prediction proved true."[41] Further, even though modern society only vaguely corresponds to that anticipated by Marx, his thought is "indispensable for understanding the present day world. In our view, it is the starting point for any such understanding, though its basic concepts have to be elaborated, refined, and complimented by other concepts where necessary."[42]

Lefebvre's attempt (after parting company with the PCF) to reconstruct Marx's thought led him to revise the marxian concepts of alienation, praxis, the state, and the nature of philosophy. By resorting to his "metaphilosophy," Lefebvre hoped to renew the link between theory and practice, between philosophy and the non-philosophical domain of everyday life, and thereby confront the problematic nature of modern society. Marxism by itself was insufficiently developed to clarify the nature of this problematic, but it was the necessary theoretical point of departure. The practical starting point would be everyday life itself. Only when philosophy could be applied to the transformation of everyday life could it be said that the link between theory and practice had been restored.

> It belongs to meta-philosophical thought to imagine and to propose forms, or rather a style that can practically construct

and realize the philosophical project by transforming daily life...The project of a radical transformation of daily life cannot be separated from the transcendence of philosophy and its realization.[43]

5. The Critique of Everyday Life

Lefebvre begins his critique of everyday life with some observations on the nature of advanced capitalist society of the latter half of the 20th century. Obviously, this society is different from that traditional capitalism which Marx describes in *Capital*. The conditions of capitalist production (production of commodities for exchange and profit) have not changed. If anything they have been consolidated. Yet the social coherence of the society is disintegrating. The meaning of Marx's conceptualizations—class, base, superstructure, praxis, etc.—have become vague because the revolutionary praxis upon which they were predicated failed to achieve its realization. Hence, "the whole structure defined by Marx a hundred years ago is collapsing for want of a revolution that would have sustained and furthered 'human totality'."[44] In its place we have Modernity, or post-traditional capitalist society. The key feature of this society is its fragmentation. "The world is fragmented...We have fragments of culture, of specialized sciences, of systems and 'sub-systems'."[45]

Classes, instead of achieving unity and coherence, have fragmented. The working class continues to exist and continues to be discontented, yet its revolutionary consciousness is fragmented and becomes a class "misunderstanding." The middle classes of white collar, technical, and professional workers gradually merge with the working class. Yet, this process occurs hardly in the manner which Marx intimated, but rather "through the obvious similarity of their everyday lives and the identical evasions from such lives in packaged tours and trips."[46] The ruling classes appear to fragment, also, into a plethora of bureacratic elites as the traditional bourgeoisie loses its social coherence. Nevertheless, through the process of bureaucratization the ruling elite consolidates a class strategy for retaining power and social domination.

Alienation increases in the age of modernity. "New types of alienation have joined ranks with the old...political, ideological, technological, bureaucratic, urban, etc."[47] This phenomenon now comes dangerously close to wiping out the vestiges of authentic human feeling: "alienation is spreading and becoming so powerful that it obliterates all traces of consciousness of alienation."[48]

Consciousness of alienation is short-circuited through ideologies of consumption. Satisfaction is promised in the act of consumption. Happiness is defined as the joy of consuming. In this context advertising ("the poetry of Modernity")[49] assumes the proportion of an ideology, indeed, a world-view and attitude toward life. Its task is to mystify the marketing of consumer goods and convince the individual of the corporations's concern for one's well-being:

> The injunctions that interrupt films and news items on American television prove the depth of this concern: you are at home in your living room in the company of the diminutive screen and you are being looked after, cared for, told how to live better, how to dress fashionably, how to decorate your house, in short how to exist; you are totally and thoroughly programmed...[50]

210557

And yet these ideologies of consumption are ultimately unsuccessful. Consumption remains unsatisfying and "a sense of unrest really prevails."[51] New contradictions emerge: loneliness in the face of overcrowding, lack of communication in a sea of signs of communication, disintegration of values and social relations (e.g., family, marriage, etc.). Modern technology has more or less solved the major problems of economic production. Yet this economic expansion was achieved at the price of stifling human development: "the *technical mastery* of material experience is not counter-balanced by the adaptation of man to his own personal experience."[52] Thus, social integration looms as a major new contradiction. Modern society is incapable of integrating its members and sub-groups except by bureaucratically transforming difference and opposition into forms of consumption (for instance, witness the tremendous growth of the market for marxist books!). This fragmented society needs new ideologies to disguise its fragmentation.

In order to be successful, modern ideologies must not appear to be ideologies at all. Rather, they must "don a scientific disguise."[53] In other words, they must eschew content in favor of method. Thus, Lefebvre sees functionalism, formalism, structuralism, scientism, and positivism all as ideologies.

> ...All parade as non-ideological. Yet, the ideologizing process is clear enough and consists in extrapolation-reduction whereby the ideology makes absolute truths of relative specific concepts.[54]

Even so these ideologies prove incapable of providing coherence to social reality. They provide fragmented explanations of fragments of the society.

Does this society form a social whole? Can it be conceptually characterized? Lefebvre calls it a bureaucratic society of controlled consumption, a society for which the principle and structure is bureaucracy and whose goal is consumption, ideologically controlled. It is a fragmented melange of subsystems whose only form of coherence is given in everyday life. The aim of this society becomes the organization and pacification of everyday life. For here is the only possible point of social integration.

The concept of everyday life is one that Lefebvre pursued throughout his career, dating back to the 1930s. In an early work, *La Conscience mystifiée* (1936), he used the term simply to refer to the dull, repetitive routines of ordinary life under capitalism, implying that socialism would bring about a spiritual and cultural renewal.

After the liberation he developed the idea in a study

called *Introduction à la critique de la vie quotidienne* (1946). Beginning with his view of marxism as a totality, Lefebvre elaborated the concept of *production* in light of Marx's early writings. It was here that he began to develop his view of *poésis* as a specific type of praxis. In producing the totality of one's existence the individual is involved in more than just the material production of one's environment. The individual is also involved in a certain form of "spiritual" production. By this Lefebvre does not necessarily mean art and culture (which traditional marxism considers part of society's superstructure), but creations like social time and space. For example, in peasant cultures there was a cyclical consciousness of time. Space was experienced in terms of the village and land tenure arrangements. In industrial cultures time is linear and cumulative; space is organized around the factory into cities. People are involved in the production of other creations as well (e.g., social networks of friendship) that are neither limited to the economic forces of production (base) nor directly concerned with the superstructure. They form an independent domain, the domain of everyday life.

Ironically Lefebvre claims that everyday life did not emerge as an independent domain until the advent of competitive captialism in the 19th century. Pre-industrial peasant society was characterized by a certain style that lent an aura and mystique to the most trivial and ordinary events. Such style provided coherence and a sense of integral unity to pre-industrial society. The advent of industrial capitalism and mass society destroyed this style and the coherence characteristic of the peasant world. Instead of being a source of constant spiritual renewal, everyday events became trivialized and routinized. Everyday life (or the *quotidien* as Lefebvre calls it) emerged as the domain of non-work relations in a milieu of alienation characterized by commodity fetishism and dissatisfaction. In a second volume of the *Critique de la vie quotidienne* subtitled, *Fondements d'une sociologie de la quotidiennété* (1961), Lefebvre elaborated these ideas further. In a third volume, *La Vie quotidienne dans le monde moderne*

(1968) he attempted to incorporate the insights of linguistics, semiology, communication theory, cybernetics, and structuralism (with his concept of everyday life) as well as criticize their ideological values.[55]

One of the most interesting aspects of Lefebvre's depiction of everyday life is his analysis of the role of language. Traditionally words have a denoting function. They are signs for something signified. The sign refers to the signified. Lefebvre claims one of the key features of modernity is the "decline of referentials." That is, "around the years 1905-1910 the referentials broke down one after another under the influence of various pressures (science, technology, and social changes)."[56] Traditional discourse gradually began to make less and less sense. The *absurd* became a practical reality filling the gap between disconnected signifiers and signifieds. Signals gradually replaced signs, and images replaced symbols as means of communication. The semiology of consumption is the chief vehicle of this process. The "smile" image in an advertisement promises us happiness if we use the accompanying product. Signals of youth, beauty, sexual fulfillment, well-being are flashed to us in the images of the young men and women who appear in many advertisements. Also, we are implicitly warned by the signals and images that if we don't use these products we will be denied self-realization. The actual use-value of the product (the signified) is subordinated to images of satisfaction and implied threats of social ostracism (e.g., "ring around the collar!"). In this process language itself is used to impart "an ideological theme to an object, endowing it with a dual real and make-believe existence. It appropriates ideological terms and links the salvaged signifiers to the re-conditioned signified..."[57] Such a form of communication attempts to reduce the consumer to a passive object responding automatically to conditioned reflexes. It is a totalitarian form of communication, much like the traffic signal which gives commands—"Stop!...Go!"—without any room for questioning. As this form of communication spreads to other domains (politics, public administration, industrial psychology) the horizon of social meaning disintegrates. People lose the ability to relate to each other because the human element has been expunged from linguistic communication. The human subject has been eliminated from language and replaced by the object-consumer (e.g., "Hey America!"—consumer addressed as an object) and the anonymity of bureaucratese (e.g., the "interdictions" of the "no longer operational" Vietnam War). To Lefebvre this points to the real meaning of structuralism: an ideological attempt to justify the elimination of the human subject from everyday life.

Historically, everyday life has become more crystalized after each failed revolution (in France—1848, 1871, 1936, 1944, etc.). Such revolutions contain within them the promise of social transformation. Yet when such transformation fails to materialize, utopian visions succumb to the routines of everyday life. Thus everyday life represents the triumph of repression over creativity and desire. But this triumph is not absolute. Creativity and desire are not completely obliterated. Rather, they find sanctuary in the cracks and fissures of everyday life. The class strategy of the ruling elite requires that it seek out such residues of human autonomy and independence and "rationally" eliminate them. In other words, they seek to provide a bureaucratic solution to the problem of the uncertainty of the human element, the problem of the unpredictable choices of free individuals. The bureaucratic solution attempts to condition the individual (primarily through the ideologies of consumption) so that one feels one is freely choosing from several alternatives which have already in fact been selected for the individual. The end result is what Lefebvre calls a "terrorist society" in which "compulsion and the illusion of freedom converge."[58]

The bureaucratic society of controlled consumption which Lefebvre describes conjures up the images of Marcuse's *One Dimensional Man*, Huxley's *Brave New World* and Bradbury's *Fahrenheit 451*. However, Lefebvre disagrees with the pessimistic view that such a society can succeed. It "cannot maintain itself for long; it aims at stability, consolidation, at preserving its conditions and its own survival, but when it reaches this end it explodes."[59] This result is because human desire is *irreducible*. It crops up again and again after each bureaucratic effort to eliminate it. Thus, along with Sartre, Lefebvre affirms the *irreducibility of the subject* as the key to revolutionary action.

The battlefield becomes everyday life itself. "Everyday life has taken the place of economics, it...prevails as the outcome of a generalized class strategy (economic, political, cultural). It is everyday life that must be tackled by broadcasting our policy, that of a cultural revolution with political and economic implications."[60] In transforming everyday life a new culture must be created that is "not an institution but a style of life...The revolution will transform existence, not merely the state and the distribution of property."[61] Sexual revolution, urbanism (the city as the creative environment of modernity), and the rediscovery of The Festival (such as the bacchanalian festival of ancient Greece) would all be elements of such a cultural revolution.

6. *Lefebvre and the French New Left*

Lefebvre's thought had turned full circle from the surrealist romanticism of the 1920s, to the stalinist orthodoxy of the 1940s, and finally back to a utopian socialist romanticism in the 1960s. His attempt to analyze the problematic nature of modern society in terms of the concept of everyday life was his central contribution to new left social theory. By expanding the analysis of alienation from the workpace to all aspects of everyday life (consumption, leisure, family life, sex roles, culture, etc.), Lefebvre brought to light arenas of oppression and dissatisfaction which were only superficially or inadequately considered by traditional marxism. Moreover, this concept could be applied to the nominally socialist countries as well. For underneath all the ideological rhetoric, the actuality of everyday life revealed a society mired in deep and manifold levels of alienation. The transformation of everyday life became a more or less programmatic goal for the French new left. Lefebvre himself suggested the slogans: "Let everyday life become a work of art! Let every technical means be employed for the transformation of everyday life."[62]

Notes

1. For an overview of this crisis see François Fejto, *The French Communist Party and the Crisis of International Communism* (Cambridge, 1967).

2. Pierre Hervé, *La Révolution et les fétiches* (Paris, 1956), p. 119.

3. For an excellent overview of French economic development 1945-1968, see John Ardagh's *The New French Revolution* (New York, 1968).

4. *L'Humanité* (25 January 1956). Jean Kanapa and four other leading communist intellectuals also wrote rebuttals in various other Party publications.

5. Sartre, "La Réformisme et les fétiches," *Les Temps Modernes* (February 1956), pp. 1153-1164.

6. Among academic philosophers Pierre Fougeyrollas, Jean Desanti, and Henri Lefebvre left the Party.

7. The bibliography on Western Marxism is vast indeed. A critical overview of the field is Perry Anderson's *Considerations on Western Marxism* (London, 1976).

8. In fact, one commentator claims the "chief merit" of the French revisionists was not their own thought, but the fact that they introduced the French public to the works of these Central European thinkers of the 1920s and 1930s. See Gombin, *Origins of Modern Leftism* (Suffolk, 1975), pp. 40-41.

9. Quoted in Morris Watnick, "Relativism and Class Consciousness: Georg Lukacs" in *Revisionism*, ed. by L. Labedz (New York, 1962), p. 146. The best work on Lukacs is Andrew Arato and Paul Breines, *The Young Lukacs and the Origins of Western Marxism* (New York, 1979).

10. Lukacs, *History and Class Consciousness*, trans. by Rodney Livingstone (Cambridge, 1967), p. xxx.

11. Perhaps because of his international reputation Lukacs received surprisingly mild punishment. He was stripped of his Party membership and exiled to Rumania.

12. Lukacs, *op. cit.*, p. 165.

13. *Ibid.*, p. 162 ff.

14. Goldmann, *Récherches dialectiques* (Paris, 1959), p. 247. He further argued that Heidegger was indebted to Lukacs for his *Being and Time* (1927) although Heidegger wouldn't acknowledge it.

15. Studies of the *Arguments* group include: Louis Soubise, *Le Marxisme après Marx 1956-1965: quatre dissidents français* (Paris, 1967); Yvon Bourdet, "Le Néo-révisionisme," in *Communisme et marxisme* (Paris, 1963), pp. 39-78; Gombin, *loc. cit.*, pp. 40-56; and Poster, *loc. cit.*, pp. 209-263.

16. Morin, *Autocritique* (Paris, 1959), pp. 117, 84. See also Chapter 2 of this study.

17. E.g., J. Duvigneaud, "Marxisme: idéologie ou philosophie," *Arguments*, 2 (February-March 1957).

18. E.g., E. Morin, "Révisions le révisionnisme," *Arguments*, 2 (February-March 1957).

19. See Heidegger's "Letter on Humanism" in *The Existentialist Tradition*, ed. N. Languilli (New York, 1971), pp. 204-245.

20. Cf. Axelos, *Marx, penseur de la technique* (Paris, 1961).

21. See Fougeyrollas, *Le Marxisme en question* (Paris, 1960).

22. See Chatelet, *Logos et praxis* (Paris, 1962). For Lefebvre, see below.

23. Lefebvre, *La Somme et Le Reste* (Paris, 1959), pp. 15-38.

24. The group included Paul Nizan, Pierre Morhange, Georges Friedmann, George Politzer, and Norbert Guterman. The first journal published by the group was called *Philosophies*. For a history of the group see Lefebvre's *L'Existentialisme* (Paris, 1946), pp. 20-33; and W. F. Redfern's *Paul Nizan* (Princeton, 1972), pp. 12-20.

25. On the relations between the *Philosophies* group and André Breton's surrealists see Robert Short, "The Politics of the Surrealists 1920-1935" in *Journal of Contemporary History I*, 2 (1966), pp. 3-26.

26. Lefebvre, "La Pensée et l'esprit," *L'Esprit*, May 1926. This journal was published by the *Philosophies* group.

27. The twofold economic thrust during the years 1929-1933 of depression in the West and socialist construction in the Soviet Union occupied the attention of Party intellectuals. They viewed marxism at this time almost exclusively as a political-economic theory, leaving little room for philosophizing.

28. Lefebvre, *Dialectical Materialism*, trans. by J. Sturrock (London, 1974). For the concept of "total man" see pp. 148-166.

29. Witness the attacks he made on Sartre and existentialism discussed in Chapter 2.

30. Edgar Morin later recalled Lefebvre's impact in his *Autocritique* (1959), p. 34. Even Roger Garaudy in 1955 recalled how Lefebvre introduced him to marxist philosophy. See his comments in his controversy with Lefebvre published in *Cahiers du Communisme* (October, 1955), p. 1216.

31. Lefebvre, "Autocritique," *La Nouvelle Critique*, 4 (1949), p. 730.

32. See his "Perspectives de la Sociologie Rurale," *Cahiers Internationaux de Sociologie* 14 (1953); and his "Les Classes Sociales dans les Campagnes," *Ibid.*, 10 (1951). He also published several works in the relatively uncontroversial field of literary criticism on Pascal, Musset, and Rabelais.

33. For the debate between Lefebvre and Garaudy on the role of intellectuals and the problems of ideological unity, see *Cahiers du Communisme* (October 1955).

34. Lefebvre, *La Somme et le reste* (Paris, 1959), p. 155.

35. Lefebvre, *The Sociology of Marx*, trans. by Norbert Guterman (New York, 1969), p. 3. Originally *Sociologie de Marx* (Paris, 1966).

36. *Ibid.*, p. 20.

37. *Ibid.*, p. 22.

38. Lefebvre, *La Métaphilosophie* (Paris, 1965), p. 28.

39. *Ibid.*, pp. 17-18.

40. Lefebvre, *The Sociology Of Marx*, p. 89.

41. *Ibid.*, p. 188.

42. *Idem.*

43. Lefebvre, *La Métaphilosophie*, pp. 118-119.

44. Lefebvre, *Everyday Life in the Modern World*, trans. by S. Rabinovitch (New York, 1971). Originally *La Vie quotidienne dans le monde moderne* (Paris, 1968).

45. *Ibid.*, p. 70.

46. *Ibid.*, p. 93.

47. *Ibid.*, p. 94.

48. *Idem.*

49. *Ibid.*, p. 107.

50. *Idem.*

51. *Ibid.*, p. 79.

52. *Ibid.*, pp. 80-81.

53. *Ibid.*, p. 96.

54. *Ibid.*, p. 97. Of course one may ask whether in fact this is what Lefebvre is doing in his own way.

55. See his *Le Langage et la Société* (1966) and *Position: Contre les technocrats* (1967).

56. *Everyday Life, op. cit.*, p. 112.

57. *Ibid.*, p. 106.

58. *Ibid.*, p. 147.

59. *Ibid.*, p. 148.

60. *Ibid.*, p. 197.

61. *Ibid.*, pp. 203-204.

62. *Ibid.*, p. 204.

/5/

Castoriadis and
Socialisme ou Barbarie:
The Gauchiste Rejection of Marxism

1. Introduction

Socialism ou Barbarie[1] was a rather obscure journal in its
time. Founded in 1949 as the theoretical organ of a small
political group of the same name, it managed to survive until
1965. Its prime movers were the ex-trotskyists Cornelius
Castoriadis and Claude Lefort.

Castoriadis is of Greek origin.[2] Born in Athens in 1922 he
was a university student (of law, economics, and philosophy)
when the war broke out. To participate in the resistance
movement he joined the Greek Communist Party. By the time
of the Athens uprising in 1944 he had broken with stalinist
politics and joined the trotskyist Fourth International, spend-
ing the balance of the war avoiding the gestapo and the
stalinist G.P.U. In 1945 he fled to Paris and continued his
study of philosophy and his trotskyist political activity. Lefort
(1924-)[3] had studied philosophy with Merleau-Ponty in the
early 1940s. Lefort was deeply influenced by him, and they
became close personal friends. It was at Merleau-Ponty's

suggestion that Lefort joined the French trotskyist organization, Parti Communiste Internationale (PCI).

When Castoriadis and Lefort met in August 1946, they found themselves to be in agreement in their opposition to the general political direction of the trotskyist movement. In particular they disagreed with Trotsky's analysis of the nature of the Russian regime. For over two years they advanced their ideas within the PCI and developed a small following. They finally left in January 1949 and published the first issue of their own journal, *Socialisme ou Barbarie*, in March 1949.

In *The Revolution Betrayed* (1937) Trotsky presented his basic analysis of the Russian bureaucracy. He argued that it was ridiculous to speak of capitalism in the USSR. The elimination of private property via nationalization and the replacement of a market economy by state planning clearly indicated that capitalism—at least as Marx knew it—no longer existed in the Soviet Union. For Trotsky a restoration of capitalism would imply the re-emergence of private ownership of capital along with a market economy. He claimed the Russian regime was essentially socialist in character since the means of production had been nationalized and capitalist market competition had been replaced by state planning.

How then did he account for inequality in Soviet society, political terror, the purges, the destruction of all socialist opposition forces including his own? Trotsky claimed inequality persisted in Russia as a consequence of the necessities of rapid industrialization. He felt (along with Stalin) that strict limitations on mass consumption were necessary to carry out "primitive socialist accumulation." Because consumer goods were scarce the bureaucracy grew to insure distribution. Through his position in the party organization Stalin was able to staff this emerging bureaucracy with loyalists who thereby formed his power base. Trotsky considered the governing bureaucracy to be a parasitic growth on Soviet society, a stratum with no historical future. It was merely a deformed or degenerated shade of a true socialist leadership. Using such reasoning Trotsky characterized the Soviet regime as a "degenerated workers' state." Stalinism had created a bureaucracy that had deformed Russian socialism but hadn't destroyed it. Socialism was still salvageable, presumably by the displacement of Stalin and his bureacracy with Trotsky and his followers. This was the point of view of the Fourth International, only slightly modified after Trotsky's assassination in 1940.[4]

Castoriadis questioned whether a trotskyist bureaucracy would be better than a stalinist one. The problem was the nature of bureaucracy itself which prevented the realization of socialism. Socialism entailed the elimination of exploitative social relations. Yet in the Soviet Union such relations continued to exist despite the nationalization of the economy and the institution of state planning. Nationalization and state planning are the essence of the communist (whether Lenin's, Stalin's, or Trotsky's) definition of socialism. To Castoriadis this was essentially a bureaucratic definition which, even though it eliminated the *form* of capitalist exploitation, preserved its content. Hence, he increasingly viewed the communist movement as a whole as a highly developed variant of capitalism (as opposed to the trotskyist view of stalinism as a deformed variant of socialism). The anti-communism of *Socialisme ou Barbarie* was thus unique in that it considered communism the highest stage of capitalism![5]

Castoriadis argued that the Russian bureaucracy was a class (in the classical marxist sense of the term) in and for itself, not just a temporary deformation. He claimed the bureaucracy replaced the bourgeoisie as the class exploiting the proletariat, and the social system was one of *bureaucratic* capitalism. This was the "highest" form of capitalism since the bureaucracy was even more centralized, concentrated, and integrated than the classical bourgeoisie.

This concept of the bureaucracy as a ruling class in the Soviet Union was supported by an analysis, done in classical marxist fashion, of the everyday relations of production in

Soviet industry between the manual workers and the managerial stratum. For when one looked behind all the ideological trappings, one found that the actual everyday work experience of Soviet factory workers was not all that different under their state than that of Western factory workers living under the yoke of the bosses' state. Neither group had much control over the conditions of employment, wages, working conditions, etc. Soviet managers were not all that different from their Western counterparts either. In both cases management of production was authoritarian and hierarchical, not democratic.[6]

Castoriadis applied this theory of bureaucracy as a class to the advanced capitalist nations as well. He interpreted the phenomena of increasing state intervention in the economy, the rise of the welfare state, and the rise of corporate and trade union bureaucracies as a sign of an emerging bureaucratic class that was in the process of engulfing the classical bourgeoisie.

In the West the state began to play a pivotal role in the economy from the 1930s on due to the inability of capitalism to resolve its crises and instability. The working class organizations, the trade union and political party structures, were gradually transformed from vehicles of challenge and opposition to capitalism as such to instruments of integration. The state bureaucracy and the workers' bureaucracy in the West shored up capitalism, which was thereby transformed into an increasingly bureaucratic system of exploitation.

The fundamental contradiction of advanced capitalism ceases to be that between the owners of private property and the propertyless laborers. It is replaced by that between the order-givers and the order-takers in the production process. The bureaucracy finds its justification in rationalization and organization of production and society at large. It makes itself indispensable as the managers of society.

The differences between the two systems were perceived as merely variations on the same bureaucratic theme. The Soviet system, however, was the more dangerous since it presented itself as the embodiment of the workers' movement, thereby creating illusions and mystifications about its essential nature.

In opposition to such bureaucratic systems, Castoriadis posited the alternative of a socialist society directly controlled by the masses of workers through a system of self-managed workers' councils (*autogestion*). This libertarian socialism drew its inspiration from the revolutionary myths of the heritage of egalitarian workers' movements—the Paris Commune, the Russian soviets of 1905 and 1917, the workers' councils movements in Italy, Germany, and Hungary following World War I, the anarchist Makhno movement, Kronstadt, and the Spanish anarchist collectives of 1936.

An authentic socialist revolution would abolish bureaucracy as well as private property. Since the abolition of private property did not bring about the liberation of the working class in the Soviet Union it cannot be considered the benchmark of socialism. It is a necessary condition for the development of socialism, but not sufficient. Only the abolition of hierarchy—the abolition of the distinction between those who command and those who obey in the production process—is the sufficient condition for guaranteeing that the working class actually controls its own destiny.[7]

As a statement of general principles, such a view is characteristic of the French new left. Yet Castoriadis had already arrived at this position in 1949, without departing from a classical (though neither orthodox nor official) marxist interpretation. However, the rejection of the practice of the communist movement brought about a significant evolution in his view of marxism. For by pursuing the critique of bureaucracy and the *autogestion* view of socialism to their ultimate conclusion, he ended by rejecting the marxism from which he developed these views. For Castoriadis it was a matter of rejecting marxism in order to remain revolutionary.

2. Overview

Initially the *Socialisme ou Barbarie* group was composed of former trotskyists. They quickly absorbed other (often quite esoteric) strands of communist dissidents. As an extremely sectarian critic of both capitalism and the communist movement, the group had a very limited appeal. Aside from some sporadic attempts of on-the-job organizing, its very existence as a revolutionary organization was generally limited to publishing the journal and holding small (30-40 people) monthly meetings to discuss its contents.[8]

The journal, however, proved significant as the only vehicle for a systematic *gauchiste* critique of the communist movement during the height of the Cold War.[9] While many leftist intellectuals (with Sartre in the lead) buried their qualms and sided with the Soviet Union against the capitalist West, *Socialisme ou Barbarie* continued a critique of both sides. Throughout the early 1950s the journal adhered to this orientation despite the lack of positive response from the rest of the French left. It presented major analyses of bureaucracy and continued to refine its *autogestion* view of socialism. The East German workers uprising of 1953 and the Polish and Hungarian revolts of 1956 were analyzed from a marxist class struggle point of view. These events were interpreted as proletarian revolts against a bureaucratic ruling class. The establishment of workers' councils in Hungary during the 1956 rebellion was proclaimed a new revolutionary model for building workers' power under socialism.

Because of the journal's uncompromising opposition to the communist movement, Sartre and others ignored its analyses, claiming the thrust of its orientation played into the hands of the political right. At times this appeared to be true. For example, in the aftermath of the Ridgeway affair of 1952 (see p. 46) *Socialisme ou Barbarie* rejoiced when the workers failed to respond to PCF calls for a protest strike.[10] Sartre thereupon entered a long and vitriolic dispute with Lefort and Castoriadis, a dispute that in fact proved instrumental in

Sartre's break with Merleau-Ponty.[11]

In the early 1950s the conjunctural factors of the Cold War made it impossible for *Socialisme ou Barbarie* to find a receptive audience on the French left. But in the wake of the Hungarian revolt, its analysis appeared to provide a rational marxist explanation of these seemingly incomprehensible events. The journal provided a great deal of coverage of the uprising, presenting opposition documents and first-hand reporting by Lefort. Castoriadis and Lefort interpreted the revolt as an authentic proletarian revolution against bureaucracy and thus a profound vindication of their own orientation. Ironically many leftist intellectuals in France now turned to *Socialisme ou Barbarie* for guidance in understanding the communist system.[12] From that time on its influence gradually increased, particularly among some who later became leaders and activists in the May 1968 upheaval.[13]

However, from 1958 on, the journal changed considerably. The advent of de Gaulle and the Fifth Republic touched off a debate over the nature of modern capitalism. The gradual modernization of French society brought into question the validity of the entire marxist ediface of Castoriadis' analysis. The traditional marxist concept of class now seemed inappropriate for describing either the bureaucracy or the working class. Bureaucratization seemed to be a process with its own dynamic, transforming the dichotonic structure of class society into a pyramidal hierarchy. While class relations as defined by relation to means of production were still discernable, they did not appear to have the same significance as attributed to them in the marxist framework.[14]

Lefort left the journal in 1958 over an organizational dispute,[15] while both he and Castoriadis proceeded to develop analyses of modern bureaucratic society which rejected marxism.[16] Other members of the group who were "against this tendency" left in 1963 after several years of controversy.[17] The journal discontinued publication in 1965 on Castoriadis' decision. He felt that since the analysis had finally found a receptive audience in the emerging new left it had fulfilled its function.

As a practical revolutionary organization the *Socialisme ou Barbarie* group proved to be a dismal failure. But as a journal representing a certain tendency of thought it proved to be surprisingly successful in anticipating the nature and scope of social conflict in advanced industrial society. Ironically their success as social theorists derived directly from their practical understanding of social processes which they acquired in their political organizing experiences.[18] They were able to bring a concreteness to their theoretical analyses which was lacking in the work of Sartre and the *Arguments* group, the other major sources of new left social theory. In the balance of this chapter we will examine more closely the three major elements of this tendency: 1) the critique of bureaucracy; 2) *autogestion*; and 3) the rejection of marxism.

3. The Critique of Bureaucracy

"Bureaucracy appears as a phenomenon that everyone talks about, feels, and experiences, but which resists conceptualization."[19] Lefort made this statement in 1960 after fifteen years of grappling with the problem. Today this remark rings even more true. Yet Lefort's and Castoriadis' analyses contributed significantly to the French new left's attempts at such a conceptualization.

The traditional marxist view of bureaucracy derived from Marx and Lenin's view of the state. In his critique of Hegel's *Philosophy of Right*, Marx faults Hegel for accepting the claims of the Prussian bureaucracy to impartial and universal representation "above" the fray of civil society. In the administration of its tasks the bureaucracy claims to represent the social whole by artificially separating itself from classes in society. In fact its administration of the state preserves and furthers the social dominance of the reigning classes in civil society.

Contrary to its claims of proficiency and expertise, Marx subscribes to the popular view of the bureaucracy as the reign of red tape and the rule of incompetence. "The bureaucracy is a circle from which no one can escape....The highest point entrusts the understanding of particulars to the lower echelons, whereas these, on the other hand, credit the highest with an understanding of the universal."[20] The bureaucracy's deification of authority and its monopoly of information (via strict secrecy) tend to mask this incompetence and its concomitant parasitic nature.

In his analysis of the Bonapartist state, Marx reiterates this claim that the state bureaucracy is parasitic: "...with a host of officials numbering half a million; besides an army of another half million, this appalling parasitic body...enmeshes the body of French society like a net and chokes all its pores."[21] According to Marx the state bureaucracy derives its very existence from the internal contradictions engendered by class conflict. The more intense this conflict becomes, the greater the need for state intervention to preserve the dominant class. Because it is *needed* by the bourgeoisie the bureaucracy may develop a certain degree of autonomy of its own, although not enough to detach itself from the bourgeoisie. After the experience of the Paris Commune, Marx drew the logical conclusion of this view: since the state bureaucracy is a parasitic growth whose existence is bound up with that of the bourgeoisie it must be destroyed. Thus, Marx did not view the bureaucracy as having a development of its own independent of the already existing social classes.

In *State and Revolution* (1917) Lenin re-examined and re-affirmed these points but with more tactical emphasis on the seizure of state power. Like his contemporary, Max Weber, Lenin perceived the similarities between the structure of production in the capitalist industrial enterprise and that of a political party in mass society. In *What Is To Be Done* (1902) he praised the military structure of production in the capitalist factory as a training ground for his revolutionary troops. In the factory, workers learn habits of discipline, efficiency, and organization—necessary experience for revolutionary militants. Such experience would be put to use in creating a new revolutionary state bureaucracy which would displace the old Czarist bureaucracy.

> Abolishing the bureaucracy at once, everywhere and completely is out of the question. It is a utopia. But to *smash* the old bureaucratic machine at once and to begin immediately to construct a new one...is the direct and immediate task of the revolutionary proletariat.[22]

In Castoriadis' view this is exactly what Lenin did: i.e., construct a new bureaucratic machine which duplicated the hierarchical and authoritarian features of capitalist industrial organization. Castoriadis claims Lenin's advocacy of piecework, Taylorism, and unquestioned obedience by the workers to "one-man-management" in the factory secured capitalist relations of production as early as 1918![23] Indeed Lenin openly advocated a system of state capitalism administered by the state bureaucracy: "At present the postal service is a business organized on the lines of a state-*capitalist* monopoly....to organize the *whole* economy on the lines of the postal service...is our immediate aim...*All* citizens as transformed into hired employees of the state."[24]

Castoriadis notes that revolutionary anti-bureaucratic alternatives were proposed by such revolutionaries as the anarchists of Kronstadt, the anarchist Makhno movement in the Ukraine, and libertarian communists within the Bolshevik Party such as the "Workers' Opposition" group. All such initial efforts to establish workers' control of production were ruthlessly suppressed by the Bolshevik leadership who were absolutely convinced that they alone could build socialism—even if they had to do it by suppressing working class protest (Kronstadt, the St. Petersburg strikes of 1921, etc.) and other socialist political groupings. In the context of 1917-1921—civil war, foreign invasion, economic chaos—the question of the positive content of socialism was suppressed. The Bolsheviks concentrated all their energy on winning the civil war, keeping themselves in power, and in securing the bureaucratic machine.[25]

To Castoriadis, Trotsky's view of bureaucracy was rooted in the same perspective as that of Marx and Lenin. Trotsky saw it as an essentially parasitic body with no historical future of its own. The only difference here is that Trotsky was willing to apply this characterization to the Soviet bureaucracy as well. However, as mentioned earlier in this chapter, he did not carry this analysis any further.

The foregoing perspective on the traditional marxist theory and practice of bureaucracy was first presented to the French new left in the numerous articles by Castoriadis in *Socialisme ou Barbarie*. Some long suppressed documents of the early anti-bureaucratic activists were also presented to the French audience in the journal.[26] This type of work profoundly changed the perception of the Russian Revolution among the students of the emerging French new left. In fact, Daniel Cohn-Bendit, one of the leading figures of the May 1968 movement, quotes liberally from these sources in his widely read, *Obsolete Communism: The Left-Wing Alternative* (1968).[27]

Under the influence of Merleau-Ponty, Castoriadis also examined Max Weber's conceptualization of bureaucracy as a form of social organization that achieves its full development in mass industrial society.[28] Based on empirical observation Weber specifies certain general traits which characterize modern bureaucratic organizations: duties based on rule-governed procedures, functions hierarchically integrated to form a military chain of command, specialization and differentiation of functions, demand of functionaries' unquestioning loyalty to the organization, information and knowledge of technique restricted according to complex division of labor. These traits are concretized according to the type of social organization: state, mass political party, trade union, etc. For Weber the social organization most conducive to bureaucratization is the capitalist industrial enterprise. Here the demands for efficiency in the rationalization and organization of technical and mechanical processes are the most explicit. Bureaucratic organization of capitalist industrial production triumphs because of its technical superiority over any other organizational form. It is efficient, accurate, clear, and uniform. Its scientific rationalization of functions tends to eliminate the human element as much as possible, thereby reducing chance, error, and other subjective elements which interfere with organizational objectives and calculations. Weber himself opposed this process. He viewed bureaucratization as a de-humanizing process of "dis-enchantment" which marches on relentlessly in spite of justifiable opposition to it. As he describes it, bureaucratic organization is the most rational means, for better or worse, of organizing mass industrial society.

While Castoriadis was deeply influenced by the Weberian view of bureaucracy, he emphatically rejected the contention that the bureaucratic project of eliminating the human element was in fact a realizable one. Indeed this was the source of its instability, a fissure which had revolutionary potential. Further, Castoriadis felt Weber overestimated the scientific rationality of bureaucracy. Instead of functioning in a smooth, reliable, uniform fashion, bureaucracies tend to foment cesspools of cliques, personal rivalries, cut-throat competition for promotions, and a profound alienation stemming from the bureaucratic destruction of work as a meaningful activity by separating the control from the execution of tasks.

To Castoriadis, the bureaucratic solution to the contradictions of capitalism is a false solution. Bureaucratic rationalization is not genuine because it contains this fundamental contradiction: it seeks to control from the outside. It is based on a fundamental opposition between those who direct and those who execute, those who command and those who obey. Thus in bureaucratic society, authoritarian hierarchy emerges as the essence of class conflict. In the production process bureaucratic ration-alization simultaneously seeks the participation of the workers (in carrying out their assigned tasks) as well as their exclusion (from decision-making). It thereby seeks to destroy the initiative, creativity, and autonomy of the workers. Yet if it actually achieved this and reduced the workers to mindless automatons or lobotomized robots, the system would collapse, for it cannot function without participation by the masses.

Castoriadis claims there is no fundamental obstacle to the continued expansion of a bureaucratic capitalist economy. But, far from solving the crisis of modern society, bureaucratization creates deeper, more profound crises. Crises move from the base (economic sphere) to the superstructure of society: from crises of exploitation (which continues to exist) to crises of alienation...crises of values and cultural crises (the family, marriage, role of women, youth, education, meaning of work, legitimacy of the political system, etc.). The essential irrationality of such bureaucratic rationalization manifests itself in sudden upheavals which question the entire bureaucratic organization of society (e.g., Hungary, 1956). Short of such explosions, all sorts of crises erupt in particular spheres (education, medical care, etc.) which belie the rationality of bureaucratic rationalization.

Castoriadis argues that such crises can be eliminated only by eliminating the separation (which is essential to bureau-cracy) between the management and execution of tasks in modern society. In the production process this would mean the elimination of a separate managerial stratum and the assumption of managerial tasks by the workers themselves. In society at large it would mean the elimination of any separate stratum (such as businessmen, professional politicians, "experts," etc.) and the establishment of a socialist society based on workers' self-management.[29]

4. Self-Management

The fundamental issue at stake in this critique of bureaucracy is the issue of elitism versus egalitarianism. Weber felt bureaucracy was a necessary evil because mass industrial society is just too complex to function without an elitist hierarchy. The implication of this view is that the experts should manage society because the masses are incapable of running things for themselves.[30] Lenin also held this conviction. He felt the masses suffered so severely under Czarist oppression that they were too backward to run the affairs of the new workers' state. The Bolsheviks, as expert revolutionaries, would run things *for* them. Thus the essence of both the liberal and communist view of bureaucracy is *elitism*.

Socialisme ou Barbarie rejected this view and held fast to the moral conviction that the masses indeed have an enormous creative potential for managing society themselves. Only by suppressing this potential can the elite (whether capitalist or communist) justify its own privileges and power. Thus, bureaucratic elitism is very destructive of human potential.

But what evidence is there of this potential? Part of it was given in the pages of *Socialisme ou Barbarie* in the form of individual workers' own descriptions of their life and work experience. Throughout the 1950s factory workers, office workers, technicians, and service workers described their everyday life in regular features on the proletarian experience. Factory workers described the monotony and alienation of the assembly-line, the daily confrontation with health and safety hazards, the speed-up, and the inescapable impact of work-tensions on family, marriage, and sex life. Office workers described the hierarchical and irrational organization of work and the lack of union opposition to management. Service workers described how the quality of their service was sacrificed to management's desire to maintain tight control over them. All claimed that initiative and creativity were stifled by management.[31]

Daniel Mothé, a Renault auto worker, joined *Socialisme ou Barbarie* in 1952 and wrote numerous articles for the journal on his own everyday experience and that of his fellow workers.[32] In a very detailed fashion he argued that the workers have an intimate knowledge of how the factory functions, while management in fact knows little. Management attempts to supervise and control the workers, but it is the latter who have the concrete knowledge of how the factory runs. In Mothé's view the management bureaucracy is superfluous—even detrimental—to the efficient operation of the factory. If it were replaced by the creative capacities of workers' *self*-management, he contends, the factory would function much more productively and harmoniously. In fact Mothé saw the everyday spirit of cooperation, collective morale, and the tendency toward self-management among the workers—even in the capitalist factory—as an already existing basis for socialism.

> In the factory and the workshop there are two laws: that of the management and that of the workers. One is written and has at its disposal a complete apparatus to make sure it is respected (supervisors, chronos, etc.). The other is tacit, without any apparatus of coercion. This is the collective law which was elaborated while no one was watching. Despite all the coercive measures of persecution that the law of the factory has at its disposal, one must admit that it is less well respected than the collective law.[33]

In addition to the proletarian experience of everyday life *Socialisme ou Barbarie* looked to the historic examples of mass revolutionary struggle mentioned previously: the Paris Commune, the Russian soviets and factory committees of 1905 and 1917, the Spanish anarchist collectives of 1936-1937, etc. *Socialisme ou Barbarie* drew its inspiration from these and numerous other examples of working people taking direct control over their own lives and attempting to restructure society on an egalitarian basis.

More than anything else the Hungarian Revolution of 1956 convinced them of the potential of workers' self-management. Surpassing the example of the Polish strikers, Hungarian workers (their hopes raised by the prospect of destalinization) occupied the factories and established workers' councils throughout the country in October 1956. Within a week a national network of federated workers' councils took over governmental functions and control of the economy. The party-state apparatus was completely bypassed. Operating on the principle of mass meetings and direct democracy, the Hungarian Workers' Councils formulated a program demanding workers' self-management in all enterprises (including governmental departments), the abolition of externally imposed work norms, a sharp reduction in income inequalities, popular control of national planning, and free governmental elections.[34]

Here was a real movement of revolution and socialism along the lines that *Socialisme ou Barbarie* envisioned. Castoriadis considered it *the* major new development for revolutionary theory: "Over the coming years *all significant questions* will be condensed into one: Are you for or against the action and the program of the Hungarian workers?"[35] Lefort had personally visited the Polish workers' councils and listened to the radio reports of the Hungarian councils. He later remarked: "All the propositions formulated by the Hungarian workers' councils, and the embryonic programs elaborated during the course of the revolution...attest to an historically unprecedented project: an anti-capitalist and anti-bureaucratic project."[36]

In the face of two Soviet interventions the workers' councils fought for their survival against overwhelming military force. It took the Russian tanks until mid-December 1956 to crush the last remnants of resistance, killing an estimated 20,000 to 50,000 Hungarians in the process. Soviet leaders claimed the movement was a counter-revolution instigated by world imperialism, thereby discounting its revolutionary significance. Many leftists in France who condemned the Soviet invasion did not see the revolutionary implications of the uprising itself. Sartre, for example, called the Hungarian Revolution a *tragedy*, an unfortunate consequence of conflicting ideals within socialism.[37] The right naturally interpreted the events as a mass revolt against socialism *per se*.

Thus *Socialisme ou Barbarie* was the only journal to present the events as a proletarian socialist revolution against the bureaucracy. It was the only journal to stress the revolutionary character of the demands of the Hungarian Workers' Councils for workers' self-management.[38]

Undoubtedly there is a kernel of truth in this view of the Hungarian events. However, the main impact of the uprising for many on the French left was to destroy the privileged status previously accorded Soviet-style socialism and its French defender, the PCF. Intellectually, marxism lost its privileged status in their eyes as well, as we saw in the case of the revisionists. This process also engulfed *Socialisme ou Barbarie* in the wake of de Gaulle's return to power.

5. *The Rejection of Marxism*

Castoriadis eventually rejected marxism by subjecting it to a "marxist" critique. That is, by applying the concepts of class analysis and class struggle he found marxism incapable of explaining the major tendencies in modern society. While this in itself is not unusual (many disenchanted marxists have come to this conclusion), the manner and direction of Castoriadis' rejection of marxism is somewhat unique. For he rejected marxism in order to remain revolutionary. Instead of abandoning the goal of social change as many disillusioned marxist intellectuals have done, Castoriadis remained committed to the revolutionary project of a socialist transformation of society. For him marxism was one of the main obstacles standing in the path of such a project. He increasingly viewed marxism as a product of capitalist society which contained in essence a capitalist worldview which stressed the work ethic, industrial production, cost efficiency, rationalization of production, and hierarchical social relations. In this "mirror of production"[39] marxism reflected the assumptions, methods, and goals of capitalist ideology—in short, the *homo economus* view of human beings. Castoriadis came to perceive the goal of revolution not merely in political and economic terms, but more fundamentally as a process of overcoming all modes of domination, and hence of alienation as well.

* * *

Socialisme ou Barbarie's initial "manifesto" of 1949—written by Castoriadis—was firmly rooted in the marxist orientation. In fact he self-consciously modeled it on Marx and Engel's *Communist Manifesto* of 1848. He considered the *Manifesto* to have launched the revolutionary workers' movement on a solid theoretical basis which laid bare the history, nature, and functioning of capitalism:

> To understand and demonstrate all this in a clear way was the inestimable merit of the *Communist Manifesto* and marxism on the whole, and at the same time it was the granite basis on which alone a solid theory could be built that was beyond question.[40]

To Castoriadis in 1949 marxism was "beyond question." The problem was that no one else—the Stalinists, Trotskyists, Ultra-Leftists, etc.—was really practicing and developing it! *Socialisme ou Barbarie*, however, would carry out this task: "We think that we represent the continuation of living marxism in contemporary society."[41]

In this 1949 statement Castoriadis displayed a certain deference toward the marxist classics. Nevertheless, it is clear that his conception of marxism precluded the scholastic preoccupation with exegesis and proofs of faithfulness to the sacred texts so common in much of official marxism. Revolutionary theory could not be static. It had to reflect a changing reality. If it didn't change it would become sterile and meaningless, and revolutionary activity would subsequently suffer from it. Therefore, Lenin's classic adage on the importance of revolutionary theory was amended to include this point: "Without the *development* of revolutionary theory, there can be no *development* of revolutionary action."[42]

In 1949 Castoriadis considered marxism to be "beyond question" and his group to be "living marxism." Yet ten years later he argued that it was necessary to reject marxism in order to remain revolutionary! This development should not come as a complete surprise if we consider what being a marxist meant for Castoriadis in 1949:

> To be a marxist means for us, to situate oneself on the terrain of a tradition, to pose problems from the same standpoint that Marx and his followers did, to maintain and defend traditional marxist positions as long as a new examination does not persuade us that it is necessary to abandon them, revise them, or replace them with other positions which better correspond to the ultimate experience and needs of the revolutionary movement.[43]

However, "posing problems from the same starting point that Marx" did led him to "abandon," "revise," and "replace" the marxist framework. Using a marxist methodology Castoriadis examined marxism and ended up rejecting it. "We started from revolutionary marxism. But we have now reached the stage where a choice confronts us: to remain marxist or to remain revolutionaries."[44]

From 1949 through 1958 *Socialisme ou Barbarie* presented a continuing marxist critique of the communist movement. Gradually it became more and more obvious that this implied a thorough critique of marxism itself. What made such a project imperative for Castoriadis was de Gaulle's accession to power with apparent massive public support. For implicit in the *Socialisme ou Barbarie* analysis of the 1950s was a view of the working class as the revolutionary agent whose aspirations were appropriated and blocked by its bureaucratic leaders. But de Gaulle's 90% favorable vote in the plebiscite of November 1958 shattered Castoriadis' faith in the revolutionary role of the French working class. De Gaulle and his constitution could not have received such a high percentage of the vote without massive support from the working class.[45] Yet for Castoriadis marxism was a revolutionary theory only insofar as it represented the aspirations of a revolutionary class. If this class was no longer engaged in the project of a revolutionary transformation of society then the theory's relevance evaporated. Castoriadis' rejection of marxism could be viewed as a response to the defeat of the French left in 1958.[46]

None of Castoriadis' criticisms of marxism are particularly novel. Most were advanced on the French left by Sartre, Lefebvre, and the *Arguments* group. Further, many of Castoriadis' objections are reminiscent of standard criticisms of marxism.

His overall critique is reminiscent of Sartre's: Marxism is objectivist, reductionist, and mechanistic. It eliminates the actions of individuals and classes from both the economic and historical process, replacing them with objective "laws." Furthermore, as a world-view marxism is merely one rationalist-materialist variation of traditional Western metaphysics and, therefore, is subject to all the general pitfalls of metaphysics.[47]

Castoriadis rejects marxist political economy, the cornerstone of the "scientific" analysis of capitalism *en bloc*. "Neither its premises, nor its method, nor its structure are tenable any longer."[48] Its chief concepts—the crises of overproduction, pauperization of the proletariat, increasing unemployment, decreasing rate of profit, etc.—do not correspond to the reality of advanced capitalism. Nor does it adequately account for such basic economic changes as: 1) the rising standard of living of the working class, 2) the relative decline of the industrial working class and the growth of new sectors of the labor force, 3) the successful strategic intervention of the state in the economy to prevent large scale depression of the 1930s type, and 4) the emergence of a consumption-oriented economy. These changes make a mockery of the technical "laws" of economic development outlined in *Capital* concerning the organic composition of capital and the rates of profit, surplus value, and exploitation. Such flaws, according to Castoriadis, stem from the fundamental error in Marx's thinking: a misunderstanding of the process of reification. For Marx (along with most economists) treats people as though they are transformed into things in the economic process. They are subsumed under economic laws that do not substantially differ from natural laws, except insofar as subjective human intention becomes their unconscious vehicle.[49]

Castoriadis also challenges Marx's conception of the historical process. The economic determinist trend in Marx's thought tends to override the importance of human autonomy, and hence of revolutionary praxis itself. On the one hand, the development of the forces of production is an objective phenomenon which proceeds independent of human will. Class struggle then appears as a subjective reflex to the development of the productive forces. Classes are seen as agents of the historical process, mediums through which the productive forces are realized. On the other hand, the view of class struggle in Marx's thought as revolutionary praxis implies that it is the actions of individuals and classes that make history, not productive forces. Thus, "economic determinism and class struggle propose mutually incompatible explanations. In marxism there is not really a 'synthesis' but a triumph of determinism over class struggle."[50]

Castoriadis also questions the validity of the base-superstructure model of analysis. This model implies that technology develops autonomously and that all social relations are but reflections of its development. Yet this is obviously an inadequate explanatory principle. It is particularly obvious when one looks at pre-capitalist civilizations which all had traditional pre-industrial technologies. The same base yields a broad variety of superstructural phenomena—a fact which marxism cannot explain.

This model also brings out the metaphysical assumptions of historical materialism. For it implies that history is governed by ideas—i.e., *technological* ideas. "In what is known as 'historical materialism' history is indeed propelled by *ideas*. But instead of being religious, philosophical or political ideas, the ideas are technological."[51] For the forces of

production are not invented blindly. Even the simplest technological innovation begins as an idea. Thus marxism elevates
one type of idea and claims all others are but reflections of it.
Hence, Castoriadis argues, it is a metaphysical system of
thought.

The crux of the matter for Castoriadis is the nature of
theory *per se*. Any theory that aims at totality tends to be
reductionistic by the very fact that it abstracts from the totality
of human experience. It cannot take everything into account,
only that which is deemed essential. Thus whole sectors of
human experience are subordinated or ignored. By its very
nature the last 2500 years of Western metaphysics is a
misleading and inadequate form of thinking! The "total-
view" is always wrong because the totality is always in the
process of becoming. This is the source of dialectical
contradiction.

Does Castoriadis mean that coherent and meaningful
thought is impossible? No, but he does mean we should
recognize the limitations on theory and the social-historical
factors that condition it. For categories and forms of thought
are themselves a product of the historical process. In ancient
Greece, for example, there was no explicit concept of ideology
or the economy. Such concepts emerge in the course of
historical development. "Historical knowledge is itself, in
essence a historical phenomenon, needing to be understood
and interpreted as such....To have an experience of history, as
a historical being is to be *in* and *part of* history, as well as *in*
and *part of* society."[52]

Marx was aware of this problem but he didn't overcome
it. His thought is strongly tainted with the categories of 19th
century European capitalist society (e.g., his praise for the
technological drive of the bourgeoisie, his contempt for the
peasants, etc.). His entire world view was based on an analysis
of a limited segment of human history—the bourgeois
revolution in Western Europe, 1650-1850.

> If in order to retain a theory we have to expunge from history
> almost everything that really happened (except what occurred

in the course of a few centuries in a narrow belt bordering the North Atlantic) the price is really too high. We had better keep this history and reject the theory.[53]

Castoriadis does not advocate a naive relativism or skepticism. Rather he argues one should become aware of the problems of social-historical centrism and attempt to eliminate their effects, while remaining deeply rooted in the particularity of one's context. Only on this basis can any serious revolutionary re-thinking begin.

As can be gleaned from this overview there are serious problems with Castoriadis' rejection of marxism. Sartre and Lefebvre make many similar particular criticisms, yet retain a marxist standpoint. Undoubtedly they have different conceptions of what marxism is. For Castoriadis marxism is obviously vulgar marxism. He argues that the theory cannot be separated from what it has become in practice, that is, the ideology of the communist movement.

> Marxism has become an ideology in the fullest meaning that Marx himself attributed to this word. It has become a system of ideas which relate to reality not in order to clarify it and transform it, but on the contrary in order to mask it and justify it in the abstract. It has become a means of allowing people to say one thing and to do another, to appear other than they are.[54]

Thus he feels that the attempts to "existentialize" or "revise" marxism serve only to further its mystifying project. He views the return to Marx as inconsistent with Marx's own contention that a theory should be judged by what it has become in practice. It would make as much sense to judge Christianity solely by the verses of the Bible and ignore its 2000 years of historical reality. To the argument that Marx has been betrayed by his followers Castoriadis claims that it is too late now to rescue a "pure" Marx. "All great theoretical discoveries have tended to become myths as soon as they sought to convert themselves into systems, marxism no less than any other."[55] Hence the only way to be true to Marx is by denouncing marxism as an ideological mystification and begin revolutionary theorizing anew.

The main issue involved in Castoriadis' rejection of marxism is the validity of his claim that marxism must be identified solely with its stalinist and trotskyist varieties—or rather caricatures. Sartre and Lefebvre reject this contention. In fact one may say that in identifying marxism with such economism, Castoriadis fails to understand its depth and profundity. For as Sartre and Lefebvre have both demonstrated in distinct ways marxism can be very useful in developing a new left social theory.[56]

Castoriadis' rejection of marxism thus remains problematic. However, his emphasis on the need for bold, new, innovative, and creative thought which bows before no authority was an important stimulus to French new left social theory. He challenged the emerging new left to think anew the very basis of revolutionary theory—its assumption, its methods and its goals. In rejecting marxism from the left Castoriadis called into question the very meaning of political discourse in a dramatic fashion:

> The absurdity of all inherited political thought consists precisely in wanting to resolve men's problems for them, whereas the only political problem in fact is this: how can people become capable of resolving their problems for themselves.[57]

It was this task which the French new left set for itself and attempted to realize in May 1968.

Notes

1. The only detailed study of *Socialisme ou Barbarie* is Alan Binstock's, "Socialisme ou Barbarie," M.A. thesis, University of Wisconsin, 1971. Dick Howard gives an overview of the group in his "Introduction to Castoriadis," *Telos* #23 (Spring 1975), pp. 117-131. Castoriadis discusses the history of the group in "An Interview with C. Castoriadis," *Ibid.*, pp. 131-155. See also Lichtheim *op. cit.* 182-192; Gombin, *loc. cit.* 32-

39 and pp. 101-105; and Poster, *op. cit.*, pp. 201-208. The most recent examination of Castoriadis is Brian Singer, "The Early Castoriadis: Socialism, Barbarism and the Bureaucratic Thread," *Canadian Journal of Political and Social Theory*, Vol. 3, no. 3 (Fall 1979), pp. 35-56; and his "The Later Castoriadis: Institutions under Interrogation," *ibid.*, Vol. 4, no. 1 (Winter 1980).

2. As an alien in France and an official of OECD, Castoriadis felt he should write pseudonymously. His articles appeared under the pseudonyms of Pierre Chaulieu, Paul Cardan, and Marc Coudray. After he left OECD and became naturalized he began to publish his collected works, most of which originally appeared in *Socialisme ou Barbarie*. Five volumes have thus far appeared. See his *La Société Bureaucratique* (Paris, 1973) 2 vols.; *L'Expérience des Mouvements Ouvriers* (Paris, 1974) 2 vols.; *L'Institution Imaginaire de la Société* (Paris, 1975).

3. A collection of his articles from *Socialisme ou Barbarie, Les Temps Modernes,* and *Arguments* appeared as *Eléments d'une Critique de la Bureaucratie* (Paris, 1971). Lefort is currently a professor of sociology at the University of Caen.

4. For a history of French trotskyism see Jacques Roussel, *Les Enfants du Prophète: Histoire du Mouvement Trotskiste en France* (Paris, 1970).

5. See Castoriadis' articles in the *Bulletin Intérieur du P.C.I.* 31 (August 1946) and 41 (August 1947). The other anti-communist critiques of bureaucracy which developed from the trotskyist movement are: The Italian Bruno Rizzi's, *La Bureaucratization du Monde* (1939); and the American Max Schactman, *The Bureaucratic Revolution* (1940) and James Burnham, *The Managerial Revolution* (1941). Politically each of these thinkers turned sharply to the right, whereas Castoriadis retained a *gauchiste* perspective and analysis.

6. Cf. Castoriadis, "Les rapports de production en Russie," *Socialisme ou Barbarie* (May 1949).

7. The foregoing is a summary of Castoriadis' worldview which he presented in his article "Socialisme ou Barbarie," *Socialisme ou Barbarie* 1 (March 1949). This article was a political manifesto defining the orientation of the journal.

8. On the internal life of the group see the articles entitled, "La vie de notre groupe" which appeared regularly in the journal.

9. As we have already seen, ex-communists like Edgar Morin were strongly influenced by the *Socialisme ou Barbarie* analysis.

10. See Chapter 2 of this study.

11. Merleau-Ponty sided with Lefort and Castoriadis against Sartre's championing of the PCF in his *The Communists and Peace* (1952). We have already mentioned Sartre's debate with Lefort on this issue in Chapter 2. Castoriadis contributed an article to the debate as well: "Sartre, le stalinisme et les ouvriers," *Socialisme ou Barbarie* 12 (August 1953).

Merleau-Ponty drew some of his arguments against Sartre's "ultra-bolshevism" from both Lefort and Castoriadis. See his *Les Aventures de la dialectique* (Paris, 1955), pp. 312-313 where he quotes from *Socialisme ou Barbarie* 10 (July-August 1952).

12. Under Morin's influence the *Arguments* group turned to *Socialisme ou Barbarie* and an informal alliance evolved.

13. We will discuss this point in Chapter 6.

14. Castoriadis pursued this analysis in a series of articles called, "Le Mouvement révolutionnaire sous capitalisme moderne," *Socialisme ou Barbarie* 31 (December 1960), 32 (April-June 1961), 33 (December-February 1961-1962).

15. In an internal debate over the form and role of political organization Lefort adopted a "spontenaicist" position while Castoriadis retained a belief in the necessity of a political party which, however, would not "lead" the working class but rather "assist" it. See Lefort's "Organisation et parti," *Socialisme ou Barbarie* 26 (November-December 1958) and Castoriadis', "Prolétariat et organization," *Socialisme ou Barbarie* 27 (April 1959) and 28 (July 1959).

16. On Lefort's rejection of marxism see his, "La Dégradation idéologique du marxisme," *Les Cahiers du Centre d'études socialistes*, 34-35 (November-December 1963).

17. J.-F. Lyotard, Maille, and Souyri disagreed with Castoriadis' rejection of marxism. They retained a marxist framework similar to the original *Socialisme ou Barbarie* orientation, which they disseminated in a journal called *Pouvoir ouvrier*.

18. There were a number of working class members of the group who engaged in on-the-job political organizing, among whom Daniel Mothé was the most notable.

19. Claude Lefort, "What is Bureaucracy," trans. by J. L. Cohen, *Telos* 22 (Winter 1974-1975), p. 31. This article originally appeared in *Arguments* 17 (1960) after Lefort left *Socialisme ou Barbarie*.

20. Marx, *The Critique of Hegel's Philosophy of Right* (Cambridge, 1970), p. 43. Originally written in 1843. Another reason for the prevalence of bureaucratic incompetence is that individual bureaucrats tend to rise in the bureaucracy to their level of incompetence. For if they do competent work at one level, they are promoted to the next. They continue to rise until their performance is deemed insufficient to warrant further promotion. Thus, incompetence prevails at every level!

21. Marx, *The Eighteen Brumaire of Louis Bonaparte* (New York, 1969), p. 121. Original edition 1850.

22. Lenin, *State and Revolution* (New York, 1943), p. 47.

23. See Castoriadis, "Le rôle de l'idéologie bolchevique dans la naissance de la bureaucratie," *Socialisme ou Barbarie* 35 (January 1964).

24. Lenin, *op. cit.*, pp. 43, 83.

25. The best study of the various oppositional tendencies within Bolshevism 1917-1921 is R. V. Daniels, *The Conscience of the Revolution* (Cambridge, 1960).

26. Such as Alexander Kollontai's, "L'Opposition ouvrière" in *Socialisme ou Barbarie* 35 (January, 1964).

27. See in particular Part IV "The Strategy and Nature of Bolshevism," pp. 199-248.

28. See Weber's *Economy and Society*, trans. by E. Fischoff *et al.* (New York, 1968).

29. Castoriadis develops this analysis of bureaucracy in advanced capitalism in the series of articles previously mentioned: "Le Mouvement révolutionnaire sous le capitalisme moderne."

30. Weber was personally sympathetic to a democratization of administration. When this possibility arose in the wake of the German Revolution of 1918 he supported it as a member of the Heidelberg Workers' and Soldiers' Council. See Marianne Weber, *Max Weber: Ein Lebenshield* (Tubingen, 1926).

31. For a sampling of such articles see: Georges Vivier, "La vie en usine," *Socialisme ou Barbarie* 17 (July-September 1955); Henri Feraud, "L'unité syndical," *ibid.*, 17, and 23 (January-February 1958); P. Guillaume, "Dix semaines en usine," *ibid.*, 32 (April-June 1961).

32. These articles were collected and published in two volumes: *Journal d'un ouvrier* (Paris, 1958) and *Militant chez Renault* (Paris, 1965).

33. Mothé, "L'Usine et la Gestion Ouvrière," *Socialisme ou Barbarie* 22 (July 1957), p. 101.

34. Issues 20 and 21 of *Socialisme ou Barbarie* were largely devoted to the Polish and Hungarian situation, including the following articles by Castoriadis, "L'Insurrection hongroise" (#20); "La révolution prolétarian contre la bureaucratie" (#20); and "La Voie polonaise de la bureaucratisation" (#21). Documents of the Hungarian Workers' Councils were also reprinted.

35. Castoriadis, "La révolution prolétarienne contre la bureaucratie," *Socialisme ou Barbarie* 20 (December 1956), pp. 277-278.

36. Lefort, "The Age of Novelty," *Telos* 29 (Fall 1976), p. 33.

37. Cf. Sartre's "Le Fantôme de Staline," *Les Temps Modernes* 129, 130, 131 (November, December 1956, January 1957).

38. Initial analyses of the Hungarian uprising are catalogued in I. L. Halasz de Beky, *A Bibliography of the Hungarian Revolution, 1956* (Toronto, 1963). Important works in French are: Balasz Nagy, *La Formation du Conseil central ouvrier de Budapest en 1956* (Paris, 1961); F. Fejto, *Budapest 1956* (Paris, 1966); and M. Molnar, *Victoire d'une défaite: Budapest 1956* (Paris, 1968).

39. Cf. Jean Baudrillard, *Le Miroir de la Production* (Paris, 1973) for an elaboration of this argument.

40. Castoriadis, "Socialisme ou Barbarie," in *Socialisme ou Barbarie* 1 (March 1949), p. 12.

41. *Ibid.,* p. 3

42. *Ibid.,* p. 7.

43. *Ibid.,* p. 4.

44. Castoriadis, "Marxisme et Théorie Révolutionnaire," *Socialisme ou Barbarie* 36 (June 1965), p. 42.

45. For a lively account of de Gaulle's return to power see Alexander Werth's, *The de Gaulle Revolution* (1960).

46. On this point cf. Binstock *loc. cit.,* pp. 80-81.

47. As noted in Chapter 4, this last point is a favorite argument of the Heideggerian marxists Axelos and Fougeyrollas. Merleau-Ponty also developed an argument along these lines in his later works.

48. Castoriadis, *History and Revolution* (London, 1971), p. 4. This is a translation of selections from "Marxisme et Théorie Révolutionnaire," published by a British offshoot of *Socialisme ou Barbarie* called *Solidarity.*

49. Of course, as Castoriadis admits, this calls *all* economic discourse into question. See Castoriadis, "An Interview," *Telos* 23 (Spring 1975), p. 148.

50. Castoriadis, *History and Revolution,* p. 24.

51. *Ibid.,* p. 10.

52. *Ibid.,* p. 27.

53. *Ibid.,* p. 21.

54. Castoriadis, *The Fate of Marxism* (London, 1966), pp. 2-3. This is a translation of more selections from "Marxisme et théorie révolution-naire," by the same group.

55. Castoriadis, "Recommence la Révolution," *Socialisme ou Barbarie* 35 (January 1964), p. 7.

56. Cf. Lefebvre: "Marx's radical criticism of political philosophy, the state, and bureaucracy...implies the objective of revolutionary praxis, namely democratic self-management, without bureaucracy or state." *The Sociology of Marx* (New York, 1968), p. 148.

57. Castoriadis, "Introduction générale," to the *Works,* in *La société bureaucratique,* Vol. I (Paris, 1973), p. 38.

/PART II/
MAY 1968

/6/
From Origins to Culmination

1. May 1968: New Left Apocalypse

For a short time in May 1968 it seemed as though the majority of the French were rejecting the alienated social order of modern bureaucratic capitalism and demanding a fundamental re-evaluation of social values.[1] This protest was initiated by Daniel Cohn-Bendit and the March 22nd Committee at Nanterre University in the Paris suburbs. The arrogant and ill-conceived reactions of the government helped the movement mushroom into a national student strike featuring university occupations and full-scale street fighting (including the street barricades of Parisian revolutionary tradition). The strikes spread to factories and offices throughout France despite the lack of official union sanction. Major elements of the managerial and professional strata joined this general strike and contested the hierarchical, overcentralized, and authoritarian structure of their respective milieux as well. Chemists contested their privileges. Even the television journalists of the government-controlled

ORTF went on strike, refusing to broadcast the distortions demanded by the government.[2] Modern bureaucratic French society came to a virtual standstill.

The deafening silence that ensued was filled with the demands and slogans of the strikers. Workers in occupied factories showed their aspirations with such slogans as "dignité du travail," "contestation du pouvoir," "contre alienation," and in some cases, "autogestion."[3] Many students expressed solidarity with the workers, while demanding control over educational institutions. Some students went further and declared a cultural revolution as well. Professionals—students, scientists, technicians, journalists—also showed solidarity and some presented demands for self-management.[4] The walls of Paris quickly filled with the slogans of the student militants:

"No to bureaucracy!"

"Consumer society must die a violent death. Alienated society must die a violent death. We want a new and original world. We reject a world where security against starvation is bought for the risk of death by boredom."

"Humanity will not be free until the last bureaucrat is strangled with the guts of the last capitalist."

"The revolution that is beginning challenges not only capitalist society but industrial civilization."

"Don't change employers, change the employment of life."

"Power to the Imagination!"[5]

Here then was a social upheaval along the lines envisioned by Sartre, Lefebvre, and Castoriadis. It was a revolt against alienation in bureaucratic society. In its variance from the traditional marxist conception of social crisis it appeared to be a profound verification of the existentialist, revisionist, and *gauchiste* critiques of marxism.

It was not a strictly economic or political crisis. Rather this was a cultural crisis with political and economic dimensions along the lines anticipated by Lefebvre and Castoriadis.[6] It was sparked by students and opposed by the traditional revolutionary organizations. In the factories the movement was led mainly by the younger workers who opposed the CGT trade union bureaucracy as well as the employers. Another novel feature was the role played by the new working class of mental workers, teachers, and technicians. Such white collar workers more frequently raised the radical demand of self-management, a demand to which the traditional marxists of the PCF leadership were opposed. It is no wonder then that they opposed this movement. For were it to succeed the PCF would appear obsolete.

Not only traditional marxist dogmas disintegrated in May 1968. The liberal myths of stability, integration, de-politicization, and consensus in advanced capitalist society exploded as well. Even after the re-consolidation of Gaullist power, who could speak of stability when it became known that at the height of the crisis de Gaulle had to sneak out of the country to confer with his generals in Germany concerning the loyalty of the Army? Who could speak of embourgeoisement and integration of the working class into modern society when ten million workers occupied the nation's factories under slogans like "contre alienation?" Who could speak of de-politicization of the youth when university students, *lycée* students, and young workers were at the forefront of a movement that almost turned society upside-down? What sense does consensus have in such a situation? A consensus against alienation and bureaucracy?

Granted, the chasm has since been filled, the breach has been closed by the triumph and re-emergence of traditional politics. Nevertheless, one cannot deny that the explosion occurred. Nor can it be explained away with facile observations about the generation gap or the archaic structure of French institutions. Even though the CGT tried to define the workers' struggle in traditional bread and butter trade union demands, and the PCF tried to define the student struggle as a movement to reform and liberalize the university, the May movement was clearly something more—something perhaps intangible. John Ardagh, an independent British commentator on the French scene, caught something of this "spirit of May."[7] He called the events:

> ...a crisis outside conventional politics...It was a strike against... the boring repetitiveness of much modern factory work which leads to "alienation"; against the rigid and bureaucratic chain of command, the refusal to delegate authority and the lack of group discussion...It was a strike against a pattern of authority.[8]

In Sartre's terms one might say it was a strike against seriality, marked by a joyous festival (in Lefebvre's use of the term) of de-alienated communication and reciprocity in a sphere of existence beyond any mode of domination (à la Castoriadis). As another commentator put it: "For a brief moment, France tasted life beyond alienation."[9]

However, this moment was just that—a moment. It passed. The new left forces lost the initiative. By calling for new elections de Gaulle succeeded in redefining the crisis in conventional parliamentary terms. The outcome was almost inevitable. The traditional left was unable to unite because the very nature of the crisis exacerbated the differences within it. Further, much of the new left extra-parliamentary opposition refused to participate in the June elections. Consequently, de Gaulle's victory was hardly surprising. For once, the parameters of alienated existence were re-established, political alienation reasserted its dominance.

2. Sartre, Lefebvre, Castoriadis and May 1968

To most observers this upheaval which shook French society to its very foundations came like a bolt from the blue. Obviously, the ideas of Sartre, Lefebvre, and Castoriadis did not cause these events. Nevertheless, it is also clear that the intellectuals did influence the climate of ideas among the student leaders who initiated the campus uprising. On this point Cohn-Bendit remarked,

> Some people have tried to force Marcuse on us as a mentor: that is a joke. None of us has read Marcuse. Some read Marx, of course, perhaps Bakunin, and of the moderns, Althusser, Mao, Guevara, Lefebvre. Nearly all the militants of the March 22nd movement have read Sartre.[11]

From the late 1950s on, Sartre's influence on the emerging new left student movement was evident. His leadership role in the Algerian war protest movements earned him the respect of the student activists. *Les Temps Modernes* became the focus of political and theoretical debate for the new left, influencing communist students as well.[12] Leaders of the national student union, the UNEF,[13] (e.g., Kravetz, Peninou, and Griset) wrote for *Les Temps Modernes* and participated with André Gorz (a close ally of Sartre and the journal's political editor in the 1960s) in working out a new left political theory.[14] Above all, Sartre's existential marxist analysis of alienation helped focus students' discontent with their life prospects in modern bureaucratic society.

Gorz's *Stratégie ouvrière et néo-capitalisme* (1964)[15] was the most comprehensive statement of new left political strategy to appear in the 1960s. Gorz synthesized and summarized the conclusions of the existentialist, revisionist, and *gauchiste* critique of marxism in a clear fashion. He began with the revisionist critique of the traditional marxist view of the working class under capitalism. As we have seen, this critique recognizes the obvious fact that in modern society the working class is no longer driven to revolt by starvation wages. It has secured its subsistence and a rising standard of living through much social conflict but without a revolutionary cataclysm. Dire poverty continues to exist in advanced capitalism for a significant minority—but not for the majority. Hence the working class could no longer be revolutionary if it was organized solely on the economic issues of poverty and exploitation.

Gorz developed the theory of a "new working class."[16] The percentage of the labor force involved in manufacturing was gradually decreasing in technologically advanced capitalist society in favor of white collar workers. This did not mean the working class was disappearing as some liberal sociologists argued. Rather it was changing in composition. Many of these new workers (technicians, researchers, teachers, journalists, social workers, etc.) received moderate incomes, and salary was not their main concern. The meaning and creativity of their work were equally important. From this Gorz concluded that the existentialist concept of alienation could provide the theoretical basis for a movement that united both the traditional and the new working class around a radical program.

This program would emphasize that the chief defect of capitalism is not economic exploitation as such, but the alienation of the worker in the capitalist production process. To overcome this alienation Gorz advocated the *gauchiste* goal of workers' self-management (*autogestion*) as the focus of the socialist movement. Workers could unite to seek structural reforms of the enterprise which would bring the process of production under their control. Such reform would be revolutionary since it would involve the transference of power in the enterprise from the capitalist managerial apparatus to the workers, and thus dissolve the alienation that arises in the separation between management and execution of work which Castoriadis highlighted.

While Gorz and the UNEF leaders developed a new left analysis of alienation in capitalist *production*, other student activists influenced by Lefebvre developed analyses of alienation in capitalist *consumption*. The *Internationale situationniste* group combined elements of surrealism and dadaism with the critique of everyday life to question the cultural values of modern consumer-oriented society. In *La Société du Spectacle* (1967), Guy Debord presented the situationist view of modern society as a spectacle of inauthenticity which is experienced as a hollow life one move away from "real" life.

The situationists did not moralistically oppose consumption *per se* but rather the "totalitarian management" of society which manipulates and conditions the individual to seek fulfillment in consumption instead of in creativity and authenticity. In the consumer society the meaning of life tends to be reduced to a quantitive expansion of material survival, leaving the question of the quality of life untouched. Everyday life is thus rendered boring and banal, an unending monotony of joyless consumption.

For the situationists, consumer society must be destroyed by a cultural revolution of free ("liberated") speech and true communication. Such a revolution would be total. It would reject the capitalist work ethic as well as the consumption ethic. It would reject all hierarchy of authority and specialization. It would affirm the realization of the revolution in art, in creativity, in desire, and in play. In short, the situationists borrowed Lefebvre's vision of the Festival as their ideal of revolution. Their strategy for achieving this revolution was to disrupt the routines of everyday life with guerrilla theatre, thereby creating outrageous situations in which people would be forced to confront the true nature of bourgeois culture.[17]

Situationist students at the University of Strasbourg committed an effective outrage in October 1966. After winning election to the student government, they declared its immediate dissolution and used its 5000 franc budget to print and distribute a pamphlet they had written entitled, "On the poverty of student life considered in its economic, political, psychological, sexual and intellectual aspects, and some means of remedying it." This pamphlet provocatively analyzed student alienation and called on students to ally themselves with the proletariat to overthrow capitalism, communism, and industrial society itself! The publicity which accompanied the criminal conviction of those situationists responsible for this "Strasbourg Scandal" guaranteed a broad distribution of the pamphlet and their journal, *Internationale situationniste*, throughout France.[18]

The situationists publicly acknowledged their intellectual debt to Lefebvre.[19] Debord participated in a study group on everyday life set up by Lefebvre, and many situationists studied under Lefebvre at the University of Nanterre where he taught sociology during the 1960s. It is not surprising that, given their orientation, the situationists were credited with the authorship of much of the provocative wall-writings that appeared in May 1968 questioning consumer society and the banality of everyday life.[20]

The situationists were not the only student activists to be influenced by Lefebvre's critique of everyday life. His work was thoroughly discussed in *Alétheia*, a student journal from the *Ecole Normale*, and in the neo-anarchist journal, *Noir et rouge*.[21]

The influence of Castoriadis and *Socialisme ou Barbarie* during the May events was realized primarily through Daniel Cohn-Bendit and the March 22nd movement at Nanterre. These students very carefully studied *Socialisme ou Barbarie* during the 1960s and based their political practice on its theory.[22] As Cohn-Bendit noted:

> From the very start, the 22 March Movement made no distinction between leaders and led—all decisions were taken in general assembly, and all reports by the various study commissions had to be referred back to it as well. This...pointed the way to the future, showing how society can be run by all and for the benefit of all. In particular, the end of the division between leaders and led in our movement reflected the wish to abolish this division in the process of production. Direct democracy implies direct management.[23]

Cohn-Bendit's book on May 1968, *Obsolete Communism: The Left-Wing Alternative* is largely based on analyses which appeared in *Socialisme ou Barbarie*. He refers explicitly to the journal and acknowledges his debt as follows:

> The readers, unfortunately far too few in number of this and other Leftist reviews, will appreciate how much this book owes to them...I am not, and do not want to be, anything but a plagiarist when it comes to preaching of revolutionary theory and practice.[24]

In reference to Castoriadis he remarked, "the views we have been presenting are those of P. Chaulieu" (one of Castoriadis' pseudonyms).[25]

Of course, Cohn-Bendit acknowledged other influences as well: Lefort, Lefebvre, the situationists, Sartre, neo-anarchism, etc. The extent to which the existentialist, revisionist, and *gauchiste* trends had merged by 1968 is revealed in the eclectic amalgam of Cohn-Bendit's new left thought.

While the overall extent of the impact of such thought on the May 1968 events themselves remains difficult to assess, it is clear that Sartre, Lefebvre, and Castoriadis had some influence on at least several groups of students—the March 22nd movement, the situationists, the UNEF—who were instrumental in detonating these events.

Like most French intellectuals, Sartre, Lefebvre, and Castoriadis supported the May movement. Sartre, Lefebvre, Gorz, and others jointly signed a manifesto which appeared in *Le Monde* depicting the student movement as a valiant effort to overcome the "alienated order" of society.[26] In other newspaper articles and radio interviews Sartre reiterated his support. For example, *Le Nouvel Observateur* carried an interview of Cohn-Bendit conducted by Sartre, who self-effacingly played Danny's straight-man.[27] Sartre also was present in the Latin Quarter throughout the strike and spoke at mass meetings in the "liberated" Sorbonne.[28]

At Nanterre Lefebvre found himself in the center of the storm. Many members of the March 22nd movement, including Cohn-Bendit, were his students. He supported their actions and allowed them to use his class as an organizing forum. In the movement which developed among his students, Lefebvre saw a protest against the totality of everyday life. He praised the students' praxis of confrontation and *contestation*: "Contestation is an all-inclusive, total rejection of experienced or anticipated forms of alienation. It is a deliberate refusal to be co-opted."[29] Lefebvre argued that this form of protest could be comprehended only in relation to an understanding of the new explosive contradictions developing in the state of advanced capitalist society which he had analyzed in his critique of everyday life. Otherwise, one would fail to see the significant novelty of this type of protest.

Castoriadis saw in May a vindication of his thought, just as he had viewed the Hungarian revolt of 1956 as such. For him both revolts confirmed the impossibility of the project of bureaucratic rationalization.[30]

3. Limitations of New Left Social Theory

May 1968 appears to the intellectual historian as both the culmination and supercession of new left social theory. This upheaval resulted in the incorporation of the new left themes of alienation, bureaucracy, and self-management into mainstream currents of thought. Marxism, liberalism, and social catholicism, were forced to recognize their significance as the problematics of modernized society.

At the same time May 1968 revealed the weaknesses of new left social theory. The new left vision of a de-alienated society failed to grant the structures of society and the practico-inert their full weight. In Sartre's terms, the serialized mass had achieved unity in a group-in-fusion. However, this unity disintegrated when the fused group refused organizational form for fear of becoming a bureaucratized institutional structure. Consequently, the previously constituted social structures which were negated during May reasserted their dominance.

This failure by the new left to develop organization and structure limited the effectiveness of its critique to the sphere of consciousness—i.e., culture. May was a revolution of consciousness without a revolution of structure, a cultural revolution without a political revolution. Hence it failed.

While Sartre, Lefebvre, and Castoriadis contributed to the strengths of new left social theory, they also contributed to its weaknesses. In rejecting the objectivist distortions of traditional marxism these thinkers tended toward the opposite pole—a subjectivist neglect of the weight of objective structures.

Methodologically, the point of unity of the different strains of new left social theory is the rejection of the positivist (both marxist and non-marxist) conception of knowledge. Positivism is based on the scientific method derived from the natural sciences. It holds that knowledge is restricted to the domain of the empirically verifiable. It analyzes the object of knowledge from the outside, externally. Such a methodology, when applied to the human organism rules out the possibility of knowledge of internal states of consciousness. In fact, it denies their very existence. Positivism reduces internal or subjective phenomena to their external or objective manifestations (forms of behavior or linguistic signs). In France the positivist trend of the 1960s known as structuralism went one step further. In addition to denying reality to subjective phenomena, the French structuralists denied the very existence of the subject! Thus Lévi-Strauss claimed, "the ultimate goal of the human sciences is not to constitute but to dissolve man."[31] Michel Foucault, another structuralist, contemptuously dismissed subjectivity and, parodying Nietzsche, claimed "Man is dead."[32] In this view the individual was not the active subject of history constituting one's own foundations, but rather the unwitting agent of social structures constituting themselves. Even language, the vehicle by which the individual believes one is expressing oneself, is actually a structure which uses the individual to express *it*self! Thus Lévi-Strauss claimed, "Language...has its reasons of which man knows nothing."[33]

In the context of French intellectual history, structuralism was a direct attack against Sartre and all the trends of thought associated with the critique of alienation: existentialism, phenomenology, humanism, historicism, etc. Levi-Strauss rejected existentialism because it promoted an "indulgent attitude toward the illusions of subjectivity. To promote private preoccupations to the rank of philosophical problems is dangerous, and may end in a kind of shop-girl's philosophy."[34] He countered this conception of philosophy with the "scientific" aim of understanding Being "in relation to itself, and not in relation to oneself."[35]

Here, then, was another classical confrontation between subjectivist and objectivist conceptions of social theory, similar to the earlier confrontation between Sartre and the PCF marxists. This earlier confrontation resulted in the adoption of existentialized versions of marxism by both Sartre and his chief opponents.[36]

The structuralists (both marxist and non-marxist) challenged this existential-marxist synthesis, claiming it was still rooted in the subjectivity of traditional metaphysics. Lévi-Strauss opposed Sartre's humanism not because he was against "man," but because he opposed the view of the individual as a self-grounding being. Similarly, he criticized Sartre's conception of the dialectical rationality of praxis and history because it claimed that social structures were the product of the praxis of the subject. Thus humanism and historicism opposed the structuralist credo of the priority of the invariant structure over the variable actions of human being.

Sartre, Lefebvre, and Castoriadis responded to the structuralist attack with an offensive of their own, focusing on its reductionist and ahistorical orientation.[37] They also questioned the structuralist claim to objectivity because it did not recognize the subjectivity of the researcher. In response to charges of historicism, the new leftists accused the structuralists of scientism. The intensity and hostility which characterized this intellectual debate ran surprisingly deep. Each side contemptuously dismissed the other, either as muddled, old-fashioned humanists, or as heartless technocrats.

The structuralist controversy of the 1960s served to highlight the weaknesses of new left thought (as well as those of structuralism). In pinpointing the limitations of structuralism, Sartre, Lefebvre, and Castoriadis appeared as unrepentent romantics whose rejection of technological rationality implied a lack of acceptance of the givens of modernity. Their "critique of the real by the possible" contained a healthy impulse to overcome the dehumanizing tendencies within modern society. The problem was that so much of the real was dehumanizing that they tended to bracket it and move on to the imaginary as an antidote. Thus, after 1968 Sartre flip-flopped back and forth between the extremes of the unreality of Maoist activism and his multi-volume "imaginary" study of Flaubert.[38] Lefebvre pursued the imaginary Festival in his study of urbanism,[39] while Castoriadis turned to a study of Aristotle to discover the roots of the social imagination and the imaginary institution of society.[40]

It is no wonder, then, that new left thought lost its coherence in the aftermath of May 1968. Since then, the political and intellectual climate has changed considerably. Ironically, for all his emphasis on the concept of scarcity in the *Critique*, Sartre and the new left achieved their broadest impact in the (relatively speaking) post-scarcity climate of the late 1960s. The re-emergence of economic crisis in the West during the 1970s, however, gave renewed impetus to a marxist economic critique of capitalism which took the form of Eurocommunism (see Chapter 8).

4. May 1968 in Perspective: The Turning Point

In retrospect one can see many elements in the May crisis: a generational conflict, a crisis within the educational system, conventional labor strife, a political crisis of the Fifth Republic, a social crisis stemming from the strains of modernization, and a cultural crisis of spiritual revolt against the alienating impact of the neo-capitalist form of modernization. Undoubtedly, all these factors helped to define the conjuncture in which this explosion took place.[41]

It is clear that there were three separate and distinct aspects of the crisis: a) the student uprising; b) the mass workers' strike; and c) the crisis of confidence in the government leading to parliamentary elections. Each of these aspects was eventually resolved in favor of the status quo. The universities reopened (somewhat modified and reformed in structure), the workers returned to work with a wage settlement of the dispute (which was soon eaten up by inflation), and the Left suffered a severe election setback with the loss of one million votes. Militants were suppressed in the universities and the factories, *gauchiste* organizations were banned, and their leaders jailed. Thus, on the political level, the defeat of the May Movement appeared complete. The revolutionaries lost.

Yet even in defeat the May Movement substantially altered the parameters of the political arena and laid the foundation for progressive politics in France in the 1970s. In this regard May 1968 was an important turning point as well as the culmination of what had come before. For May opened up new possibilities in both political practice and social theory.

In the domain of political practice two new paths were opened up: the Union of the Left electoral strategy and the proliferation of a whole range of new social movements.

No political party can claim real leadership of the amorphous and spontaneous May revolt. Various trotskyist and maoist grouplets participated in the movement and unsuccessfully attempted to place themselves at its head. The P.S.U. (Parti Socialist Unifié) was the only established party to fully support the movement, but it couldn't win many votes for its efforts since most of the militants did not consider electoral politics a legitimate strategy for change in the aftermath of mass revolt. As we have seen, the PCF denounced the movement and attempted to restore order as quickly as possible. The defeat of the left in the June 1968 elections clearly demonstrated that the left parties did not gain any immediate benefits from May.

Yet, May had demonstrated there was a substantial constituency in France for large-scale change. The formation of a renovated Socialist Party (Parti Socialiste or PS) in the early 1970s was a direct result of the appearance of this constituency for progressive change which May revealed.

Founded on a strategy of alliance with the PCF, the PS helped to create the conditions in the 1970s in which a left government seemed to be a real possibility in France.

This constituency, however, did not necessarily see electoral politics as the only arena in which to seek such change. All sorts of new groups emerged around a variety of issues which traditional marxism had considered secondary (and therefore inconsequential) to the class struggle, narrowly defined as the trade union movement. Tenants' rights, consumer protection, health care, public transportation, prison reform, gay rights, immigrant workers' rights, mental patients' rights, and regional autonomy all became focal points of controversy after May 1968. The most significant of these new movements were self-management, feminism, and ecology.

These movements emerged outside the sphere of traditional politics—of parties, trade unions, and elections. What they represent is an attempt to redefine politics so that it encompasses all aspects of everyday life. In this regard, May 1968 may be said to have opened up an era of universal contestation of all aspects of society. This may prove to be its most significant legacy.

In the domain of social theory the defeat of the new leftists, with their emphasis on voluntarism, tended to give greater credibility to structuralism, which accentuated the inability of individuals to change social structures. For their part many of the structuralists sympathized with the May Movement and sought to identify themselves with it to maintain their avant-garde image. Thus, structuralism experienced a resurgence in the 1970s by abandoning some of its most strident rhetoric and identifying itself with the goals of May 1968 (see Chapter 7).

New developments in social theory also emerged from the new social movements. Self-management, feminism, and ecology each continued to develop aspects of new left social theory and its critique of traditional marxism. In fact, I will argue that they represent the legacy of new left social theory.

In conclusion, one may say that May 1968 represents the end of one era and the beginning of a new one. It was the crucial turning point in the transition from the new left criticism of traditional marxism to a new vision of an egalitarian and libertarian society that begins to emerge in the 1970s around the themes of self-management, feminism, and ecology.

In Chapter seven we will examine the resurgence of structuralism, and in particular, the structuralist-marxism of Louis Althusser. In Chapter eight we will analyze Eurocommunism and the electoral strategy for change adopted by the Union of the Left political parties. And finally, in Chapter nine we look to the new social movements of self-management, feminism, and ecology as the legacy of new left social theory.

Notes

1. The literature on May 1968 is vast. A good starting point is L. Wylie, F. Chu, M. Terrall, *France: Events of May-June, 1968: A Critical Bibliography* (Pittsburgh, 1973). I also found the following works helpful: J. Ardagh, *The New French Revolution* (London, 1968), R. Johnson, *The French Communist Party vs. The Students* (New Haven, 1972), C. Posner, ed., *Reflections on the Revolution in France: 1968* (Baltimore, 1970), Schnapp and Vidal-Naguet, *The French Student Uprising* (New York, 1970), and D. Singer, *Prelude to Revolution* (New York, 1970).
2. Office de radio et de télévision françaises.
3. Cf. Ardagh, *op. cit.*, p. 465 and Singer, *op. cit.*
4. See Posner, *op. cit.*, pp. 172-184.
5. Cf. J. Besancon, *Les Murs ont la parole* (paris, 1968) for more of the wall-writings.
6. For Lefebvre's analysis of May see his *L'Irruption de Nanterre au sommet* (Paris, 1968) translated by A. Ehrenfeld as *The Explosion* (New York, 1969). Castoriadis, Lefort, and Morin each wrote essays on May which were published together as *Mai 1968: La Brèche* (Paris, 1968).
7. For a somewhat different analysis of this spirit, see J. J. Servan-Schreiber, *The Spirit of May* (New York, 1971). Many liberals saw the May movement as a healthy movement for reform and modernization.

8. Ardagh, *op. cit.*, pp. 462, 465, 468.

9. Poster, *loc. cit.*, p. 386.

11. Cohn-Bendit, *The French Student Revolt*, trans. by B. Brewster (New York, 1968), p. 58.

12. For Sartre's influence on the Union des étudiantes communistes (UEC) see Richard Johnson, *op. cit.*, pp. 11-26, 48-54.

13. Union nationale des étudiants de France.

14. For example, see Marc Kravetz, "Naissance d'un syndicalisme étudiant," *Les Temps Modernes* (February 1964).

15. Translated by M. Nicolaus and V. Ortiz as *Strategy for Labor* (New York, 1967).

16. Other similar analyses of the new working class are Pierre Belleville, *Une Nouvelle class ouvrière* (Paris, 1963) and Serge Mallet, *La Nouvelle classe ouvrière* (Paris, 1963). Belleville's book was published in the *Les Temps Modernes* collection and Mallet received financial support from Sartre while he researched and wrote his book. Thus Sartre played a definite role in proliferating this concept. Gorz later reconsidered and pointed out serious limitations in this notion. See his, "Techniques, techniciens, et la lutte des classes," *Les Temps Modernes* 27:301-302 (August-September 1971), pp. 141-180.

17. Cf. R. Vienet, "Les Situationnistes et les nouvelles formes d'action contre la politique de l'art," *Internationale situationniste* 11 (October 1967).

18. See "Nos buts et nos méthodes dans le scandale de Strasbourg," *Internationale Situationniste* 11 (October 1967).

19. *Ibid.*, p. 11.

20 See R. Vienet, *Enragés et situationnistes dans le mouvement des occupations* (Paris, 1968).

21. Cf. Poster, *op. cit.*, p. 257.

22. *Ibid.*, p. 205. See also Schnapp and Vidal-Naquet, *op. cit.*, pp. 3, 65-67.

23. Daniel and Gabriel Cohn-Bendit, *Obsolete Communism: The Left-Wing Alternative*, trans. by A. Pomerans (New York, 1968), p. 199.

24. *Ibid.*, p. 18.

25. *Ibid.*, p. 133.

26. *Le Monde*, 10 May 1968 in Contat and Rybalka, *Les Ecrits de Sartre* (Paris, 1970), p. 463.

27. *Ibid.*, p. 464.

28. *Ibid.*, p. 465.

29. Lefebvre, *The Explosion* (New York, 1969), p. 67.

30. Castoriadis, "La révolution anticipée," in *La Brèche, op. cit.*

31. Lévi-Strauss, *The Savage Mind*, trans. G. Weidenfeld (Chicago, 1966), p. 247.

32. Cf. his "L'homme est-il mort?" *Arts* 38 (June 1966). Also see his *The Archaeology of Knowledge*, trans. by A. Smith (New York, 1972) and *The Order of Things* (New York, 1970).

33. Lévi-Strauss, *op. cit.*, p. 252.

34. Lévi-Strauss, *Tristes Tropiques* trans. by J. Russell (New York, 1965), p. 62.

35. *Ibid.*, p. 62.

36. Even Roger Garaudy, the PCF's leading philosopher after Lefebvre's expulsion and the only intellectual ever to serve on the Party's politburo, assimilated existentialism within his marxist humanism of the early 1960s.

37. See Sartre's "Replies to Structuralism," trans. by R. D'Amico in *Telos* 9 (Fall 1971), pp. 110-115 and Lefebvre's *Position: contre les technocrates* (Paris, 1967) and *Au-delà du structuralisme* (Paris, 1971). For the controversy between Sartre and Lévi-Strauss see Lawrence Rosen, "Language, History, and the Logic of Inquiry in Lévi-Strauss and Sartre," *History and Theory* 10:3 (1971), pp. 269-294.

38. An interesting critique of Sartre's post-1968 stance can be found in Ronald Aronson's articles, "Sartre's Individualist Social Theory," *Telos* 16 (Summer 1973), pp. 68-91; and "*L'Idiot de la famille: The Ultimate Sartre?*" *Ibid.*, 20 (Summer 1974), pp. 90-107.

39. See his *La révolution urbaine* (Paris, 1970) and *La production de l'espace* (Paris, 1974).

40. See his *L'Institution Imaginaire de la Société* (Paris, 1975).

41. An excellent bibliography of the explanations of May is Benton and Touchard's "Les Interpretations de la Crise de Mai-Juin 1968," *Revue Française de Science Politique* 20:3 (June, 1970), pp. 503-544.

/PART III/

BEYOND MAY 1968:
THE LEGACY OF
THE FRENCH NEW LEFT

/7/
Althusser and the Resurgence of Structuralist-Marxism

1. Introduction

Louis Althusser was born in Algeria in 1918. In 1948 at the age of 30 he received his doctoral degree in philosophy, began teaching at the *Ecole Normale*, and joined the PCF. His major works (*For Marx* and *Reading Captial*) appeared in the mid-1960s as part of the structuralist critique of humanism. Althusser presented his structural marxism as a scientific or theoretical anti-humanism. Like Lévi-Strauss and Foucault, Althusser wished to combat what he considered to be the metaphysical assumptions of the subjectivist philosophy of "man," and his work received significant attention at the time.[1]

May 1968 interrupted the structuralist debate with humanism. For the most part, structuralists remained silent during May, giving little public support to the strikers.[2] In fact, Lévi-Strauss pessimistically viewed May as the death-knell of structuralism and the triumph of existential-marxism:

"In France you know structuralism is no longer in fashion. Since May 1968 all objectivity has been repudiated. The position of the youth corresponds to that of Sartre."[3]

Yet the political defeat of the May Movement carried a different message for many of its activists. In their minds May demonstrated that a revolutionary situation was indeed possible in an industrial society. The May revolt failed because it lacked organization. What was needed then was a revolutionary party to provide that organization. Even new leftists like André Gorz claimed, "the need for a new vanguard party is clearer than ever."[4] The new leftists were discovering they needed a structure of their own to combat the structures of bourgeois society. They also needed to understand the structures of bourgeois society in order to combat them more effectively. Thus, many of the May activists now turned to the structuralists to acquire such an understanding. For their part, the structuralists now claimed that this was their goal all along. Foucault put it this way:

> What the students are trying to do...and what I myself am trying to accomplish...is basically the same thing...What I am trying to do is grasp the implicit systems which determine our most familiar behavior without our knowing it. I am trying to find their origin, to show their formation, the constraints they impose upon us; I am therefore trying to place myself at a distance from them and to show how one could escape.[5]

After Roger Garaudy's expulsion from the party in 1970,[6] Althusser assumed the undisputed role of leading party intellectual. As the most prominent structural marxist, his theories were of particular interest since he united marxism's concern for social change with the structuralist analysis. Thus, it wasn't until after 1968 that Althusser's intellectual political influence assumed its broadest dimensions.[7]

From the late 1960s to the mid 1970s we witness a distinct resurgence of Althusser's structural marxism. In this chapter we will first look back to the origins of his problematic, then examine the broad strokes of Althusser's effort to renovate traditional marxism, and finally assess the impact of his project.

2. *Althusser's Problematic*

Althusser's lifelong project has been to preserve what he judged to be the revolutionary integrity of marxism, to prevent marxism from being "contaminated" with bourgeois ideologies that inevitably deflect it from its revolutionary goals, and to save marxism from the twin evils of reformism and revisionism. Althusser believed this contamination of marxism arose within the communist movement itself as an over-reaction to Khruschev's 1956 denunciation of Stalin:[8]

> The criticism of Stalin's errors was formulated...in terms such that there inevitably followed what we must call an unleashing of bourgeois ideological and philosophical themes within the Communist Parties themselves.[9]

What Althusser is referring to here is the emergence after 1956 of a marxist humanist stance among communist intellectuals basing itself on Marx's early writings and particularly (as we saw in Chapter one) the *1844 Manuscripts*. Althusser condemned this humanism as a bourgeois ideology because its emphasis on the common interests of all has traditionally served to obscure the fundamental marxist concepts of class and class struggle.

For instrumental political reasons, however, the post-1956 atmosphere was conducive to the spread of this marxist humanism. On the one hand, Soviet leaders declared that classes had been eliminated in the Soviet Union. On this basis they claimed a dictatorship of the proletariat was no longer necessary and proclaimed in its stead a "State of the Whole People."[10]

On the other hand, PCF leaders sought to break out of their political isolation by building bridges to other groups in

French society. Marxist humanism served the political function of opening a dialogue with humanist liberals, socialists, and particularly, catholics. Roger Garaudy, at this time the party's leading philosopher[11] (and central committee and politburo member) developed the marxist humanist trend. He was so successful that he helped to effect not only the acceptance of marxist humanism as a serious intellectual and ethical endeavor among these groups, but he also helped legitimize humanist themes for party intellectuals. In fact, by the early 1960s, the gulf separating Garaudy's humanist marxism and Sartre's existential-marxism was disappearing.

One final political phenomenon conditioned the conjuncture in which Althusser's problematic took shape.[12] That, of course, was the developing Sino-Soviet dispute. The Chinese leaders viewed Khruschev's denunciation of Stalin and the ensuing abandonment of the concept "dictatorship of the proletariat" with alarm and hostility. They saw in these developments the emergence of a modern form of revisionism. For Mao and his followers the concept of the dictatorship of the proletariat was the essence of communism. To abandon it was to abandon the very heart and soul of revolutionary marxist-leninist ideology. To the maoists, the "State of the Whole People" concept was an open admission of the ascendency of bourgeois ideology that would ultimately lead to a full scale restoration of capitalism.[13]

Althusser never publicly sided with the maoists, but it was clear from numerous references to Mao in his work that he was privately receptive and sympathetic to their analysis. Thus he set upon the task of combatting revisionism in philosophy by adhering to a strictly orthodox interpretation of marxism. Orthodoxy required the denunciation and rooting out of humanism and all other bourgeois, revisionist tendencies: empiricism, voluntarism, and historicism. This he made his life's work and proudly proclaimed, "I am the defender of orthodoxy" against "the threat of bourgeois ideology."[14]

If Althusser can be characterized as a dogmatist, he can

hardly be considered a vulgar marxist, and therein lies the source of the Althusser sensation. For he had been able to assimilate and synthesize the most advanced intellectual trends (structuralism, Freudianism, linguistics, system theory) with an encyclopedic knowledge of Western philosophy (Spinoza, Kant, Hegel, Nietzsche, Husserl, and Heidegger all turn up in his analyses) in defense of his interpretation of marxism. And while this interpretation is orthodox, it is hardly conventional. For Althusser has invented a series of concepts and a new vocabulary in which to express his highly sophisticated "symptomatic reading" of the classic texts. In short, he has created an intellectual *tour de force* which is overwhelming in its scope and pretension.

3. Theoretical Anti-Humanism

Althusser's critique of marxist humanism hinges on what he calls an "epistemological break" (*coupure épisto-mologique*) in Marx's work. A concept derived from the philosopher, Gaston Bachelard,[15] such a break or *rupture* is said to occur in a "leap" from pre-scientific ideas into the realm of science. It involves a complete break with the previous pattern of thought and the creation of a whole new problematic. Althusser sees such a break occurring in Marx's work in 1845 when he supposedly abandons Hegelian idealism and begins to construct a science of historical materialism. Althusser argues that in *The Theses on Feuerbach* and *The German Ideology* (1845) Marx "settles his accounts" with philosophy proper and then spends the rest of his life developing the science of marxism, concentrating his attention on the critique of political economy, which is the subject of *Capital*. In other words, Althusser is claiming that until 1845 Marx himself was not a marxist and therefore his writings before that date are not marxist either. In particular, Althusser claims that the crucial *1844 Manuscripts* is not really a marxist (i.e., "scientific") text![16] Rather, Marx is still under the influence of Hegel. Such notions as alienation, negation of the negation and the themes of humanism are really only remnants of Marx's adolescent philosophical idealism. It is only when in his maturity that Marx turns to developing such concepts as mode of production, forces of production, relations of production, infrastructure and superstructure, is he expressing the materialist science of marxism. Consequently, Sartre and others (Lefebvre, Garaudy) who present the humanist interpretation of Marx are not only wrong, "they are an obstacle to knowledge. Instead of helping it to progress, *they hold it back.*"[17]

Paradoxically, by asserting that Marx's theory of alienation is in fact a marxist theory, Sartre is an "obstacle" to knowledge. He has fallen into the trap of "empiricism," claims Althusser. Althusser dismisses empiricism as a bourgeois ideology because it is a theory of knowledge which assumes that the "real" is directly accessible to us through observation, when in fact what we are observing is conditioned by our assumptions about the nature of reality.[18] The humanist reading of Marx is empiricist because it implies an underlying conception of knowledge that takes at face value Marx's discussion of alienation. For Althusser, this is just an Hegelian "residue" from which Marx is in the process of freeing himself. There is no such thing as an "innocent" reading of a text since the reader always brings to it an underlying conception of knowledge.[19]

Only a "symptomatic" reading of Marx which has a scientific conception of knowledge (i.e., Marx of *Capital*) will reveal (disclose) the true objective meaning of the text. To achieve such a reading Althusser adopts the structural linguistic technique of a "superreader" to "reread" the text[20] and "decode" its true meaning by discovering the new problematic Marx unconsciously adopts in his scientific discovery of history.[21] "The age Marx lived in did not provide him and he could not acquire in his lifetime, an adequate concept with which to think what he produced: *The concept of the effectivity of a structure on its elements.*"[22] (In other words,

Althusserian structuralism!)

To flesh out this reading two further preconditions are necessary. One is the Freudian conception of the unconscious (interpreted by Jacques Lacan[23]) as a way of understanding how Marx's personality affects the development of the hidden, unconscious structure of his problematic (i.e., "adolescent" Marx, "mature" Marx). The other is Lévi-Strauss' concept of structuralism[24] as a framework for analyzing the structures Marx discovered (e.g., mode of production, superstructure).

Only when fully prepared, then, with an understanding of *Capital*, Freud (à la Lacan), Lévi-Strauss, and Althusser can we reread the *1844 Manuscripts* without falling into the trap of empiricism![25]

Voluntarism and historicism are two further ideological "errors" of the humanist reading of Marx. Voluntarism is the assumption that human subjects create the social world in which they live by intentional acts. As a structuralist, Althusser claims that the social structure has no subject who creates it. Rather, it is a system of objective processes without subjects. Human agents are simply the bearers of social structures, not *free* agents.

Historicism is a corollary assumption of voluntarism.[26] It holds that history is made up of the conscious acts of the individual (as subject) pursuing the fulfillment of one's projects over time.[27] Althusser argues, on the contrary, that "man" has no history since there is no such thing as "man" (i.e., a subject of history). Only classes have a history as they develop and come into conflict in a specific mode of production. Thus, there is a history of feudalism and a history of capitalism, but there is no history of the human subject. Althusser comes to the structural determinist conclusion that "man does not make his own history" in spite of the fact that Marx himself wrote (*after* 1845, in the *18th Brumaire*) that men make their own history, but they do so on the basis of prior conditions.

What emerges from the sophisticated opaqueness of

Althusser's structuralist renovation of traditional marxism is a consistent pattern of an almost transmogrified form of Hegelian essentialism. That is, those parts of Marx's *corpus* which are in agreement with the traditional orthodox view are considered essential elements of marxism, whereas those parts which don't fit in with this view are considered non-essential. They are considered to be part of the bourgeois ideology from which Marx (as a member of bourgeois society) was struggling to free himself. As such, they are not part of Marx's dramatic scientific "discovery," but represent the alchemy and phlogiston of the pre-scientific world which his discovery rendered obsolete.

Here we come to the crux of the matter: the marxist conception of knowledge and its relation to science. Althusser tells us time and again that a pre-condition for understanding the novelty of Marx's scientific discovery is a marxist theory of knowledge. What is such a theory of knowledge? It is one based on a view of reality which sees structures as primary knowledge objects while subjects are considered non-existent. In other words, Althusser assumes that a marxist theory of knowledge is necessarily based on a structuralist conception of the nature of reality. This is the source of Althusserian scientism. By restricting knowledge to a very narrow positivist conception of science based exclusively on the natural sciences, he has foreclosed in advance the very possibility of knowledge about human being as self-grounded subject.[28]

The irony here is that the entire Althusserian ediface is self-grounded, and Althusser himself admits it!

> That the precondition of a reading of Marx is a Marxist theory of the differential nature of theoretical formations and their history, that is, a theory of epistemological history, which is Marxist philosophy itself; that this operation in itself constitutes an indispensible circle in which the application of Marxist theory to Marx himself appears to be the absolute precondition of an understanding of Marx and at the same time as the precondition even of the constitution and development of Marxist philosophy, so much is clear.[30]

While so much may not be "clear" to all, the operative phrase here is "an indispensible circle." For what Althusser is saying is that a precondition for understanding Marx is an understanding of marxist theory. We already know what he means by marxist theory: that is, his own structuralist interpretation. This "indispensible circle" reveals the circularity implicit in his position: marxism is scientific. The way we know it is scientific is by a "scientific reading" of Marx. Where does this scientific reading come from? From Althusser, of course! Thus we find that Althusser's "theoretical anti-humanism"—whose purpose was to refute the claim that man is a self-grounded being—is itself self-grounded!

4. Althusser and the PCF

Despite its weaknesses, Althusser's prodigious intellectual counter-attack on marxist humanism had a considerable impact on the French intellectual scene. The structuralist challenge to humanism was mounted on many fronts: anthropology (Lévi-Strauss), semiotics (Barthes), history of science (Foucault), psychoanalysis (Lacan). In this context, Althusser's structural marxism exercised a strong attraction for intellectuals of the left. Since he was both an eminent professor of philosophy at the *Ecole Normale* and a long time member of the PCF, the Party began to bask in the reflected glory of Althusser's prestige and gained a new intellectual respectability. Its theoretical journals, *La Pensée* and *La Nouvelle Critique*, enjoyed increasing circulation and greater intellectual esteem.[31]

Yet Althusser's relationship with the Party was marked by conflict. As we have seen, his "theoretical anti-humanism" in fact ran counter to the dominant Party position as expressed by Roger Garaudy in his *De l'anathème au dialogue* (1965) and *Marxisme de XXe siècle* (1966). In these works Garaudy rejected the dogmatism of stalinism, took a favorable view of existentialism and stressed the similarity of the humanistic goals of communists and catholics alike. The controversy became so intense[32] that a special meeting of the PCF central committee strongly rebuked Althusser for his deviation and forced him to make a self-criticism, while Garaudy's humanism was upheld.[33]

One of the key points of conflict was over the relationship between science and ideology. Althusser's view was that science was the domain of true, immutable laws which are not dependent on empirical verification. Mathematics was his model for the science of marxism:

> No mathematician in the world expects that his theories have to be applied before they are declared verified by the facts. The truth of its theorems are completely furnished by the internal criteria of mathematical practice. We could say the same of all the sciences.[34]

Ideology, on the other hand, was a system of ideas dependent on an empirical analysis of the facts of the social world.

Traditional communist theory made no such distinction between science and ideology. Proletarian science was true because it was rooted in proletarian ideology. Its truth could be verified by empirical social practice. In fact, communist leadership based its claim to legitimacy on its superior knowledge and practice of the marxist-leninist "science" of revolution. Althusser's views were perceived as a serious political challenge by the Party leadership. Party secretary-general, Waldeck Rochet published a work to publicly attack Althusser's theory.

> Comrade Althusser explains that in order to be scientific a theory must be verified by purely internal criteria, such as those that are applied in a mathematical demonstration, so as to be beyond all ideology. It seems that according to this conception, Marxist theory must be elaborated and developed by specialists in philosophy, well trained in abstract reasoning but without any real ties with social practice.[35]

In addition to usurping the role of the Party leadership, Althusser's view of science is rooted in intellectual elitism.

Garaudy made this point more clearly when he said that for Althusser "ideology is good enough for maneuvering the masses about, but that theory should be reserved for the technocrats of philosophy."[36]

Althusser discreetly accepted the criticism to avoid a break and attempted to preserve his autonomy by developing his argument on the relative autonomy of different spheres of practice. He claimed that theoretical practice is distinct from and autonomous of political practice. Conversely, political practice—the sphere of expertise of the Party leaders—is not subject on the political level to the criticism of theoretical practice. Philosophy, he now claimed, was the "theory of theoretical practice."[37]

The Party leadership, however, did not accept this obtuse formulation and was only satisfied when Althusser admitted falling into a "theoreticist deviation" and failing to discuss the "union of theory and practice."[38]

Within the context of inner Party struggle, the PCF leadership had good reason to feel threatened by Althusser's theoretical peregrinations. For his students attacked the Party leadership as opportunist and revisionist and attempted to take over the Party's student organization, the Union des étudiantes communistes de france (UEC) in the mid-1960s. Althusser never publicly criticized the PCF's political line, but as mentioned above it is clear from the numerous references in his writings that he was sympathetic to maoist theory.[39] His followers were openly pro-Chinese and threatened to split the Party along the ideological lines of the Sino-Soviet dispute.[40] Thus the political implications of Althusserian theory represented something which could develop into a formidable challenge to the Party leaders.

Althusser's self-criticism and the expulsion of over six hundred of his followers from the Party in the fall of 1966 ended the immediate crisis in the PCF. Those expelled went on to form a maoist grouplet determined to denounce the theoretical shortcomings of the Party of which their mentor was still the most prominent marxist philosopher.[41]

Significantly, Althusser maintained a discreet silence about the whole affair.

It is interesting that one of the goals of Althusser's symptomatic reading of Marx was to uncover the "silences" in the texts. That is, to explain the significance of what is left unsaid. If we were to apply such a technique to Althusser's own work, we would need to explain the significance of his silence on the expulsion of the Althusserites from the PCF, his silence on the Soviet invasion of Czechoslavakia in August 1968, and his silence on the expulsion of Garaudy from the PCF for "too vigorously" criticizing this invasion.

Evidently, the threat of expulsion from the Party and the prospect of being branded a renegade after many years of loyal service was too high a price for him to pay to maintain his intellectual integrity. The psychological hold the Party had on its members, and particularly intellectuals, is difficult to grasp. Years later when Althusser partially broke that hold, he described its effects as follows:

> The PCF leadership morally broke and crushed men under the weight of base accusations...There were real "Moscow Trials" right here in France. The death sentence was missing, but you can also make a man die of dishonor, by torturing him with the charge of being a "police-agent," "crook," or "traitor"; by forcing all his comrades-in-arms to condemn, shun, and calumniate him, renouncing their own past. That happened in France between 1948 and 1965.[42]

It was undoubtedly out of fear of such approbation that he shrank back from the role of Party "Luther" and instead assumed that of Party "Galileo."[43]

From the late 1960s through the mid-1970s, Althusser appeared to be pursuing a policy of tactical retreat in order to enhance his long term strategic influence. (This may be another reason for his silences). In a certain sense this policy appeared to be paying off. For after Garaudy's break with the Party in 1970, he assumed the undisputed role of leading Party intellectual. His essays on Lenin written in the late 1960s (incidentally, simultaneous with the Chinese Cultural Revolution) carried a much simpler, clearer, and politically "correct" message. Philosophy is no longer viewed as the "theory of theoretical practice." Rather it is a "revolutionary weapon," "class struggle in the field of theory." Its function is *to draw a dividing line* between true ideas and false ideas...between the people (the proletariat and its allies) and the peoples' enemies."[44] If such formulations smack of stalinism, they fulfill two important functions for Althusser. One, they are straightforwardly orthodox without any theoreticist trimmings and thus win him the approval of the PCF leadership; and two, they are leftist and hardly distinguishable from the maoist mass line on philosophy.[45] These essays thus represent a finely honed synthesis of political orthodoxy and philosophical radicalism. It also helps to explain how in the early 1970s Althusser was able to win the approval of both the PCF leadership and the dissident communists of the grouplets.

5. Althusser's Stalinism

As we have seen, Althusser's self-description of his problematic places him beyond the crudities of stalinist economism on the one hand and the anti-stalinist reformism of marxist humanism on the other. And yet, even though he does make a few critical remarks about stalinism, it is clear that the bulk of his life work has been devoted to attacking humanism. In 1975 he was quoted in *Le Monde* as saying:

> I would never have written anything were it not for the 20th Congress and Khruschev's critique of Stalinism and the subsequent liberalization...My target was therefore clear; these humanist ravings, these feeble dissertations on liberty, labor, or alienation which were the effects of all this among French Party intellectuals.[46]

Nevertheless, he did also attack stalinism, even if only sporadically and superficially. In fact he duly notes in his

Essays in Self-Criticism (1976) that "already" in 1965 he had raised the issue of Stalin[47] and in 1972 placed himself at "personal risk" by proposing to open up discussion of the "Stalinist deviation."[48] However, he doesn't actually develop an analysis of stalinism here. He merely points out that Khruschev's critique was non-marxist in that he denounced the "cult of personality" and "violation of Socialist legality" under the Stalin regime. To Althusser, such notions as personality and legality are part of bourgeois ideology which Khruschev and the Soviet leadership fostered.

> If you take...Communist "intellectuals" and set them officially on a bourgeois ideological...line, in order to "criticize" a regime under which they (and others) have suffered deeply, you must not be surprised when the same Communist...intellectuals go straight forward on the road of bourgeois philosophy.[49]

The "bourgeois philosophy" referred to here is humanism; Althusser has subtly turned the effort to critique stalinism back to a critique of humanism! Instead of analyzing the cause of stalinism, which he claims has been improperly diagnosed, he again denounces the effect. This time, however, he does mention (and only mentions without actually doing it) what a marxist analysis of stalinism would entail: analysis of the Soviet superstructure, the state and party in particular, and of the infrastructure, "namely the relations of production, class relations, and the class struggle in the USSR."[50] It is clear from a reading of Althusser that he did not consider it as important to combat stalinism as it was to combat humanism since he hasn't produced such an analysis.

This "softness" on stalinism can be gleaned not only from his reluctance to pursue a thorough-going critique of stalinism, but also from the scattered appreciative references made to Stalin himself in Althusser's writings. There is no mention before 1978 of Stalin's role in mass purges, show trials, grotesque bureaucratization, arbitrary abuse of power, etc. These are mere empirical facts and Althusser is concerned with theory. Stalin may be guilty of a "deviation," but he still has made a contribution to marxism. In his essay, "Contradiction and Overdetermination," Althusser tells us that Stalin's *Problems of Leninism* is a text that is "excellent in many ways."[51] In another essay he tells us that Stalin's rejection of the Hegelian "negation of the negation" was "evidence of real theoretical perspicacity."[52] Althusser seems capable of appreciating Stalin's theoretical "brilliance" and yet is incapable of carrying out an analysis of why stalinism resulted in the total perversion of all the egalitarian and liberating ideals of marxism.

It is no wonder then that numerous critics see Althusser himself as a stalinist or neo-stalinist. Alex Callinicos, for example, in his *Althusser's Marxism* refers to his "closet Stalinism";[53] while Alvin Gouldner sees him "providing a theoretical storm-cellar for Stalinism."[54] E.P. Thompson, in a scathing polemical denunciation, regards Althusserianism as "a manifestation of a general police action within ideology, as an attempt to reconstruct Stalinism at the level of theory."[55]

Is neo-stalinism, then, Althusser's legacy? In large part, yes. Yet there is one area in which Althusser made a decisive break with stalinism: that of economic determinism (or as Althusser called it, "economism"). As we have seen in Chapter 1, stalinist diamat claimed that the economic base directly and totally determined the superstructure of society, including its political institutions and its ideology. Althusser rejected this simple determinism and argued instead for the relative autonomy of politics and ideology. He claimed that Marx's concept of a mode of production involved three distinctly articulated structures or levels (the economic, the political, and the ideological) that were intimately and internally combined to form the matrix of the mode of production. While the economic structure was always "determinate in the last instance," any one of them could be the "structure in dominance" in a particular mode. What this means is that the economic, the political, or the ideological could be the dominant structure in a given social formation, but the *economic structure would determine which of the three would be dominant.* In feudalism, for instance, the economic structure determined that the *political* structure would be dominant.[56]

It is also clear that his rigorous analyses spurred on the intellectual renewal of marxism in France. By demonstrating that the most avant-garde intellectual trends (structuralism, linguistics, systems theory, Freud) could be synthesized with traditional marxism, he contributed (perhaps inadvertently) to the opening up and fleshing out of a more flexible *neo*-marxism that flourished in the wake of the rise of an independent Eurocommunism.

By the late 1960s he began to re-examine the work of Antonio Gramsci, the Italian marxist. Despite the prevalence of humanist and historicist themes in Gramsci's work, Althusser found much to praise in his analyses of ideology, hegemony, and the state.[57] In his essay, "Ideology and Ideological State Apparatuses," Althusser notes that "Gramsci is the only one who went any distance on the road I am taking."[58] Did he thus abandon structuralism?

By the late 1970s the insights of structuralism had been integrated into a broader framework. Althusser and other structuralists (e.g., Poulantzas, Foucault) now denied that in fact they were structuralists. They claimed they merely wanted to expose the metaphysical confusion and lack of conceptual rigor of humanism. Once this task had been accomplished, they were ready to criticize structuralism, to move beyond it into the era of "post-structuralism."[59]

The advent of Eurocommunism in the 1970s contributed to this surpassing of structuralism. For it raised new issues of political theory and strategy in a context in which a left electoral victory appeared possible.

Notes

1. *La Pensée*, the PCF theoretical journal published several critical articles: Guy Besse, "Deux questions sur un article de Louis Althusser," (February 1963); Roger Garaudy, "Les Manuscrits de 1844," (February 1963); Gilbert Mury, "Matérialisme et hyperempiricisme," (April 1963). *Les Temps Modernes* published three articles in its May 1966 issue (Vol. 21, #240) and André Glucksmann's critique, "Un structuralisme ventriloque," in March 1967.

2. See Mark Poster, *Existential-Marxism in Postwar France* (Princeton, 1975), p. 386.

3. *New York Times*, 31 December 1969. Quoted in Poster, *ibid.*, p. 386.

4. André Gorz, "What are the Lessons of the May Events?" in Charles Posner (ed.), *Reflections on the Revolution in France: 1968* (Baltimore, 1970), p. 264.

5. J. Simon, "A Conversation with Michel Foucault," *Partisan Review* 2 (1971), p. 201.

6. The PCF position during the May 1968 events and the Soviet invasion of Czechoslovakia soured Garaudy considerably. His strong criticism of PCF and Soviet policy served as grounds for his expulsion.

7. In fact, outside of France (particularly in England) Althusser was distinctly a 1970s' phenomenon because translations of his works were not readily available until then.

8. See Chapter 4 above.

9. Althusser, "Response to John Lewis (Self-Criticism)," in *Marxism Today* (November 1972), p. 348. This work originally appeared in two succeeding issues of *Marxism Today*, the British CP theoretical journal. Further citations will be referred to as *Response* with page references.

10. Althusser himself discussed the terms of this political situation in the Preface to the English edition ("To My English Readers") of *For Marx* (New York, 1970), pp. 9-15. Further references to *For Marx* will be abbreviated, *F.M.*

11. After Henri Lefebvre's departure in 1958.

12. It should be noted that Althusser was responsible for spreading the use of the concepts, "conjuncture" and "problematic."

13. For the Chinese analysis see Mao Tse-tung's, *On the Historical Experience of the Dictatorship of the Proletariat* (Peking, 1960).

14. *Response*, p. 312.

15. See his *La Formation de l'esprit scientifique* (Paris, 1963). Althusser was a student of Bachelard's at the Ecole Normale in the late 1940s.

16. See his essays in *F.M.*, "On the Young Marx," pp. 49-86; and "The '1844 Manuscripts' of Karl Marx," pp. 153-160.

17. *Response*, p. 343. Althusser's critics regard such charges as indicative of an underlying stalinism.

18. See Althusser, *Reading Capital* (London, 1970), pp. 34-40. Further references to this work will be abbreviated *R.C.*

19. *Ibid.,* p. 34.

20. See Edith Kurzweil, "Louis Althusser: Between Philosophy and Politics," *Marxist Perspectives* 6 (Summer 1979), p. 11.

21. Althusser discusses what he calls the three continents of science in "Philosophy as a Revolutionary Weapon," in *Lenin and Philosophy, and other essays* (New York, 1971), pp. 15-17. Further references to this work will be abbreviated *L.P.*

22. *R.C.*, p. 29.

23. See Althusser's, "Freud and Lacan," in *L.P.*

24. See Chapter 6 above.

25. We will spare the reader further explication of Althusser's lexicon if it is duly noted that we have only scratched the surface here.

26. See "Marxism is not a Historicism," in *R.C.*, pp. 119-144.

27. This, of course, is exactly Sartre's argument on the nature of the dialectic in the *Critique.* No wonder then that he is accused of both voluntarism and historicism by the structuralists.

28. See Chapter 6 above.

30. *F.M.*, p. 38. On this point see A. Callinicos, *Althusser's Marxism* (London, 1976), p. 34.

31. See Pradeep Bandyopadhyay, "The Many Faces of French Marxism," *Science and Society*, 36:2 (Summer 1972), p. 145.

32. The matter was hotly debated in Party journals. *Cahiers du Communisme* devoted a whole issue to the topic of marxist humanism in May-June 1966. *La Nouvelle Critique* also published several articles.

33. For a more detailed discussion of the inner-party conflict see Richard Johnson, *The French Communist Party Versus the Students* (New Haven, 1972), pp. 57-64, 67-71.

34. *R.C.*, p. 75.

35. Waldeck Rochet, *Le Marxisme et les chemins de l'avenir* (Paris, 1966), p. 20.

36. Roger Garaudy, *Peut-on être communiste aujourd'hui?* (Paris, 1968), p. 271.

37. See discussion in "On the Materialist Dialectic," in *F.M.*, pp. 164-174.

38. *F.M.*, pp. 14-15.

39. See, for example, his analysis of Mao's *On Contradiction* in "On the Materialist Dialectic," in *F.M.*, pp. 161-217.

40. See, for example, Claude Harmel, "Vers la création d'un parti français pro-chinois," *Est et Ouest*, December 1967.

41. Union des jeunesses communistes (marxistes-leninistes) or UJC(ML).

42. Althusser, "What Must Change in the Party," *New Left Review* (June 1978), p. 39. This is a translation of the articles Althusser published in *Le*

Monde (24-27 April 1978) criticizing the PCF leadership after the electoral defeat of the Union of the Left in March 1978.

43. Martin Luther was excommunicated for criticizing the Church leadership and demanding a return to pure Christian principles; while Galileo recanted his claim that the earth revolved around the sun rather than face torture by the Inquisition.

44. *L.P.*, p. 21.

45. See Mao's, "Where Do Correct Ideas Come From?" in his *Selected Works, Vol. I* (Peking, 1967).

46. Quoted in *Radical Philosophy* (Winter 1975), p. 12.

47. Althusser, *Essays in Self-Criticism* (London, 1976), p. 36. He is referring to *F.M.*

48. *Ibid.*, p. 89. He is referring to *Response.*

49. *Response*, pp. 348-349.

50. *Ibid.*, p. 349.

51. *F.M.*, p. 97n.

52. *Ibid.*, p. 200n.

53. Alex Callinicos, *op. cit.*, p. 102.

54. Alvin Gouldner, "Louis Althusser, Essays in Self-Criticism," *Theory and Society* IV (1977), p. 450.

55. E. P. Thompson, *The Poverty of Theory and other essays* (London, 1978), p. 323. Thompson also states: "If I thought that Althusserianism was the logical terminus of Marx's thought, then I could never be a Marxist." p. 381.

56. See, for example, *R.C.*, pp. 216-218.

57. See *Essays in Self-Criticism* and *L.P.*, p. 12.

58. *L.P.*, p. 142n.

59. From lecture by Denis Donoghue, "French Structuralist Theories," Boston University, 14 September 1979. Also, see remarks by Poulantzas on this point in Chapter 8 below.

/8/

Eurocommunism and The Crisis of Marxism

1. Introduction: The Rise of Eurocommunism

The term "Eurocommunism" is used to connote the political changes in Western European communist parties (particularly the Italian, Spanish, and French) during the 1970s.[1] Basically these changes involve the rejection of the Soviet model of socialism as inappropriate for Western Europe and the commitment to the Western values of democracy and civil liberties as essential components of the socialist ideal. What distinguishes Eurocommunism from traditional social democracy is commitment to the long-term goal of achieving "socialism" (i.e. nationalization of the means of production) rather than merely assuming the management of a capitalist society as social democrats have done in West Germany, Sweden, and Great Britain.

Santiago Carrillo, the general-secretary of the Spanish Communist Party, presented the general themes of Euro-communism in his *Eurocommunism and the State* (1976). In this work he argued that the overwhelming differences between Czarist Russia and contemporary advanced capitalist societies render the Bolshevik Revolution of 1917 obsolete as a model for transition to socialism in Western Europe. Instead, a viable strategy should be based on Europe's democratic traditions. He claimed that the working class should develop alliances with other sectors of the population which would give it a leading role in advancing democratic control over all spheres of public life. This alliance would prepare the ground for socialism by demonstrating that the advance of democracy is incompatible with, and in fact obstructed by, capitalism, thereby destroying capitalism's legitimacy in the minds of the people.

The primary but not only means for carrying out this strategy would be election of a left government with communist participation to implement programs that weaken capitalist power over society at large. While this would not be a fully socialist government, it would pave the way for a future transition to socialism. To make this strategy effective the Eurocommunists have agreed to accept the rules of parliamentary democracy. That is, in principle they reject the one-party political system and agree to step down from power should the electorate vote them out. In summing up what Eurocommunism stands for Carrillo has stated,

> The parties included in the "Eurocommunist" trend are agreed on the need to advance to socialism with democracy, a multi-party system, parliaments, and representative institutions, sovereignty of the people regularly exercised through universal suffrage, trade unions independent of the State and of the parties, freedom for the opposition, human rights, religious freedom, freedom for cultural, scientific, and artistic creation, and the development of the broadest forms of popular participation at all levels and in all branches of society.[2]

Such a characterization of socialism obviously precludes considering the Soviet Union as the model since it lacks all of these attributes. In fact Carrillo plainly states that "the

October Revolution has produced a state which is evidently not a bourgeois state but neither is it...a genuine workers' democracy."[3]

Eurocommunism can be viewed, in a certain sense, as a delayed reaction to Khruschev's 1956 de-stalinization campaign. For it was in the wake of the Twentieth Congress of the CPSU that Italian CP leader Palmiro Togliatti advocated "polycentrism"[4] and began developing an independent strategy for socialism critical of the Soviet Union.

The Sino-Soviet dispute and the emergence of Third World socialisms further weakened the legitimacy of Soviet claims to be *the* model of socialism. Also, the emergence of a mass new left in the 1960s strongly critical of the Soviet Union was an obvious indication of the lack of popularity of this model for the West. And finally, the actions of the post-Stalin regime itself (invasion of Hungary and Czeckoslavakia, wholesale repression of dissenters, lack of democratic evolution) further discredited "real, existing socialism" (as Soviet leaders came to call their social system) as a model for others to follow. It is no wonder that even the French party with its long history of staunch pro-Sovietism finally began to criticize certain Soviet policies.

Another major factor contributing to the emergence of Eurocommunism was the general political situation in Europe in the 1970s. On the one hand, we witness the passing of a generation of older authoritarian, conservative figures (de Gaulle, Franco, Salazar) and the collapse of dictatorships in Spain, Portugal, and Greece. This apparent decline of the right was accompanied by the emergence of radical mass movements for democracy (again in Spain, Portugal and Greece) and working class militancy (in France, Italy and Great Britain). In this context the Western CPs grew in both membership and electoral strength. In parliamentary politics they became forces to be reckoned with, and they began to consider participating in coalition governments in alliance with non-communist parties. Most notably, the popular Italian party under Enrico Berlinguer, reached an "Historic

Compromise" with the Christian Democrats under which the PCI agreed to support (and, they hoped, participate in) the government.[6]

In France, Eurocommunism appeared to be consistent with the electoral strategy of the PCF. Since 1964, when French communists supported François Mitterand's presidential candidacy, the PCF has sought an electoral alliance with the socialists. Prior to the 1960s, the French socialists were suspicious of communist overtures and reluctant to ally themselves with the PCF. During the Fourth Republic (1946-1958) the SFIO allied itself with parties of the center and thereby insured itself a governmental role. But the coming of de Gaulle to power in 1958 based on a center-right coalition effectively shut the socialists out of power. Thus, though still suspicious of communist designs for a single party dictatorship, the socialists proved more receptive to PCF overtures in the 1960s, as witnessed by their acceptance of support for Mitterand's 1964 candidacy.

May 1968 interrupted this process of accommodation. It also led to the collapse of the old SFIO and the birth of a new, rejuvenated Socialist Party (PS) in 1969, as many of the May participants filled its ranks. Rescued from extinction by this participation, the new PS surged with dynamic energy and radical ideas, appropriating many new left themes. The left-wing of the new party advocated an *autogestion* view of socialism and allied itself with the radicalized CFDT labor federation.

On the whole, the PS represented a loosely affiliated broad array of socialist opinion. Old-style social democrats and left technocrats reluctantly rubbed shoulders with militant *autogestionnaires* and activists from many of the new unaffiliated movements of feminism, ecology, migrant workers, gay rights and prison reform.

This renovated Socialist Party still had reservations about an electoral alliance with the PCF. But its leaders accurately surmised the existence of a large constituency in the electorate who would vote socialist if the PS was part of a credible Union of the Left with the PCF. Mitterand and the socialist leadership hoped to dominate the Union of the Left on the strength of a larger vote and thus prevent PCF domination. On this implicit basis the PS leadership agreed to an electoral alliance based on the Common Program.[7] (As we will see later, the PCF leadership seemed to have a similar hidden agenda.)

As a campaign platform, the Common Program is an interesting document. It calls for nationalization of most of France's major industrial and financial corporations (about half the economy), democratization and decentralization of management, the social security system (including health insurance), educational institutions and housing. It calls for full employment, a rising standard of living, an end to wage discrimination, a greatly increased minimum wage, and new health and safety standards in the workplace. There are provisions for the equality of women, maternity leave, day care, and legal abortion. Sections on preservation of the environment include anti-pollution regulations and encouragement of new non-polluting technologies. Overall it is a fairly enlightened document, although cynics may correctly see in it a lot of election promises and campaign rhetoric.[8]

One reason for scepticism is that many of the platform's provisions appear at odds with traditional PCF theory and practice. Yet at some level the PCF did experience a Eurocommunist transformation in the 1970s in line with the principles of the Common Program.

The Eurocommunism of the PCF was formalized at the Party's 22nd Congress in 1976. At this Congress the PCF reversed all of its long held orthodox leninist positions and adopted the Eurocommunist stance. For the first time the PCF claimed that the transition to socialism may be peaceful and democratic, and the preservation—and expansion—of civil liberties and human rights is essential to socialism. But most dramatically, without any prior public discussion, Party general-secretary Georges Marchais announced on national television that the PCF henceforth was abandoning the slogan "dictatorship of the proletariat." French communists would loyally accept the alteration of governments in a parliamentary democracy, and the PCF would not seek a one-party dictatorship in France.[9]

Thus, in 1976 the PCF presented itself to the world as a Eurocommunist party working for Union of the Left with the socialists on the basis of the Common Program. Public opinion polls indicated that the Union of the Left could win the 1978 legislative elections. With electoral victory close at hand, the Eurocommunist strategy appeared vindicated.

Yet left critics voiced the concern that the PCF's sudden conversion was based primarily on electoral opportunism and could easily lead to "social-democratization" (i.e. reformism) unless the party based its practice on a rigorous and scientific theoretical analysis of advanced capitalist society. One such critic, Nicos Poulantzas, attempted to provide such an analysis and give solid theoretical underpinnings to Eurocommunism.

2. Poulantzas and the Theory of Eurocommunism

a. Introduction

More than anyone else, Nicos Poulantzas (1936-1979) contributed to the development of a Eurocommunist political theory. An emigré from Greece, Poulantzas studied under Althusser in Paris in the 1960s and adopted his general problematic. Beginning with the Althusserian conception of a mode of production as a combination of the economic, political, and ideological, Poulantzas took it upon himself to develop a "regional" theory of the political—i.e., a theory of the State. The state, for Poulantzas, is not an independent social institution but a "regional structure" constitutive of a particular mode of production. Therefore, there can be no general theory of the state, but rather a theory of the state in a particular mode—i.e., a feudal state, a capitalist state, etc. This latter "knowledge-object" (as he calls it) is Poulantzas' prime concern and the whole of his *Political Power and Social*

Classes (1968) is devoted to constructing a rigorous and scientific theorization of the capitalist state in the Althusserian structuralist tradition.

The major thrust of Poulantzas' work is to establish the theoretical basis for the relative autonomy of the state vis-à-vis the economy within a marxist framework. Marxism long lacked any developed theory of the state. Even the classic texts of Marx and Lenin, though they stress the importance of the state, don't express an explicit and developed theorization because the structuralist foundation required hadn't been laid. So Poulantzas proposed to follow Althusser and conduct a symptomatic reading of the classic texts in order to tease out a theory of the capitalist state with the aid of structuralism.

Marxists have long viewed the state simply as a tool or instrument which the ruling class uses to exert its domination over society. In this traditional view the capitalist state is seen simply as the reflection in the superstructure of society of the dominance of the bourgeoisie in the relations of production, or in the base of society. In other words, the political is simply a reflection of the economic. It is determined by the economic, and it is economic dominance alone which determines the role of the capitalist state as an instrument of bourgeois power.

Poulantzas considered this determinist characterization of the state incorrect. Relying on the Althusserian concepts of "structure in dominance" and "determination in the last instance" he hoped to demonstrate that the capitalist state is not an instrument reflecting bourgeois dominance in the relations of production. Rather, as a regional structure of the capitalist mode of production it is constitutive of these very same relations of production. That is, one of its main functions is to constitute and reproduce the relations of production. Therefore the state is *not* a superstructure wholly determined by the economic base. If the state is said to constitute and reproduce the relations of production, then it would be a superstructure "determining" the base. Thus the implications for traditional marxism of Poulantzas' analysis are radical indeed. For it would involve throwing overboard the whole base-superstructure schema. On this point he later stated:

> The constructivist image of "base" and "superstructure"...
> cannot in fact provide a correct representation of the articu-
> lation of social reality...It has even proved disastrous in more
> ways than one, and there is everything to be gained from not
> relying on it.[10]

Poulantzas attempted to replace it with a conceptualization that emphasized the relative autonomy of the state and
the determination "in the last instance" of the economic
instead of viewing it as universally dominant. In granting such
autonomy he was able to provide the foundation for a theory
of the capitalist state which is neither instrumentalist (state as
instrument of ruling class domination) nor neutralist (the
view that the state is neutral in the relations of social classes).
Instead, Poulantzas' theory presents the contemporary "interventionist" state as the *condensation* of class antagonisms.
As such it becomes a "site" of class struggle. The implication
of this theory for Eurocommunist strategy is that it is not
necessary to destroy the state (since it is not an instrument of
the bourgeoisie) but to conquer it through democratic popular
struggle. Just as marxists seek not the destruction of the
factories but the seizure of control by the working class within
them so it is with the state. In this context social-
democratization will be avoided only by demands for
structural reforms which, short of outright expropriation,
directly challenge capitalist power. Such demands include
workers' self-management of the production process, social
control of investment and profits and expansion of social
welfare programs.

b. The Theory of the Capitalist State

Poulantzas anchors his analysis of the state in the social
formation. He considers a mode of production "an abstract-
formal object which does not exist...in reality," whereas a
social formation is for him a "real-concrete object" which is

"historically determined." It "constitutes a complex unity in which a certain mode of production dominates the others which compose it."[11] In other words, social formations are actual existing (or historical) societies at a particular point of development. Bismarck's Germany, for example, "is characterized by a specific combination of capitalist, feudal, and patriarchal modes of production."[12]

Every social formation is divided into classes as an *effect* (cf. Althusser's "the effectivity of a structure on its elements") of the social division of labor implicit in the modes of production. Classes as such are not "things-in-themselves" that exist independent of one another and then come into conflict. Rather they come into being as diachronic *relations of conflict*. A bourgeoisie cannot exist without a working class from which to extract surplus value. A dominant class cannot exist without a dominated class. Thus, conflict is implicit in the very character of classes and thereby in every social formation.

The state's function is to hold this conflict-ridden formation together; to prevent, as Marx put it, "the common ruin of the contending classes." It is by virtue of this function that there is a correlation between the capitalist state and the power of the bourgeoisie. In preserving the cohesion and unity of a social formation riddled with class conflict, the state preserves the dominance of the dominant classes. Hence, it is not merely an instrument the dominant classes use to preserve their power in society. The cause-effect relation is just the opposite: in preserving society, the state preserves the power of the dominant classes.

One might argue that such a fine point is irrelevant since either way there is a close correlation between capitalist state power and the interests of the bourgeoisie. For Poulantzas, however, this point is crucial since it demonstrates the basis of the state's autonomy as an institution derivative of the social formation (civil society) as a whole and not just from the dominant classes.

Further, because it is derivative of the totality of civil

society, the state represents a condensation of its relationships (i.e., class conflicts) and not just the interests of the
dominant classes. Class conflict in the social formation is
refracted through the state. The contemporary capitalist state
becomes a "site" of class struggle where competing interests
of various classes and class fractions come into conflict with
one another in the form of competing and conflicting state
policies within and between different state agencies. The state
itself is thereby infected with the conflicts plaguing civil
society.

To preserve its own cohesion, then, the state must plan
policy around organizing a "power-bloc" of classes and class
fractions who agree with policy because it protects their basic
interests vis-à-vis other classes. A power-bloc inevitably will
consist of an alliance of the dominant classes and class
fractions in which the "hegemonic fraction" is most powerful
by virtue of its dominant role in the economy.

In addition to organizing the power-bloc, the state must
prevent the dominated classes and class fractions from
achieving cohesion and unity, playing them off against one
another by ideological means or by selective concessions. It is
in this manner that specific state agencies and bureaus become
the sites of class conflict over the implementation of alternative policies. Some state agencies will in fact attempt to
promote the interests of the dominated groups and thereby
come into conflict with other state agencies. Also, this conflict
will rage within various state bureaus and offices over specific
policies (such as welfare policy, industrial growth policy,
energy policy). In this manner the capitalist state comes to
represent a condensation of the relationship of class forces.

In contemporary advanced capitalist social formations
the hegemonic fraction of the bourgeoisie is composed of the
monopoly capitalists of the large multi-national corporations
tied to the world market and American monopoly capitalism.
In France the power-bloc is centered around this hegemonic
fraction and includes the rest of the owners of medium and

large businesses as well as upper management, large landown-
ers, and fractions of the traditional petit-bourgeoisie. The
dominated classes consist of the industrial working class, agricultural laborers and farmers, and new fractions of the petit-
bourgeoisie.

Poulantzas' analysis of class boundaries conforms to
traditional marxism.[13] He takes issue with the new working
class theories of Mallet and Gorz (discussed above in Chapter
6), arguing that white-collar workers, mental workers, technicians, etc. are part of a new petit-bourgeoisie, not a new
working class.[14] The significance of this terminological
dispute lies in the area of political strategy. Gorz viewed these
"new workers" as the vanguard of the working class and their
demand for self-management to overcome alienation as the
most advanced revolutionary demand. Poulantzas, on the
other hand, considered the "new petit-bourgeoisie" to be, at
best, a possible ally of the working class but hardly its
vanguard, thereby preserving the privileged role of the
communist party as the vanguard of the working class. Also,
since he considered them petit-bourgeois, their demand for
self-management was also "petit-bourgeois" and not revolutionary. It is in this area that the differences between the
Eurocommunist and new left social theory are clearest.

Trying to provide a marxist explanation for the rise of
the welfare state, Poulantzas distinguishes between different
phases of development of capitalism. He argues that the
change from competitive to monopoly capitalism was paral-
leled by the transformation of the liberal (laissez-faire) to the
interventionist capitalist state. The major consequence of this
transformation is that, while the state and the economy
remain separate, the state takes on more and more economic
functions. The state takes on responsibility for maintaining
the economy through government regulation, and takes on
responsibility for reproducing the economy through planning, investment, education, and training for the labor force,
etc. It is in this sense that Poulantzas claims the state helps to
constitute and reproduce the relations of production. This is

why he disagrees with the base-superstructure model.

But the contemporary interventionist state is in crisis, which may open opportunities for the working class and its allies to challenge the power-bloc. More and more, the state's economic functions appear contradictory and seem to be in conflict with elements of this power-bloc. Yet unless the state pursues its economic functions, the interests of the power-bloc will be hurt in other ways. This leads to conflict within the bloc over what strategies and policies to adopt. It leads to conflict between the state and the dominated classes as state policy appears more openly to be formulated with power-bloc interests in mind. And it leads to conflict between the state and sectors of the power-bloc whose immediate interests may be sacrificed for the interests of the hegemonic fraction.

The end result is a crisis of democracy and a drift towards authoritarian statism. Faced with opposition from within the power-bloc and from the dominated classes, the state seeks to justify itself on the basis of superior knowledge and technical expertise. Such a technocratic solution, however, is both elitist and undemocratic, and creates further strains for democracy. This opens the way for the working class to seek hegemony in a democratic alliance with the other dominated classes and fractions. In particular, the new petit-bourgeoisie of mental and technical employees are receptive to such an alliance because they find themselves in conflict with the power-bloc.

Poulantzas argues that an alliance between the working class and the new petit-bourgeoisie is possible if it is based on seeking an "advanced democracy" in which the hegemonic power of monopoly capital is destroyed and the drift toward authoritarian statism is reversed. The working class would be the hegemonic class in this alliance. It would lead the struggle for democratic structural reforms that are revolutionary because they challenge the logic of capitalist power.

It is this theory of the state which provides the foundation for the Eurocommunist strategy of a democratic transition to socialism. For if the capitalist state is a site of class struggle, then a revolutionary transformation of the

state can be achieved without—to use the leninist term—
"smashing" it. Reformism or social-democratization will
always be a risk with such a strategy, but it is a risk that
Poulantzas says must be taken since the only alternatives are
variants of authoritarian statism (whether stalinist or fascist).

c. Retreat from Structuralism

Poulantzas arrived at these conclusions only after a long
and tortuous odyssey through structuralism. He began his
sojourn with the intention of placing the marxist theory of the
state on a scientific basis by his own "symptomatic" reading of
the classic texts. The major purpose of such a reading was to
continue the structuralist crusade against humanism, historicism, and the "problematic of the subject," and extend it into
the field of political theory. While the chief concepts he
employs (mode of production, social formation, relative
autonomy, structure in dominance, determinate in the last
instance) have already been introduced by Althusser,
Poulantzas nevertheless presents a distinct contribution to
structuralist marxism as well as a sophisticated theory of the
state. Even an unsympathetic critic has remarked: "grimly
professional, rigorously logical...he seems to have read practi-
cally everything produced in this century."[15] His thorough
discussion of the marxist classics and 20th century political
theory (e.g., Weber, Schumpeter, Parsons, Lasswell, MacIver,
and Dahrendorf) seem to bear out this remark.

Yet numerous critics of all persuasions repeat that his
work suffers from abstractionism, formalism and a lack of
empirical data.[16] One critic considers his Political Power and
Social Classes to be the marxist equivalent of Talcott Parson's
The Social System.[17] In 1976 Poulantzas (in the tradition
established by Althusser) made a self-criticism of his early
work for "theoreticism," "formalism," "needlessly difficult
language," and "neglect of concrete analyses."[18]

The substance of his analyses has been equally contro-
versial. Various marxists have criticized his work for a lack of
theorization of class struggle, an inability to account for

historical change, inconsistency in his general theoretical framework, a spurious identification of ideology with culture, a mechanistic and reductionist analysis of fascism, a narrow and dogmatic taxonomy of social classes, an inaccurate analysis of Bonapartism, and numerous other sins. In fact, one critic questions the validity of his core concept (capitalist state) as an erroneous ideological conflation of the state and society that has totalitarian overtones—i.e., the appropriation of the totality of civil society by the state.[19]

In short, Poulantzas' work has provoked a deluge of criticism that is often as contentious and polemical as his own contributions. He has, however, shown the ability to accept criticism and change accordingly. His later work is much less abstruse, and as Eurocommunism became more of a reality we witness a decisive shift away from the structuralist problematic. In his 1976 self-criticism he made the remarkable statement, "I have attempted to break definitively with structuralism."[20] In 1979 he stated,

> There are some remnants of structuralism in Althusser and in the rest of us [i.e. the Althusserians]. In the theoretical conjuncture in which we were working it was structuralism against historicism, it was Lévi-Strauss against Sartre. It has been extremely difficult for us to make a total rupture from these two problematics. We insisted that for Marxism the main danger was not structuralism but historicism itself. So we directed all our attention against historicism—the problematic of the subject; against the problematics of Sartre and Lukacs, and as a result we "bent the stick"; and of course this had effects in our theory itself.[21]

This retreat from structuralism should not be confused with a reconciliation with the "problematic of the subject." Rather it represents a recognition that Lévi-Strauss' conceptualization of "timeless, invariant, structures" neglects the importance of class struggle in history and cannot account for historical change. It is part of the shift to a more open "post-structuralist" position (alluded to at the end of the last chapter) that emerged in the late 1970s.

In Poulantzas' case this shift also involves an appropri-ation of the new left themes of structural reforms and self-management. For Poulantzas did not advocate Eurocom-munism merely as an electoral strategy or an alliance "at the summit" between socialist and communist party leaders. Rather he argued that an electoral victory would be significant only in the context of a broad mass movement in which the masses could seize power "at the base" via self-management. Further, he argued that the new social movements (feminism, ecology, etc.) should be taken seriously by marxists as new forms of popular revolt and not be considered as secondary to the workers' movement. Thus, the later Poulantzas appears to have undergone a decisive intellectual and political evolution away from orthodox structural marxism toward an open, flexible neo-marxism which has incorporated new left themes. The extent of his Eurocommunist conversion to a democratic socialism is reflected in the conclusion to his last book, *State, Power, and Socialism* (1978):

> History has not yet given us a successful experience of the democratic road to socialism: what it has provided—and this is not insignificant—is some negative examples to avoid....But one thing is certain: socialism will be democratic or it will not be at all.[22]

Finally, Poulantzas' commitment to democratic socialism was tempered with a dose of realism and a tone of pessimism about the previous failures of the socialist experience. Nevertheless he felt that the goal of a democratic socialism was necessary and realizable despite the risks involved. "At worst, we could be heading for camps and massacres as appointed victims [as in Chile]." But this would be far preferable to "massacring other people only to end up ourselves beneath the blade of a Committee of Public Saftey or some Dictator of the proletariat [i.e. Stalin].[23] In spite of socialism's grim stalinist legacy (from which Eurocommu-nism sought to free itself), Poulantzas hoped that its realization in a democratic setting would unleash its full potential for human liberation.

Others, however, who also participated in the Althusserian trend of structural marxism experienced disillusionment in the 1970s and drew very different conclusions about socialism just when the Eurocommunist strategy appeared to be nearing fruition in France.

3. The New Philosophers

Marx's quip about historical events occurring twice—first as tragedy, then as farce—may very well apply to that curious movement known as the "new philosophers" which burst upon the French intellectual scene like a dazzling fireworks display just prior to the decisive 1978 legislative elections. What was "new" about this phenomenon was not the "philosophy" (mostly cribbed from Karl Popper and Albert Camus) but rather the triumphal reception with which it was greeted by the media. Its chief proponents, André Glucksmann and Bernard-Henry Lévy, became overnight celebrities complete with radio and television appearances, interviews in *Le Monde* and *L'Express*, and full-page color photographs in *Paris-Match*. Lévy was even offered a part in a movie! With all this media-hype their books became instant best-sellers. Meanwhile, their intellectual critics, scandalized by such blatant commercial exploitation, responded with a torrent of vituperation.

What was this new philosophy that it should provoke such an electrifying response? Its central thesis is disillusionment prompted first of all by Solzhenitsyn's gripping portrayal of Soviet camps in *The Gulag Archipelago*. But more deeply it is a despair born of the unfulfilled hopes of May 1968.

Both Lévy and Glucksmann were students of Althusser, 68ers, and maoists. Lévy was twenty years old in 1968 and a student militant. Glucksmann is the son of German Jewish refugees from Nazism. He is also a former member of the PCF[24] and the author of *Le Discours de la Guerre* (1967) and *Stratégie et Révolution en France, 1968* (1968). He and Lévy were among the *gauchistes* in the streets of Paris during the May events. They became leaders of a maoist grouplet that fancied itself the beginning of a new "Resistance" in a France "occupied" by the bourgeoisie. They advocated guerrilla warfare and "peasant" revolution to overthrow the "fascist" Pompidou regime.[25] Very few activists heeded their call to "take to the countryside" to build guerrilla bases. Even fewer French "peasants" joined their "long march," and this political fantasy disintegrated in short order.

At this point they read Solzhenitsyn and were suddenly enlightened as to why their efforts failed. They failed because, as Solzhenitsyn demonstrated to them, socialism is an impossible dream. The effort to overcome domination and oppression ultimately creates new forms of domination and oppression. Witness the Gulag. Here is the true meaning of socialism, the true meaning of marxism. Here is the true meaning of human existence. It is impossible to liberate humankind because the very essence of human existence is domination in one form or another. If one understands this one understands that all visions of a free and just society can serve *only* to promote the power of a new form of domination over an older one. That is why marxism is responsible for the Gulag. "The Soviet camps are Marxist, as Marxist as Auschwitz was Nazi."[26]

In *La Cuisinière et le mangeur d'hommes* (1975) Glucksmann presented his initial reaction to Solzhenitsyn's account of the Gulag and this inspired several others to join in. Many of these authors—Maurice Clavel, Christian Jambet, Guy Lardreau, Jean-Paul Dolle, Jean-Marie Benoist—were also former 68ers and former maoists. As an editor at Editions Grasset, Lévy arranged to publish their works in a series entitled "les nouvelles philosophes"—and thus the movement was christened.[27] In 1977 Lévy published his own book, *Barbarism with a Human Face* and Glucksmann published

The Master Thinkers.[28] These last two works thrust Lévy and Glucksmann to the fore as the major spokesmen of this anti-marxist philosophy just as the French were to decide whether or not to vote for the marxist parties of the Union of the Left.

While there are differences in emphasis and scope between the two works, they complement one another in such a way as to form a common project. Glucksmann's is the more serious intellectual endeavor of the two, although its main thesis comes directly from Karl Popper's, *The Open Society and Its Enemies* (1946). This can be summarized as follows: 20th century totalitarianism has its roots in 19th century German philosophy, particularly in the works of Fichte, Hegel, Nietzsche, and of course, Marx. Lévy's book is less analytical and more an emotional expression of his disillusionment with marxism, although he attempts to place it in the wider context of historical pessimism. "I have attempted nothing in this book but to think through to the end the idea of pessimism in history," he tells us.[29]

Both Lévy and Glucksmann are deeply influenced by Nietzsche. "We should reread Nietzsche..." Lévy advises us.[30] Glucksmann, although more critical of Nietzsche, finds much that is liberating: "Nietzsche's 'frankness' frees us."[31] Further, he tells us, "In the anarchist workers' libraries of the early part of this century Nietzsche occupied a place of honor. He still occupies this place..."[32] Nietzsche is clearly the role model of the new philosophers. They portray themselves as smashing the idols of accepted thought as Nietzsche presented himself in his last work, *Ecce Homo* (cf. chapters "Why I am a Hammer," "Why I Am So Clever"). Glucksmann self-consciously "apes" the style of this work by titling his chapters: "Why I Am So Revolutionary," "Why I Am So Clever," etc. (Could it be that Glucksmann is one of Zarathustra's apes whom Nietzsche warned against in *Thus Spake Zarathustra?*) Lévy, for his part, adopts the poetic prose of Zarathustra: "If I were a poet, I would sing of the horror of living and the new Gulags that tomorrow holds in store for us. If I were a musician, I would speak of the idiot laughter and impotent tears, the dreadful uproar made by the lost, camped in the ruins. If I had been a painter...But I am neither painter nor musician, nor poet. I am a philosopher."[33]

While Solzhenitsyn and Nietzsche are the brightest stars in the new philosophers' firmament, these ex-Althusserians also speak approvingly of the post-structuralist work of Foucault and Lacan.[34]

The unreality of their former maoism may help explain the new philosophers' political reaction against socialism. Similarly, the "unreality" (i.e., theoreticism and over-abstractionism) of their Althusserian structuralism may help explain their intellectual reaction against marxism. The source of the pretentiousness, however, remains a mystery. Lévy, nevertheless, considers his book to be of such world-historical import that it is literally; a "prolegomena to any philosophy taking on the task of looking at evil face to face."[35]

If we have the patience to wade through the poetry, the moral outrage, and the un-self-critical pretension, we find that the new philosophers present an analysis of power on three interrelated levels: that of political practice, theory of knowledge, and ontology.

As a political practice they find socialism to be an utter abomination. Its practice is that of one party political dictatorship; elimination of democracy, civil liberties, and human rights; suppression of all dissent; and a massive system of concentration camp (i.e., slave) labor with which much of the infrastructure of socialism was built. In this indictment of the Soviet Union the new philosophers are on firm ground. The rare pro-Soviet sympathizer in the West today may point to the economic growth, the low cost of housing and medical care, job security, and the apparent approval by the Soviet majority of their social system. (The almost complete lack of public strife and protest is interpreted by apologists as a sign of approval for the regime.) Yet such a case is obviously weak. The Soviet Union is a totalitarian society. On this point the new philosophers are absolutely correct.

However, their sudden discovery of this fact in the mid-1970s after reading Solzhenitsyn somehow rings false as a reason for rejecting socialism. Most non-PCF intellectuals had been critical of the Soviet Union for years. The May 1968 rebellion was as equally opposed to authoritarian, bureaucratic communism as it was to Western capitalism. Why then this startling revelation?

Presumably, when they were maoists, Lévy and Glucksmann knew about the Soviet system. Maoism itself is already a rejection of the Soviet Union as a revisionist, fascist dictatorship. If they were consistent maoists they presumably didn't believe that the Soviet Union even *was* socialist. Hence, why become disillusioned with socialism on the basis of a non-socialist dictatorship?

Of course the Soviet leaders call their system "real socialism" and the new philosophers are in their right to accept this self-description because it is an historical reality. But it still rings hollow for former maoists to lose their faith in socialism based on the political practice of a social system they previously claimed was not socialist at all. However, if they said they had become disillusioned with China then their rejection of socialism would make more sense. But precious little is said about China and maoism in their works. Curiously though, Lévy makes the strange claim that the "Maoist adventure (is) one of the very great pages in the recent history of France."[36] Why? Presumably because *he* was a part of it!

In addition to rejecting socialism on the basis of Soviet political practice Lévy and Glucksmann also reject marxism as the ideology used to justify this oppressive system. Borrowing from Lefort and Castoriadis, they argue that marxism must be judged on the basis of the practice it has inspired and which it serves to legitimate.[37] That is, it is used to justify a dictatorship *over* the working classes and disguises it as rule *by* them. Also, it serves to justify a new imperialism and masks it as internationalism. As a closed body of dogma it claims to be beyond criticism since it is "scientific truth." In short, it functions as the state religion of totalitarian dictatorships.

The new philosophers explain that in the hold marxism has over the minds of its adherents lies the basis of its power to dominate. Far from being a philosophy of liberation, marxism—with its iron logic of historical necessity—has functioned as a mode of ideological domination; as a rationale for "voluntary servitude."[38] Lévy makes much of Stalin's show trials of the 1930s in which Bukharin and others confessed to crimes they did not commit because the logic of marxism convinced them that the Party is always correct.[39] "Princes had never discovered how to teach resignation and acceptance so effectively," Lévy claims.[40]

But it is not just marxism's effects and consequences to which the new philosophers object. It is the very intent of marxism as a theory of knowledge, they claim, to dominate the world. Just as Castoriadis argued that marxism is imbued with a "Western rationalist metaphysic" of domination, so do Lévy and Glucksmann. The "Master Thinkers" desire to master the world with their thought. For as Francis Bacon said, "Knowledge is Power," and as the master thinkers acquire knowledge of the world, they acquire mastery over it. They acquire power. The Soviet Union then, is an example of "philosophy in power."[41]

Power, thus, is the crucial issue for the new philosophers; power in its deepest ontological meaning. The ultimate philosophical question is not why is there being rather than nothing. No, it is why is there *power* rather than nothing.[42] For power *is* being:

> Power is not a foreign body in society, but an integral part of it: it is the *founder of social conditions*...it is *the means by which a society organizes itself*...it is the demiurge without which society and its health would not exist.[43]

Power is not just the organized force of the state. In fact it is not a *thing* at all. Its reality is more fundamental than its material instruments, for its origins are found in the very fact of social relations. It is more fundamental than desire, language, and time (history), also. The power of desire, the power of language, the power of history are not the ultimate reality of power.[44] Rather they are expressions of power. Power creates desire. Power creates language. What, then, is power? Following Lacan's Freudianism, Lévy tells us power is an "ego ideal" that is the necessary condition for the survival of the human species. Power "means nothing but the 'will to live' or the 'will to survive.'"[45]

Thus power—and domination—are inescapably rooted in the souls and minds of humankind. We cannot survive without it. This traditional pessimistic view of human nature is presented by Lévy as a basic ontological fact which makes optimism about the human condition unthinkable. For him, it shatters all prospects of the perfectibility of the social order. It explains why both capitalism and socialism are barbarisms. In short, Lévy concludes: "life is a lost cause, and happiness an outmoded idea."[46]

This pessimism is the major thrust of the new philosophers' message. Politics is a dead-end. There remains only the domain of ethics. For the committed "anti-barbarian intellectual" is both a metaphysician and a *moraliste* who, like Solzhenitsyn and the Soviet dissidents, will stand up and denounce evil even though Satan is fated to triumph.

> Yes, we know that the world is subject to the law of the Master, and we *do not believe* that that law will ever give way to our desires. But we will continue *to think...without believing it* the impossible thought of a world freed from lordship.[47]

Thus, like Camus' rebel who pursues the myth of Sisyphus, the new philosophers abandon politics as such and opt for metaphysical rebellion: because without it, "the world would be even worse than we say it is."[48]

There are numerous problems of the logic and consistency of the new philosophy. The main problem is that which we encountered with Castoriadis: the total identification of marxism as a theory of knowledge with the political practice of communist movements. This logic would lead us to judge Christianity on the basis of the Inquisition, the massacre of the Huguenots, and the pogroms against East European Jewry. It would lead us to judge Nietzsche on the basis of Auschwitz and Nazism.

Closer to home, Glucksmann accuses contemporary French marxists with partial responsibility for the Cambodian holocaust of the 1970s: "The miseries of the world are sometimes of French origin. For example, the Khmer Rouge leaders who are responsible for one or two million dead were often educated in Paris."[49] If we follow Glucksmann's logic, perhaps these leaders read his own *Le Discours de la Guerre* (1967) and applied his theory in their military operations! Would not Glucksmann himself share some of the responsibility for the bloodbath? Would he hold himself responsible for this Cambodian Gulag?[50] What for that matter are the effects of the new philosophy itself? Could it not be argued—as its critics do—that its anti-marxism has the effect of strengthening capitalist domination?

The problem, of course, is that it is misleading to claim that a theory by itself produces social reality. What we have here is but another form of theoreticism. The Soviet experience, for example, is obviously conditioned by a host of historical, social, economic, and cultural factors as well as the impact of marxism. To consider a theory as the sole cause of social reality implies that reality is a construction of our minds in the way that fantasy is. In fact this is consistent with the previous political and theoretical efforts of the new philosophers: i.e., maoism and Althusserianism. What we see then is a progression from one fantasy type of thinking to another.

This is not to deny the importance of the phenomenon of the new philosophy or the issues with which it is concerned. For disillusionment, despair, and pessimism about the prospects of authentically liberating social change was indeed a significant trend in the 1970s. The failure of May 1968 to bring about an immediate and thorough transformation of France was very discouraging for those with high hopes of a de-alienated, self-managed, liberatory society. Further, the

Soviet invasion of Czechoslavakia, the conservative turn in China, the overthrow of Allende's Chile, the Cambodian holocaust, war among communist states in Southeast Asia, the Vietnamese boat people, and the Soviet invasion of Afghanistan provided meager inspiration for the international socialist cause in the 1970s. The new philosophy was significant in that it captured and crystalized this mood of discouragement which was an undercurrent in all segments of the left to one degree or another.

In its rejection of marxism, however, the new philosophy seems to have backfired. With Castoriadis the rejection of marxism contributed to developing new left theory and social activism. This was so because his anti-marxism was coupled with a continuing effort toward social transformation. Since the new philosophers' rejection of marxism was coupled with a cosmic pessimism it failed to jolt the left out of its dogmatic slumbers and probably had the effect of reinforcing older habits of thought. In this respect Castoriadis is probably correct in calling them "diversionists."[51]

4. The Crisis of Marxism

The inadequacies of the new philsophers' critique, however, could in no way obscure the fact that marxism was indeed in crisis during the 1970s. To a certain extent the advent of Eurocommunism masked this crisis because it represented a positive model of socialism when other models appeared discredited. It is no wonder, then, that many French leftists invested their hopes in it despite serious reservations about the extent of the PCF's de-stalinization or the PS's radicalization. And as mentioned above, the Common Program of the Left appeared to embody in many ways the legacy of May 1968. Thus when the electoral alliance broke down and the left was defeated in the crucial 1978 elections, the ensuing political demoralization laid bare the theoretical confusion and conceptual lethargy of contemporary marxism.

The breakdown of left unity was initiated in September 1977 when PCF leaders tried to get the PS leaders to agree, prior to assuming office, to specific income redistribution and nationalization goals for actualizing the Common Program. Fearing an investment "strike" and economic sabotage by the business sector in the wake of a left electoral victory—which could lead to chaos and possible civil war or a military coup as in Chile—the socialists insisted on cautious and moderate goals for implementation of the Common Program. PCF leaders sharply attacked the socialist position as a "turn to the right" towards typical social-democratic "management of capitalist crisis." Therefore, they broke ranks with the PS and conducted their own electoral campaign around the theme of "soaking the rich" in order to eliminate "poverty and misery."

In spite of this split in ranks opinion polls predicted the two parties would win a majority of the vote. When in fact the left lost the election despite a last minute unity effort, PCF leader Georges Marchais further attacked the socialists, claiming the defeat was totally their fault.

Others, however, argued that it was the PCF leadership who was responsible for the defeat since they provoked the split in left unity. Because the PS was winning more votes than the PCF—and probably *from* the PCF—critics claimed that communist leaders preferred to lose the election (thereby scuttling any prospect of immediate reform in France) rather than allow the PS to emerge as the dominant party in a left government. In this sense the 1978 election was a "victory" for the PCF leadership, for they prevented the PS from overtaking their role as the dominant force on the left.[52] *

In the wake of this electoral defeat, disillusionment and demoralization swept through the ranks of the left. Within the PCF itself there was a storm of protest and widespread confusion. However, the Party leadership refused to allow any criticism of its policies published in the Party newspaper, *L'Humanité*. Critics within the Party therefore sought publi-

*As this book went to press, PS candidate François Mitterand won the 1981 French presidential election. He immediately called new legislative elections in which the PS won enough votes to govern without PCF participation if it so desired.

cation of their opinions in *Le Monde*. Prominent intellectuals, led by Jean Ellenstein (a well known communist historian) and Louis Althusser, denounced the PCF leadership in strong terms. Hundreds of other Party members signed petitions criticizing the lack of open discussion.

After thirty years of loyal party service, Althusser was bitterly disillusioned. In April 1978 he published a series of articles in *Le Monde* in which he claimed that "the leadership's habits...are rooted in the whole Stalinist tradition surviving within the Party apparatus.[53] He accused the leadership of fostering bureaucratic authoritarianism, cynically manipulating the rank-and-file, and undermining the prospect of progressive change in order to perpetuate their own power. He also claimed that their shabbily disguised stalinism literally destroyed marxism in the PCF: "Marxist theory, which was barely alive within the Party, has never recovered from this voluntary servitude (sic!)...Marxist theory has reached zero-point in the Party. It has disappeared.[54]

When the most prominent French marxist philosopher can make such a statement, it is a clear indication that marxism is again in the midst of a serious crisis. Even before the electoral defeat Althusser and other marxist intellectuals were talking of a "crisis of marxism." For Althusser this crisis stems from the fact that "there no longer exists in the minds of the masses any 'achieved ideal', any really living reference to socialism."[55] Lucio Colletti, a prominent Italian marxist, agreed with Althusser that marxism is in crisis because it "has produced a reality totally distinct from that which it first envisioned."[56] Fernando Claudin, the Spanish Eurocommunist, sees this crisis as an unanticipated result of the October Revolution. "Lenin, Trotsky, and a long series of authentic Marxists, while thinking they were building socialism, in fact contributed to laying the foundation of a new society of dominant and dominated classes."[57]

At this point Althusser might do well to read Sartre's *Critique of Dialectical Reason* on how the individual's projects come back to one as the opposite of one's intentions

(See Chapter 3 above). In this sense Althusser himself might be viewed as a kind of tragic existential figure whose life project (to preserve the revolutionary purity of marxism from contamination by bourgeois forms of thought) has turned into its bitter opposite. Along the way he sacrificed much of his personal integrity (abandoning his maoist students in the 1960s, abandoning the "dictatorship of the proletariat" concept) for a Party that measured success by getting a few more votes in bourgeois elections.[58] His revolutionary principles were shattered on the reefs of the PCF's electoral opportunism.[59]

While the future of marxism in France is difficult to predict, it was clear by the late 1970s that marxism was in a serious crisis. Due to the break-up of the Union of the Left and its subsequent electoral defeat, Eurocommunism failed to meet the expectations it raised. In rejecting marxism, the new philosophers caused a big splash and underscored the fact that many others were having their doubts. Even Sartre, though now quite old, declared his own break with marxism and joined with his old nemesis Raymond Aron to seek aid for the Vietnamese boat people.[60] The major marxist theorists (Althusser in France, Colletti in Italy, Claudin in Spain) were all aware of the crisis but could offer no solutions.[61] Marxism was left floundering.

While the immediate prospects for a rejuvenation appeared slim, the development of several new social movements in the 1970s pointed the way toward a possible resolution of this crisis in radical social theory.

Notes

1. Eurocommunism has not been accepted by all West European CPs. In fact, it has provoked splits in the Greek, Swedish, and British parties, while the Irish and Portuguese, for example, remain staunchly pro-Soviet. For a sympathetic view of Eurocommunism see the collection of articles edited by Carl Boggs and David Plotke, *The Politics of Eurocommunism: Socialism in Transition* (Boston, 1980).

2. Santiago Carrillo, *Eurocommunism and the State* (Westport, CT, 1978), p. 111.

3. *Ibid.*, p. 164. Carrillo conjectures that perhaps the Soviet state is an intermediate phase between a capitalist and socialist state such as an absolute monarchy was intermediate between feudalism and modern bourgeois democracy.

4. By use of this term Togliatti meant to convey his view that the international communist movement should not be led by a single center (i.e., the Soviet Union), but rather that there should be many centers and many paths to socialism.

5. For the development of the PCI in the 1950s and 1960s see Donald Blackmer, *Unity in Diversity: Italian Communism and the International Communist Movement* (Cambridge, 1965).

6. For the recent development of the PCI see Joanne Barkan, "Italian Communism at the Crossroads," in Boggs and Plotke, *op. cit.*, pp. 49-75.

7. For a Eurocommunist view of the politics of the French left in the 1970s see George Ross, "The PCF and the End of the Bolshevik Dreams," and Andrew Feenberg, "France: The New Middle Strata and the Legacy of the May Events." Both are in Boggs and Plotke, *op. cit.* For a critical view of French Eurocommunism see C. Castoriadis, "The French Left," in *Telos* 34 (Winter 1977-78), pp. 49-73.

8. See *Programme commun de gouvernement du parti communiste et du parti socialiste* (Paris, 1972). For a sympathetic analysis of the Common Program see Andrew Feenberg, "Socialism in France? The 'Common Program' and the Future of the French Left," in *Socialist Review* 19 (1974), pp. 9-38.

9. Even Althusser defended this position despite the fact that he spent the previous twenty years attacking it as reformist and revisionist! See his, "On the 22nd Congress of the French Communist Party," in *New Left Review* 104 (July-August 1977), pp. 3-22.

10. Poulantzas, *State, Power, and Socialism* (London, 1978), p. 16. Poulantzas' major works (in English translation) are: *Political Power and Social Classes* (1968), *Fascism and Dictatorship: The Third International and the Problem of Fascism* (1970), *Classes in Contemporary Capitalism* (1974), *Crisis of Dictatorships: Portugal, Greece, Spain* (1975), and *State, Power, and Socialism* (1978).

11. Poulantzas, *Political Power and Social Classes* (London, 1973), p. 15.

12. *Ibid.*, p. 15.

13. See his *Classes in Contemporary Capitalism* (London, 1974). For a critique of Poulantzas' class taxonomy see Erik Olin Wright, "Class Boundaries in Advanced Capitalist Societies," *New Left Review* 97 (July-August 1976), pp. 3-42.

14. For an analysis of this debate see George Ross, "The New Middle Classes: French Marxist Critiques," *Theory and Society* (March 1978).

15. George Lichtheim, *From Marx to Hegel* (New York, 1974), p. 150.

16. Much of this criticism emerged in a debate between Poulantzas and the English marxist Ralph Miliband in the pages of *New Left Review*. See Poulantzas, "The Problem of the Capitalist State," 58 (November-December 1969); Miliband, "Reply to Poulantzas," 59 (January-February 1970); and "Poulantzas and the Capitalist State," 82 (November-December 1973). Ernesto Laclau attempted to mediate the controversy in his, "The Specificity of the Political: the Poulantzas-Miliband Debate," *Economy and Society*, Vol. 5, #1 (February 1975). Poulantzas had the final word in "The Capitalist State: Reply to Miliband and Laclau," *New Left Review* 95 (January-February 1976).

17. Abercrobie et al., "Class, State, and Fascism: The Work of Nicos Poulantzas," *Political Studies*, Vol. 24, #4 (December 1976), p. 517.

18. Poulantzas, "The Capitalist State: Reply to Miliband and Laclau," *op. cit.*, pp. 66-68.

19. See Lichtheim, *op. cit.*, p. 151.

20. Poulantzas, *op. cit.*, p. 73.

21. Stuart Hall and Alan Hunt, "Interview with Nicos Poulantzas," *Marxism Today* (July 1979), p. 198.

22. Poulantzas, *State, Power, and Socialism* (London, 1978), p. 265.

23. *Idem.*

24. Glucksmann quit the PCF in 1956 at the age of 19.

25. See Glucksmann's "Le fascisme qui vient d'en haut," *Les Temps Modernes* (February 1972).

26. Levy, *Barbarism with a Human Face* (New York, 1979), p. 155.

27. E.g., Jean-Paul Dolle, *Voie d'accès au plaisir* (Paris, 1974); Guy Lardreau and Christian Jambet, *L'ange* (Paris, 1976).

28. Although Editions Grasset also published Glucksmann's book, it was not part of the "nouvelles philosophes" series edited by Lévy. On this basis Glucksmann claims—true to the form of French intellectual individualism—that he is not one of the new philosophers. However, the English translation of this work is subtitled, "The Manifesto of the 'New Philosophy' from France."

29. Lévy, p. xi.

30. *Ibid.*, p. 41.

31. Glucksmann, *op. cit.*, p. 244.

32. *Ibid.*, p. 245.

33. Lévy, pp. ix-x.

34. See Levy, pp. 17, 30 and Glucksmann, pp. 189, 218, 221, 278. Foucault in turn wrote a favorable review of Glucksmann's book for *Le Nouvel Observateur*, 9 May 1977.

35. Levy, p. 27.

36. *Ibid.*, p. 205.

37. Lévy profusely acknowledges his debt. See *ibid.*, p. 204.

38. Recently the 16th century work of Etienne La Boétie, *Discours de la*

servitude voluntaire has received a great deal of attention among French intellectuals. La Boétié addresses the issue of why people voluntarily accept domination as necessary. For a recent review of his work see *Telos* 43 (Spring 1980), pp. 215-229.

39. Arthur Koestler's *Darkness at Noon* (1941) of course captures this psychology quite clearly.

40. Lévy, p. 157.

41. *Idem.*

42. *Ibid.,* p. 1.

43. *Ibid.,* p. 25.

44. Here Lévy is attacking positions put forth by Felix Guattari and Jacques Deleuze in *Anti-Oedipus* (Paris, 1974).

45. Levy, p. 18.

46. *Ibid.,* p. 2.

47. *Ibid.,* p. 195.

48. *Ibid.,* p. 196.

49. Max Gallo, "An Interview with André Glucksmann," *Telos* 33 (Fall 1977), p. 99. Translated from *L'Express* 18 July 1977).

50. When asked a similar question Glucksmann lamely replied that he was sure the Red Khmer leaders left Paris before his work was published! See *Ibid.,* p. 99.

51. C. Castoriadis, "The Diversionists," *Telos* 33 (Fall 1977), pp. 102-106. Translated from *Le Nouvel Observateur,* 30 June 1977.

52. For an analysis of the 1978 election that is sympathetic to the PCF position see George Ross' article in Boggs and Plotke, *op. cit.* For a critical analysis see Louise Beaulieu and Jonathan Cloud, "Political Ecology and the Limits of the Communist Vision," also in Boggs and Plotke.

53. Althusser's *Le Monde* articles are translated as "What Must Change in the Party," in *New Left Review* 109 (July 1978), pp. 19-43.

54. *Ibid.,* p. 35.

55. Althusser, "The Crisis of Marxism," in *Marxism Today* (July 1978).

56. Quoted in Fernando Claudin, "Some Reflections on the Crisis of Marxism," *Socialist Review* 45 (May-June 1979), p. 137.

57. *Ibid.,* p. 138.

58. Georges Marchais stated as the PCF's goal in the 1978 elections: "25 percent would be good, but 21 percent is not good enough." Quoted in Althusser, *op. cit.*

59. Althusser's personal tragedy took an even more bizarre turn. In November 1980 he confessed to strangling his wife and was committed to a mental asylum.

60. See M. Rybalka, "Introduction to 'La Nouvelle Philosophie,'" *Telos* 33 (Fall 1977), p. 94.

61. For an interesting effort by U.S. theorists to confront this crisis, see Michael Albert and Robin Hahnel, *Unorthodox Marxism* (Boston, 1978).

/9/
The New Social Movements of the 1970s

The formation of a viable and dynamic Socialist Party in the 1970s was one of the major consequences of May 1968. As we have seen, this development made possible Eurocommunist strategy for the PCF and a credible Union of the Left electoral alternative. The collapse and defeat of the Union of the Left in 1978 left both parties temporarily in a state of disarray and made it possible for the new social movements of the 1970s to emerge in their own right and not just as background to electoral politics.

These movements are the backbone of the legacy of the new left. They may ultimately provide the basis for a renovation of radical social theory now caught up in the crisis of marxism and the surpassing of structuralism. For the core ideas of the new left—self-management, critique of alienation and bureaucracy in everyday life—form the basis of much of their practice. They focus on mass action (as opposed to electoralism) to achieve specific goals and share an anti-technocratic vision of an autonomous, decentralized, self-managed society.

In the wake of May 1968 single-issue movements sprang up to contest many aspects of everyday life—tenants' rights, prison reform, mental health reform, gay rights, immigrant workers' rights, etc. In this chapter we will concentrate on three particular movements—self-management, feminism, and ecology: for while they may appear to be single-issue or constituency-oriented movements like the rest, they each contain the seeds of a general vision of society. From a synthesis of these three the elements of a new radical social theory may emerge.

1. Self-Management

As we have seen in chapter 5, the theme of self-management was introduced in France in the 1950s by the *Socialisme ou Barbarie* group. In attempting to recover the democratic and egalitarian core of the socialist ideal they looked to three sources: a) the historical experience of mass revolutionary action such as the Paris Commune of 1871, or the Russian workers' councils of 1905 and 1917; b) the workers' struggle for control of the industrial production process itself in the factory; and c) the anti-bureaucratic Hungarian Revolution of 1956. What was significant in each of these instances was that workers exercised their power directly without the mediation of a hierarchical leadership superimposing its own will (and hence domination) on them.

In Chapter 6, we saw that autogestion appeared in May 1968 both as a general political slogan to indicate the movement's independence from the traditional left political parties and as part of a vision of society in which individuals are empowered to control all aspects of their own lives. In this sense there was much discussion during May of a self-managed society as a model of socialism which avoided the bureaucratic domination associated with the Soviet model. In a statement distributed by the March 22nd Committee at Nanterre, the revolutionary meaning of the term was explained as follows:

> Practically, self-management consists in the worker comrades operating their factories by and for themselves and, consequently, the suppression of the hierarchy of salaries as well as the notions of wage-earner and boss. It is for them to constitute the workers' councils, elected by themselves and executing the decisions of the whole.

> These councils must be in close relation with the councils of other enterprises on the regional, national and international plane.

> The members of these workers' councils are elected at a determinate time and their tasks are rotated. It is in fact necessary to avoid the re-creation of a bureaucracy which would tend to set up a leadership and re-create oppressive power.[1]

Such a vision is consistent with the anarchist goal of abolishing the state since the councils could take over the state functions. It is also consistent with council communism as opposed to party communism. The councils as the direct voice of the workers would replace the party which is supposed to represent the workers in the governing of a communist society. The point, obviously, of a self-managed society is that it would eliminate the separation between the workers and the rulers of society. Instead of a communist party (or any other grouping) ruling *in the name of* the working class or *on behalf of* the working class, the working class would rule *in its own right*. Thus slogans for "workers' power" and "workers' control" sprang up as corollaries of the self-management theme.

In addition to this general vision of a self-managed society, the demand of self-management was raised during May by various groups of strikers who sought specific decision-making powers in their jobs from the most basic issues of working conditions (e.g., work schedules: starting time, break times, quitting time), to questions of technique (e.g., *how* to perform a certain operation), to fundamental policy issues (e.g., what kinds of products should be produced). Wresting control from management of the actual everyday process of production was seen by many militants as the first step toward creating workers' control over society at large.[2]

While such reforms could prove to be the beginnings of a general social transformation, they also could be the basis for a co-optation of such change. In fact in the years after May 1968 there was a major effort to restrict the meaning of self-management to a modest set of proposals for greater "employee input" and "job enrichment." From de Gaulle's offer of "participation" to the PCF's concept of "democratic management" (that is, *some* management personnel to be elected by the workers) there have been numerous efforts to co-opt and water down the radical demand for a self-managed society raised in May 1968. In fact, some employers view limited forms of self-management (job rotation, small work teams, flexible working hours) as ways of effectively raising productivity—and profit—by boosting worker morale.

The social-democratic model of self-management—as practiced in Sweden and West Germany in the 1970s—consists of union representation in the management of the capitalist firm. In the system of co-determination (*Mitbestimmung*) practiced in West Germany union officials are given token positions on a company's board of directors and thereby represent labor's viewpoint in management. Whether this is what French socialist leaders have in mind when they speak of self-management is not clear. Obviously such a system is far removed from one in which workers' directly manage their factory.

Another practice which has been called self-management in the 1970s is that of workers (either directly or through their union) buying up their factory when the owners plan to shut it down. Generally, there is little radical intent in this kind of situation. It is primarily a defensive act on the part of workers trying to save their jobs. As the new owners, the workers have a say in the management of the plant. In most of these situations the firm eventually fails despite the fact that workers usually take a pay cut and increased workloads to try to keep things going. This model of self-management as a failed capitalist enterprise hardly makes it a desirable goal on which to base a vision of society.

There is at least one nation which claims to be a model of self-managed society and that, of course, is Yugoslavia. Critics, however, claim that Yugoslav self-management is a sham since the communist party exercises all power in the economy and in the government.

Such co-opted and deformed practices have raised a certain scepticism about self-management as the panacea its advocates claim it is to all the problems raised historically with socialism. Critics note that during May 1968 the self-managed councils and action committees that sprang up tended to be dominated (and some claim manipulated) by articulate speakers or "big talkers." The council form thus masked the domination of the articulate (or even demagogic) over the inarticulate by the power of speech. Critics of Yugoslav practice note a similar phenomenon. They claim that technical and administrative personnel dominate the work councils in Yugoslav enterprises because of the unequal distribution of education and knowledge. Self-management thus may mask the domination of mental workers over manual workers in the technical division of labor.

Advocates of self-management who recognize these problems agree that there is much to learn about how to avoid the re-creation of relations of domination in a self-managed society. But they also note it is preferable to learn this by trial and error than to fall back on bankrupt and discredited models of socialism or resign oneself to the inevitability of capitalist domination.

In France there have been several developments in the 1970s which continue to foster the democratic and egalitarian vision of a self-managed society. On the theoretical level the journal *Autogestion et socialisme* picked up the thread where *Socialisme ou Barbarie* left off. After the demise of *Socialisme ou Barbarie* in 1965, Yvon Bourdet and others who had been influenced by it founded *Autogestion et socialisme* in 1966.

They continued the attempt to develop a libertarian socialism in the workers' council tradition of Pannekoek, Luxemburg, and Gramsci.

In 1977 they helped organize the Second International Conference on Participation, Workers' Control, and Self-management which was held in Paris.[3] Representatives from 28 countries analyzed and discussed self-management in its various forms as an idea, a movement, and a practice. They also established an international coordinating center to develop a sense of an international movement for self-management.[4]

As a social movement in France self-management has been identified primarily with the CFDT union confederation. During May 1968 the CFDT leadership endorsed the demand for self-management raised by the students:

> The student struggle to democratize the university and the workers' struggle to democratize industry are one and the same....Industrial and administrative monarchy must be replaced by democratic institutions based on self-management.[5]

After May thousands of militant workers joined the CFDT and made self-management the programmatic goal of the confederation at its 1970 national convention.

Under the leadership of Michel Rocard, the PSU also supported the demand for self-management in May and its aftermath. Eventually both the PS and even the PCF made a gesture of support for this demand. The PCF went so far as to include "autogestion" on the banner above the speakers' platform at its 23rd National Congress in 1979. This happened after years of denigrating the slogan. Militant *autogestionnaires*, however, viewed such gestures as opportunistically inspired attempts to increase electoral strength by co-opting a popular slogan.

Undoubtedly the biggest impetus given to the French self-management movement in the 1970s was the strike at the LIP watch factory which began in the summer of 1973. LIP, a watch manufacturing firm, decided to streamline its operation by shutting down a production plant. Such a move would have left hundreds of workers unemployed with few immediate job prospects. Angered by the cavalier manner in which the firm was deciding their fate, the LIP workers took matters into their own hands by occupying the factory, ejecting the management and continuing the production of watches to build their strike fund. Inside the occupied plant they established an egalitarian community and similarly reorganized production on an egalitarian basis.

This seizure of the means of production by the workers and the egalitarian reorganization of the production process captured the imagination of the French left and served to revitalize the revolutionary meaning of self-management. It also served to further the commitment of the institutional left to self-management since the strikers were led by members of the CFDT, and the PS and PSU vigorously supported them. In fact the PS' reputation as a militant, revolutionary party grew because of its identification with the LIP strike. This forced the PCF to support the action despite the fact that it conflicted with Party policy, for PCF leaders were afraid of losing the revolutionary halo (and left votes) to the PS.

Eventually the LIP strikers were forced out of the plant, but the action did serve to galvanize the *autogestionnaires* and continues to be a model for the revolutionary potential of self-management in contemporary France.

2. Simone de Beauvoir and the New French Feminism

An unexpected consequence of May 1968 was the emergence of the women's liberation movement in France.[6] In the fall of 1968 women activists began to form their own informal small groups, initially as a reaction to the sexism of men activists they experienced during May, but primarily as a continuation and deepening of the revolt against hierarchy and domination that May unleashed.

The first explicitly feminist organization, "politique et

psychanalyse" was also formed in 1968. Founded by the Lacanian psychoanalyst Antoinette Fouque, this group quickly established itself as the intellectual and cultural center of the emerging movement.[7] Its goal was to provide a feminist synthesis of historical materialism and psychoanalysis—Marx and Freud. They established a feminist bookstore, newspaper (*Le quotidien des femmes*) and a publishing house (*Editions des femmes*) as vehicles for spreading their ideas.

In August 1970 a small group of women (including the feminist writers Christiane Rochefort and Monique Wittig) placed a wreath on the Tomb of the Unknown Soldier inscribed: "to the unknown wife of the soldier." The media was scandalized by this sacrilege committed against the symbol of French patriotic heritage and railed against its perpetrators, whom they dubbed as members of the "Mouvement de Libération des Femmes" (Women's Liberation Movement) or MLF. Thus was born the new French feminist movement.

Feminists argue that the dependent and subordinate role of women in society is not a natural condition. Rather, the inequality of the sexes is the result of a social mode of domination of women known as patriarchy or phallocracy. The near universal prevalence of this domination is not an argument for its biological necessity but rather an indication of its deep-rooted pervasiveness in all previous and contemporary social systems, including both capitalism and socialism. Radical feminists argue that the institution of marriage and the family, as the locus of women's oppression, should be abolished or radically transformed; and that women should have independence in society at large equal to that of men—politically, economically, and sexually. Ultimately the goal of feminism is to abolish sex roles altogether and create an egalitarian society in which individuals are not defined by their gender or sexual preference. In such a society one's sexuality would not be denied but gender would be inconsequential *as a determinant of social distinction* as is, say, the color of one's eyes today.

This new feminist movement has numerous social roots in France: women's role in the Resistance, the granting of formal legal equality after World War II, the role of women in the labor force, and the impact of the American and British feminist movement. But the basic starting point for contemporary feminist *theory*—not only in France, but worldwide—is Simone de Beauvoir's *The Second Sex* (1949).

In this work, as we saw in Chapter 2, de Beauvoir elaborates her view that "One is not born, but rather becomes a woman." "Woman" is a product of a socialization process in which female infants are taught one set of behaviors associated with a feminine identity and male infants are taught a different set of behaviors corresponding to a masculine identity. Thus, girls *learn* to be passive, dependent, and subordinate, while boys learn to be active, independent, and dominating. Woman's lot, thus, is not the inevitable result of biology (woman as child-bearer, woman as physically weaker than man). Rather, woman is a product of society. Her subordination to man in an hierarchical social relation is a man-made phenomenon, not something originating in nature.

After its initial publication, *The Second Sex* seemed to disappear from public discussion. This was due not to its irrelevancy but rather to the lack of any existing forum for feminist thought. When a new generation of English-speaking authors (Betty Friedan, Kate Millet, Germaine Greer, Shulamith Firestone, Juliet Mitchell) emerged in the 1960s, they all viewed *The Second Sex* as the essential starting point. Remarkably this work sold 750,000 copies in the United States in 1969—a full twenty years after its initial publication. Such a fact is ample testimony that *The Second Sex* was truly a work ahead of its time.

Ironically, while the new French feminists of the 1970s looked to de Beauvoir for leadership, they also looked with a sharply critical eye at *The Second Sex*. Much of this had to do with the influence of Lacan's structuralist interpretation of Freud among the feminist theorists of "politique et psychanalyse." They looked favorably upon Lacan's re-reading of Freud as an antidote to conventional Freudianism and economic determinism. Further, because of the sexist assumptions implicit in language and grammar French feminists were attracted to structural linguistics and semi-otics. Consequently they accepted much of the structuralist attack on existentialism, humanism, and the problematic of the subject. Some French feminists argued that de Beauvoir's existential phenomenology was incapable of sustaining feminist theory.

Michèle Le Doeuff, for example, claimed, "we need a different problematic than that of the Subject" as a basis for feminist theory.[11]

Based on a reading of *Being and Nothingness* that emphasizes Sartre's "incredibly fierce sexist fantasies" as "indispensible" to existentialism, Le Doeuff argued that it is an inherently "phallocratic discourse."[12] She rejected what she calls de Beauvoir's Sartrean metaphysics as an inadequate explanatory principle of woman's lot.

Other feminists have noted with unease that lack of a feminist viewpoint in many of de Beauvoir's writings. In her memoirs she appears emotionally and intellectually dependent on Sartre. For example, she states quite unselfconsciously: "Ever since Sartre and I had met, I had shuffled off the responsibility for justifying my existence on him."[13] In fact she tells us that it was he who encouraged her to write *The Second Sex*.[14] Other women appear in her memoirs either as "the wife of so and so" or are referred to only by their first name, while men are referred to by last names. Her novels don't provide feminist role models, and at least one of her essays, "Must We Burn Sade?", has shocked feminists because of her qualified defense of this misogynist as a "philosopher of liberty."

Defenders of de Beauvoir emphasize that she was a member of a generation for which there was no feminist movement. It is little wonder then that her work reflects that fact. What is remarkable, they claim, is that she was able to make the groundbreaking contribution that *The Second Sex* represents.

When the new feminist movement emerged in France after 1968 she joined in without hesitation. In 1971 her name was at the top of the "Manifesto of the 343," a list of women who publically declared they had illegal abortions and demanded its legalization. She participated in numerous feminist demonstrations and activities in the 1970s, lending her celebrity status to the causes of women's reproductive rights (birth control and abortion), legal rights (divorce law reform), economic rights (equal opportunity, equal pay, childcare) and protection against physical violence.

As an editor of *Les Temps Modernes* she opened the journal to the feminist movement. In April/May 1974 an entire issue was devoted to feminism, and a regular feature on "everyday sexism" was instituted. (Incidentally, the latter tends to be very critical of Lacanian theory.) In 1975 the journal *L'Arc* devoted an entire issue to "Simone de Beauvoir et la lutte des femmes" (Simone de Beauvoir and the woman's struggle).

She served as first president of Choisir, the pro-choice organization which emerged from the Manifesto of the 343, and also of the Ligue du droit des femmes (League of Women's Rights). She also assumed the title of "directrice de publication" of the League's newspaper, *Nouvelle feministe*, and the the feminist theoretical journal, *Questions feministes*. Thus, both as its theoretical inspiration and as its leading figure, the new French feminism is unthinkable without Simone de Beauvoir.[15]

The French feminist movement is not monolithic, nor is its theory homogeneous. A variety of political and intellectual trends co-exist within the movement. Politically, there are five general tendencies: 1) establishment feminist, 2) reform feminist, 3) socialist feminist, 4) radical feminist, and 5) lesbian radical feminist. Establishment feminists do not seek to change the social order or society's basic attitudes towards women. They assume the values of bourgeois society and seek a greater role for women in such a society. Thus, they desire more positions of power and prestige for women (including themselves) such as in corporate management, government, and the professions. The liberal or reformist feminists have a much broader perspective. They also seek greater employment and career opportunities for women, but they go much further in demanding equal rights for women in all areas of life. They are reformist in that they seek to achieve these goals within a framework that does not challenge the present social system. Socialist feminists, on the other hand, claim that women's true liberation can only be achieved in a socialist society. They see capitalism and the profit system as the basic cause of women's oppression. Only when capitalism and the economic basis of women's oppression are eliminated can women be free.

Radical feminists, however, claim that even in the so-called socialist countries the relations between the sexes haven't changed very much. Socialism, then, is not the panacea for women's problems. Rather, what is necessary is to root out patriarchy in its most elemental forms. Sexism is the primary conflict in society, not class conflict or anything else. To eradicate sexism most radical feminists believe it is necessary for women to organize themselves independently of men. Some carry this separation into their sexual preference and advocate lesbianism as a political choice. Such lesbian radical feminists argue that homosexuality is the only way to escape from the male-defined role of woman.

There are various intellectual trends also. As we have already seen, structuralism has been very influential. So too has post-structuralism with its emphasis on "de-constructing" texts and modes of discourse. A new generation of feminist writers—Hélène Cixous, Luce Arigaray, Julia Kristeva, Annie Leclerc, Monique Wittig—has emerged to explore the implications of feminism in literature, psychoanalysis, philosophy, sociology, and literary criticism.[16]

A recurring theme in much of the feminist writings, as with the new philosophers, is the issue of power. In order to achieve liberation some feminists argue it is necessary for women to seek power—political power. Others, however, argue that power as the source of domination is an exclusively male phenomenon. They see it as something to be destroyed by disrupting the symbolic order (à la Lacan) instituted by language within the individual. Such feminists have criticized the activists who hold demonstrations as imitators of male power, but ignore the fact that their theory is dependent on a male model (Lacan).

In fact, one of the major problems of feminist theory is that for the most part it has attempted to fit women's oppression into prior theoretical models—Marx, Freud, Sartre, Lacan, or Levi-Strauss. Recognizing this fact, some feminist theorists attempted to "re-think the world" from a feminist perspective that definitively surpasses such prior models. De Beauvoir has stated that were she to rewrite *The Second Sex* she would "provide a materialistic, not an idealistic, theoretical foundation."[17] Feminists associated with the journal, *Questions feministes*, have taken up this project and in the process have attempted to critique other tendencies of feminist theory as well as social theory in general.

Christine Delphy, in particular, has argued that no prior social theory is adequate to explain social reality if it ignores women's oppression as its central feature. "A feminist—or proletarian—science wants to succeed in explaining oppression; in order to do this, it has to start with it."[18] The analogy here with marxism does not compromise her project. Rather, in seeking to place women's oppression at the center of social theory, Delphy surpasses marxism by broadening the scope of the examination of social domination. Her feminism is materialistic in that "its premises lead it to consider intellectual productions as the product of social relationships, and to consider the latter as relationships of domination."[19]

If knowledge ("intellectual productions") is a product of social relationships of domination, then it is implicated in the fact of social oppression. Either this fact can be recognized and made the starting point of social theory, or it can be ignored and thereby denied. But, "all knowledge which does not recognize, which does not take social oppression as premise, denies it, and as a consequence objectively serves it."[20] Thus any social theory that does not take women's oppression as a premise, Delphy implies, is not only inaccurate in its depiction of reality but serves the continuation of such oppression by presenting a false image of reality.

Now it is a fact that *no* prior social theory—materialist or otherwise—takes the oppression of women as its major premise. Thus *all* the accumulated knowledge of the science of "man" and society is thereby distorted and ideological in the sense of presenting a view of reality which masks oppression. Thus a feminist materialism is a necessary precondition for the development not only of feminist theory but of general social theory. In this way it may prove instrumental in resolving the antinomies of egalitarian social theory expressed in the current crisis of marxism.

3. Political Ecology and the "Greening" of André Gorz

The growth of a mass ecology movement in France in the 1970s was another major yet unexpected consequence of May 1968.[21] Radical ecology organizations such as *Les Amis de la Terre* and publications such as *Charlie-Hebdo*, *Gueule Ouverte*, and *Le Sauvage* sprang up in the early 1970s out of the remnants of the May Movement. René Dumont's 1974 presidential campaign on the left-ecology platform and the substantial vote for ecology candidates (12% or 2.3 million votes) in the 1977 municipal elections indicated that *les verts*—or "the greens" as the ecology proponents are called—had sensitized a significant segment of the French to the ecological crisis.[22]

One of the more important developments in this regard, from the perspective of egalitarian social theory, was the "greening" of new left theorist, André Gorz. More than anyone else Gorz has drawn together the various threads of new left social theory with the new social movements it has spawned in the 1970s into a coherent theoretical framework. A French journalist of Austrian birth (b. 1924), Gorz brings together in his lifework all of the themes of radical social theory that have emerged in the course of this study.

As a student of philosophy just after the war, Gorz immersed himself in Sartre's existentialism. In fact he met Sartre in 1946 and began a life-long association. Simone de Beauvoir has described their meeting in her memoirs:

> At a party in Laussane, Sartre had met a young man called Gorz who knew all his writings like the back of his hand and talked very knowledgeably about them. In Geneva we saw him again. Taking *Being and Nothingness* as his starting point, he could not see how one choice could justifiably be given preference over another, and, consequently, Sartre's commitment troubled him. 'That's because you're Swiss,' Sartre told him.[23]

Sartre's joke of course did not resolve the ambiguity of his existentialist ethics (as we saw in Chapter 2), and Gorz was instrumental in challenging him to confront his political commitment.

Like Sartre, Gorz moved closer to marxism in the early 1950s only to be disenchanted by the 1956 events. Like Lefebvre he then attempted to revise marxism in light of the changes taking place in modern society.[24] Like Castoriadis he looked to self-management as a vehicle for resolving the dilemmas of socialism created by the Soviet experience. Unlike Castoriadis, however, he looked to the Italian marxists Vittorio Foa and Bruno Trentin for versions of self-management (designed to reform and revitalize the existing trade union movement) and combined them with the existential-marxist analysis of alienation in Sartre's *Critique*. His major work of the 1960s, *Stratégie ouvrière et néocapitalisme* (1964), reflects this effort, and, as we saw in Chapter 6, provided the basis for the French new left's political strategy. It also won him international recognition as a major strategist for a militant working class movement.

As a journalist Gorz made significant contributions to new left social theory. In 1961 he became a co-editor and regular contributor to *Les Temps Modernes* and took responsibility for its political direction. In particular, he initiated the journal's "Italian" period in the early 1960s by popularizing the unorthodox marxist work of Bruno Trentin and Lucio Magri, which dealt with the issues of alienation at work and in consumption.

Under the pseudonym Michel Bosquet, Gorz became the economics editor and a regular contributor to *Le Nouvel Observateur*, an independent socialist weekly news magazine. Over the years his articles on specific aspects of everyday life (à la Lefebvre) have served to concretize and illustrate various points of radical social theory. In 1973 he published a collection of these articles in book form under the title, *Critique du capitalisme quotidien*. When *Le Sauvage*, the first serious theoretical journal of political ecology, was founded in 1973, Gorz became a regular contributor. He collected the political ecology articles he wrote in both *Le Nouvel Observateur* and *Le Sauvage* and published them in two volumes as: *Ecologie et liberté* (1977) and *Ecologie et politique* (1975). In 1977 he published the essay, *Ecologie et liberté*.[25]

In the aftermath of May 1968, Gorz's political thought began to move in what might be called a Luxemburgist direction.[26] The political failure of May led him to the conclusion that a revolutionary party is needed to organize and lead a successful revolutionary movement. This should not be a leninist vanguard party, but rather a mass party. In order to guarantee that it truly be a mass party, Gorz advocated workers' control at the point of production as its basis. Self-management by the workers in their factory councils was the only way for the working class to maintain control of the factory, the party, and society at large. Accordingly, in the early 1970s, he began to look more closely at the actual process of production in the factory and the social division of labor evident there.[27]

This investigation, however, led him into an analysis of technology which, on the one hand, appeared to foreclose his working class strategy of social change, and on the other hand, opened up for him the domain of political ecology as the arena of the fundamental contradictions of advanced industrial society. It is in this sense then that we can speak of a "greening" of André Gorz. We will briefly trace the process Gorz went through and then examine its implications for radical social theory.

In his *Strategie ouvrière et néocapitalisme* (1964) we saw (in Chapter 6) that Gorz advocated self-management to overcome alienation in the factory and in society at large. This could be achieved by structural, revolutionary reforms which he said, "require a *decentralization* of the decision-making power, a *restriction on the powers of State or Capital*, an *extension of popular power.*"[28] This popular power must be exercised by the workers themselves and not subordinated to management or the government. In this sense it is an *autonomous* power. Decentralization and workers' autonomy, then, were essential to Gorz's concept of self-management.

How is power to be decentralized? How is autonomy to be exercised? In May 1968 when these questions were raised most urgently, the proposed solution seemed to lie in the workers' council tradition. Gorz endorsed the efforts to achieve workers' control and workers' power at the point of production that followed in the wake of May in both France and Italy.[29]

However, such experiments seemed to be hampered by the existing division of labor. Within a factory the division between manual and mental workers hindered efforts to abolish hierarchy. But more fundamentally the advanced degree of specialization in the international division of labor and centralization of decision-making power above the plant level precluded real decentralization and autonomy. When the entire factory produced only one or several parts of a product (as is often the case, for example, in the automobile industry), it was dependent on others hundreds of miles away in such a manner as to undermine workers' autonomy.

Gorz thus moved on to examining the capitalist division of labor and concluded as the young Marx did, that it was "the source of all alienation."[30] But what was the source of this division of labor? Technology. "It is the technology of the factory that imposes a certain technical division of labor, which in turn requires a certain type of subordination, hierarchy, and despotism. Thus, technology is apparently the matrix and ultimate cause of everything..."[31]

But the "tyranny of the factory" is not an absolute requirement of technology. Rather, *capitalist* technology has been designed with a double aim in mind: to maximize production *and at the same time* to dispossess the worker of his/her skill and thereby of his/her control over production. Adam Smith, with his famous pin factory example, was the first to note that specialization in the division of labor results in increased workers productivity. The subdivision and fragmentation of production involved in assembly line technologies, however, not only yield greater productivity, but they also result in the destruction of the craftsman's skill. At one and the same time work is rendered meaningless by its minute subdivision, and the worker is robbed of autonomy in the performance of his/her tasks. S/he must conform to the requirements of the machine which is not designed with workers' needs in mind but with those of the accumulation of capital.

> As a whole, the history of capitalist technology can be read as the history of the dequalificaiton of the direct producers....The most qualified production worker's professional skills are carved up into sub-specializations shorn of autonomy.[32]

Thus, technology is not a neutral tool to be used regardless of the type of society one seeks. The type of technology a society chooses will largely influence the quality of social relations in the production process and in society at large. On this point Gorz wholly agrees with Marx.

Where Gorz disagrees with marxism is in his assessment of the significance of industrial technology for contemporary society. Marx was impressed primarily with the immense productive capacity of industrial technology vis-a-vis pre-industrial technology. It promised a world free of scarcity, free of misery and want. What he objected to was not industrial technology itself, but the private appropriation of the socially produced wealth it made possible.

> The contradictions and antagonisms inherent in the capitalist use of machinery exist because they have sprung not from the machine itself, but from the capitalist application to which it has been put. Machinery considered on its own shortens the working time....intrinsically it is a victory of mankind over the forces of nature, but used for capitalist ends it employs the forces of nature to enslave man.[33]

Marx was sensitive to the alienation of the laborer in the production process, which "degrades him so that he is but an appendage of the machine."[34] He claimed that the overthrow of capitalism would eliminate alienation. But for Gorz, the historical experience of 20th century socialism indicates that this in fact has not occurred. Instead, alienation appears even more intense (for example in Eastern Europe) when the domination of the laborer is justified by the very discourse that proclaims his liberation. For, if the language of revolt against alienation is used to justify it and the means of expressing it is thereby appropriated, then the worker's anguished cry of protest is stifled even before it leaves his throat.

Probing further into the nature of industrial techno-logy, Gorz argued that traditional marxism had taken its decisive wrong turn when it adopted a superficial analysis of capitalist technology and accepted its militarization (i.e., hier-archical chain of command) of the production process in the factory.

For Gorz, two very important consequences follow. First, "it is difficult to see how 'collective appropriation' of the means of production carrying the imprint of this technology would be able to change anything in the order of the factory, in the mutilation and oppression of the workers."[35] In other words, nationalization of the means of production will not alter the everyday social relations of production as long as the factory still functions with tools marked with the logic of capitalism. For this reason socialism has thus far failed to bring the working class to power. For Gorz—following Castoriadis—the workers cannot have power in society without control over the production process.

The other consequence of this superficial analysis is that an open-ended technology is an *essential* and *necessary* precondition for the realization of human liberation. Capitalist technology is based on a rationality of domination: domination of the worker and domination of nature. An open-ended technology, however, could repudiate domination and respect the rhythms of the worker and of nature as its basis.

This conclusion was the significant turning point in Gorz's theoretical development. For in examining "alternate" technologies, he was led by the dynamic of his new left problematic—the overcoming of alienation via self-management—into the problematic of ecology.

In the 1960s Gorz advocated self-management to overcome the existential problem of alienation. Self-management implied decentraliztion of decision-making power and workers' autonomy. But as Gorz saw in the workers' control and workers' power experiments of May 1968 and beyond, the capitalist division of labor frustrated decentralization and autonomy. This division of labor was rooted in a capitalist technology based on a logic of domination. To overcome the capitalist division of labor, to create the conditions for the decentralization of power and autonomy, to implement self-management, to overcome alienation: it would be necessary to reject an industrial technology based on the domination of the individual and nature and to create in its place a "post-industrial" technology based on cooperation between individuals and cooperation with nature.

To develop this position Gorz was forced to step outside of marxist and new left social theory and assimilate the work of the radical social ecologists who emerged in the 1970s in the United States and Great Britain. Ivan Illich's work[36] had the biggest impact on his thought, although the influence of Barry Commoner, E.F. Schumacher and Amory Lovins is also evident.[37]

The ecological perspective is concerned broadly with four interrelated sets of problems: economic growth, exhaustion of natural resources, pollution of the environment, and population growth. Historically, economic growth has been the motor of development of capitalism and industrial society generally. Proponents argue that growth is essential for the functioning and well-being of society, that the history of the human species is one long effort to achieve growth in order to overcome scarcity.

Ecologists, however, claim that we have reached the limits of growth.[38] Considerable evidence indicates we are on the verge of exhausting the natural resources (fossil fuels in particular plus numerous mineral resources) on which the technology of our economic system is based. In addition, industrial pollution of our air, water, and soil which accompanies economic growth is destroying the ecological systems of our natural environment upon which all life on this planet depends. In particular, the threat of radioactive pollution implicit in the existence of nuclear weapons and nuclear power could render the planet uninhabitable for thousands of years.

This crisis of a growth-oriented consumer society is further complicated by world population increases. Population growth rates indicate that world population will probably double in the next twenty years (particularly in the Third World), at the same time that natural resources like oil run out and pollution chokes the cities. Thus, ecologists warn that a monumental worldwide calamity is in the making that is literally of earth-shattering proportions.

They therefore argue that the only chance of avoiding such doomsday predictions is to halt economic growth, radically transform our lifestyle to limit consumption, and make the transition from non-renewable energy sources (oil, nuclear fission) to safe renewable sources (solar, tidal, wind, biomass).

Gorz was deeply influenced by this ecological perspective, as were millions of others in France in the 1970s. Whereas marxism was in crisis and Eurocommunism was enmeshed in traditional electoral politics, ecology raised issues that were conducive to a new left interpretation. For Gorz, "the ecological perspective is incompatible with the rationality of capitalism. It is also incompatible with authoritarian socialism..."[39] The ecological critique of growth also fit in with the new left cultural critique of consumer society since it calls for drastic change of consumption patterns and lifestyle (see Chapter 6). Further, its emphasis on alternate technologies to solve the problems of pollution and scarce resources complements Gorz's political critique of capitalist technology as the source of social domination. Finally, both the new left and the radical ecological perspective are anti-technocratic, and both stress decentralization, autonomy, and self-management as desirable social values. Thus it is not surprising that many of the former activists of May 1968 found in the ecology movement an expression of the aspirations of the May revolt.

Initially, the French ecology movement concentrated on the issue of pollution—industrial pollution, automobile pollution, and the "throw-away" pollution of mass consumption. But soon the issue of nuclear power became its focal point. Because France has no domestic oil or natural gas resources, the French government committed itself to an energy policy heavily dependent on the development of nuclear power. The OPEC oil price increases of the 1970s increased the government's commitment to the nuclear option in spite of the dangers involved and the lack of public input on the issue. This policy provoked massive anti-nuke demonstrations in France throughout the 1970s. In 1972 10,000 demonstrated against the construction of a nuclear power plant at Fassenheim in Alsace. In 1975-76 activists from all over Europe occupied the plant site. In the late 1970s the center of the anti-nuke movement shifted to Brittany where thousands of Breton villagers organized against a government proposal to build a nuclear plant on the Breton coast.

Critics of nuclear power argue that it is not safe.[40] A major accident could cause thousands of deaths and render thousands of square miles of land uninhabitable. Even when it is functioning smoothly, critics claim, nuclear plants emit low-level radiation which could cause thousands of cancer deaths per year. After 35 years of trying, the nuclear industry has not developed a workable solution to the problem of long-term storage of nuclear wastes. Some of this material will remain deadly radioactive for literally several hundred thousand years. Critics further point out that nuclear fuel (uranium) is a non-renewable resource which will soon become exhausted. Even if fusion reactors which create their own fuel are perfected—at best a longshot gamble—all the currently planned multi-billion dollar fission reactors could be obsolete within 20 years. And finally, the actual performance of nuclear power indicates that it is a poor investment even from a business point of view.

Gorz, Commoner, Lovins, and others point out that nuclear technology represents an authoritarian political choice. By its very nature it is a highly centralized technology with huge plant facilities which leads to the concentration of decision-making power in the hands of a few. Moreover, because of the security risks involved (employee sabotage, theft of radioactive materials, terrorist attack) nuclear power requires greater government control over the population. "The all-nuclear society is a society full of cops. I don't like that at all. There can't be the slightest self-management in a society based on such an energy choice."[41] Such is the opinion of Louis Puiseux, a critic of nuclear power within the management of Electricité de France (EDF).

Renewable energy sources such as solar, tidal, or wind power use decentralized technologies on a human scale, subject to control by all. Until someone figures out how to meter the sun or bottle the wind, such energy sources are free.

They cannot be sold and they cannot yield profits. (Though the equipment needed to convert such sources into usable energy can be monopolized to yield profits.) These renewable energy technologies are potentially democratic and anti-capitalist, whereas nuclear technology has a decidedly authoritarian and capital-intensive bias.

For all these reasons, nuclear power has become the central issue of the ecology movement. For Gorz it involves "the choice of the kind of society and civilization we want."[42] We can choose between a society based on an authoritarian centralized technology of domination of both the individual and of nature, or one based on a democratic, decentralized technology which promotes individual autonomy and co-operation with nature.

Within the socialist heritage the obvious forebearer of the latter choice would be the utopian socialist, Charles Fourier. Gorz's effort in the 1970s to develop a vision of a decentralized, autonomous, and self-managed society is reminiscent of Fourier's utopian socialism. Although he avoids the precise blueprints of Fourier's "phalanxes," Gorz does present us with a detailed and realistic model of an ecological, post-industrial, utopian socialist society.[43]

Gorz's utopian vision is based on the premise that in post-industrial society it is possible to work less if we consume better. Such a policy would result in a vast expansion of free time for all to pursue autonomous activities and re-integrate culture into everyday life.

Gorz claims that most worktime in post-industrial consumer society is spent in producing and selling commodities we don't absolutely need. Such commodities (e.g., cosmetics, toiletries, many electronic gadgets, the private automobile) meet socially produced and conditioned needs which other societies have done without quite well. Gorz argues that if we "consume better"—use durable products of good quality that satisfy basic needs for food, clothing, and shelter—we could work less. Specifically, he claims that if everyone in France worked at most 24 hours per week, all basic social needs could be satisfied. Eventually, socially necessary labor time could ideally be reduced to two hours per day![44]

In the vast amount of free time thereby created individuals could pursue autonomous activities of their own design. For example, in every neighborhood there would be centres in which individuals could learn crafts and skills to produce goods beyond the basic necessities. Instead of being a passive observer of the "society of the spectacle,"[45] individuals would actively fulfill their creative desires: play music instead of just listening; play sports instead of just watching; work with their hands instead of always buying prefabricated items.

Gorz's utopia would be ecologically sound. The growth syndrome would be abandoned, natural resources husbanded and recycled. Pollution would be stopped by recourse to "soft" technologies. The countryside would be reclaimed with organic farming and repopulated to reverse the trend toward over-urbanization. An effective free mass transportation system of buses, trains, bicycles, and "driverless taxis" would make it possible to go anywhere quickly and greatly reduce air pollution caused by the mass-produced private automobile.

The political structure of Gorz's utopia is that of a democratically-elected government that views its role as eliminating the functions of the state by providing optimal conditions for individuals, neighborhoods, communities, and work groups to develop self-reliance and take the initiative in meeting their own needs. While there would still be the need for some centralized national planning, the state would work to minimize its own role and maximize the realm of decentralized, autonomous planning. Thus Gorz's utopia would be a society of self-management in which the state begins to "wither away." In this sense it might be more appropriate to call his vision one of utopian communism to distinguish it from 19th century utopian socialism

Feminism and the women's movement would play a vanguard role in bringing about this society by virtue of its roots in cooperative and non-economic values:

...In the posing of autonomous activities and non-economic values as essential and economic values and activities as subordinate...the women's movement becomes a component force of the post-industrial revolution, and in this respect its vanguard...Post-industrial socialism, i.e., communism, will be *feminine* or it will not be. It presupposes a cultural revolution, which at the level of both individual and social behavior, extinguishes the principle of efficiency, the ethic of competition, of accumulation, and the struggle for existence; in order to affirm the supremacy of the values of reciprocity, of tenderness, of the appreciation and love of life in all its forms.[46]

Overall, Gorz's vision is one that combines the values of the new left analysis of alienation in contemporary bureaucratic society with the themes of the new social movements of the 1970s: the themes of self-management, feminism, and ecology. Above all, it is a bold and innovative attempt to concretize and specify the ideals which have been at the heart of all authentically revolutionary movements—liberty, equality, and community—in terms of the conditions of life in advanced capitalist society entering the 1980s.

Notes
1. Quoted in Feenberg, "Socialism in France?..." *op. cit.,* p. 17.
2. See André Gorz, "Workers' Control is More Than Just That," in *Workers' Control,* ed. by G. Hunnius et al.
3. See Sharon Zukin, "The Paris Conference on Self-Management," *Telos* 34 (Winter 1977-78), pp. 148-157.
4. Centre Internationale de coordination de recherches sur l'autogestion.
5. Quoted in C. Posner (ed.) *Reflections on the Revolution in France: 1968* (Baltimore, 1970), p. 144.
6. For a discussion of the emergence of contemporary French feminism see Maite Albistur and Daniel Armogathe, *Histoire du feminisme français* (Paris, 1977); and Elaine Marks and Isabelle Courtivron (eds.) *New French Feminism* (Amherst, 1980), pp. 23-38.
7. Because French surnames are of patrilineal derivation, she generally

chose not to use hers and is known in the feminist movement simply as "Antoinette."

11. Michèle Le Doeuff, "Operative Philosophy, Simone de Beauvoir and Existentialism," paper presented at The Second Sex Conference, New York University 27 September 1979.

12. *Idem.*

13. De Beauvoir, *Prime of Life* (New York, 1962), p. 316.

14. De Beauvoir, *Force of Circumstance,* Vol. I (New York, 1977), p. 185.

15. De Beauvoir discusses her activities in the feminist movement in *All Said and Done* (New York, 1975), pp. 458-473, as does Marks and Courtivron, *op. cit.,* and Axel Madsen, *Hearts and Minds: The Common Journey of Simone de Beauvoir and Jean-Paul Sartre* (New York, 1977), pp. 270-286. See also "Simone de Beauvoir et la lutte des femmes," Special Issue, *L'arc,* no. 61 (1975); and Jane Leighton, *Simone de Beauvoir on Women* (Rutherford, NJ, 1975).

16. See Hélène Cixous, "Le rire de la méduse," *L'arc,* no. 61 (1975), pp. 39-54; Luce Iragaray, *Ce sexe qui n'en est pas un* (Paris, 1977); Julia Kristeva, *Des chinois des femmes* (Paris, 1974); Annie Leclerc, *Parole de femme* (Paris, 1974); and Monique Wittig, *Les guerillères* (Paris, 1969).

17. De Beauvoir, *All Said and Done* (New York, 1975), p. 462.

18. Christine Delphy, "Pour un matérialisme feministe," *L'arc,* no. 61 (1975).

19. *Idem.*

20. *Idem.*

21. For a general discussion of the rise of the ecology movement in France see Beaulieu and Cloud, "Political Ecology and the Limits of the Communist Vision," in Boggs and Plotke, *op. cit.,* pp. 221-250.

22. In Alsace some anti-nuke candidates received over 65% of the vote.

23. De Beauvoir, *Force of Circumstance, Vol. I,* p. 92.

24. See his *La morale de l'histoire* (Paris, 1959). He also published a novel in this period, *Le traître* (Paris, 1958) for which Sartre wrote a preface.

25. These last two works were updated and republished as one volume in 1978.

26. Dick Howard emphasizes the parallels between Gorz's thought and that of Rosa Luxemburg. See his "New Situation, New Strategy: Serge Mallet and André Gorz," in the collection of articles Howard edited with Michael Klare, *The Unknown Dimension* (New York, 1971), pp. 388-413.

27. See his articles, "The Tyranny of the Factory" and "Technology, technicians and class struggle" in his (editor) *The Division of Labor: The Labor Process and Class Struggle in Modern Capitalism* (London, 1976).

28. Gorz, *Strategy for Labor* (Boston, 1967), p. 8n.

29. Gorz, "Workers' Control is More Than Just That," in Hunnius et al., *op. cit.*

30. Gorz, *The Divison of Labor*, p. vii.

31. *Ibid.,* pp. viii-ix.

32. *Ibid.,* p. 57.

33. Quoted in Jurgen Kuczynski, *The Rise of the Working Class* (New York, 1967), p. 41.

34. Quoted in *Ibid.,* p. 40.

35. Gorz, *The Divison of Labour*, p. ix.

36. See Ivan Illich, *Tools for Conviviality* (New York, 1971), *Deschooling Society* (New York, 1974) and *Medical Nemesis* (New York, 1976).

37. See Barry Commoner, *The Poverty of Power* (New York, 1976), E.F. Schumacher, *Small is Beautiful* (New York, 1977) and Amory Lovins, *Soft Energy Paths* (New York, 1977).

38. See Donella and Dennis Meadows et al., *The Limits to Growth* (1971); and Mesarovic and Pestel's *Mankind at the Turning Point* (1974). These two works were commissioned by the Club of Rome, an international body of "enlightened" businessmen and futurology scholars. Accordingly, the traditional left attempted to discredit ecology as a diversion from the class struggle concocted by the big bosses and their intellectual lackies. Gorz, however, disagreed. He argued that ecology is a real, indeed fundamental, crisis which can be resolved either in the direction of democratic socialism or that of authoritarian capitalism. See his "Socialism or Ecofascism," in *Ecology as Politics* (Boston, 1980), pp. 77-91.

39. *Ibid.,* p. 18.

40. For a thorough analysis of all aspects of nuclear power see Anna Gyorgy and friends, *No Nukes: Everyone's Guide to Nuclear Power* (Boston, 1979).

41. Quoted in Gorz, *Ecology as Politics*, p. 109.

42. *Ibid.,* p. 102.

43. See Mark Poster (ed.), *Harmonian Man: Selected Writings of C. Fourier* (New York, 1971).

44. Cf. Adret, *Travailler deux heures par jour* (Paris, 1977).

45. See Guy Debord, *Society of the Spectacle* in Chapter 6 above.

46. Gorz, *Adieux au prolétariat: Au delà du socialisme* (Paris, 1980), p. 120.

Epilogue:
Marxism and Autonomous Society

Is Gorz's vision of an autonomous, egalitarian society marxist, anti-marxist, or what? In the mid-1970s he was willing to concede that for him marxism had "lost its prophetic value."[1] That is, changes in advanced capitalist society did not inspire belief in the inevitable and messianic triumph of a downtrodden working class over its oppressors. Nor did communist practice or "authoritarian socialism" as he called it, inspire a belief that socialism would automatically produce a good society. Nevertheless, Gorz still viewed marxism as "irreplaceable as an instrument of analysis."[2] In fact, he gave a convincing interpretation of the economic origins of the ecology crisis using such traditional marxist economic concepts as crisis of overaccumulation, increasing organic composition of capital, declining rate of profit, and a crisis of reproduction of the means of production:[3]

> We are dealing with a classic crisis of over-accumulation, aggravated by a crisis of reproduction which is due, in the final analysis, to the increasing scarcity of natural resources. The

> solution to this crisis cannot be found in the recovery of economic growth, but only in an inversion of the logic of capitalism itself.[4]

Thus he based his analysis of the ecology crisis on marxist premises. But is his conclusion marxist? Evidently not. For in denying that the solution to the crisis of capitalism lies in economic growth, is he not implying an "inversion" of the productivist logic of marxism also? If that is the case, then marxism is Gorz's springboard from which he leaps "beyond" into the unknown.

Indeed, in his most recent work, *Adieux au proletariat: au dela du socialisme* (Paris, 1980), this appears to be the trajectory of his thought—a leap beyond marxism, "overcoming" it in a dialectical sense of simultaneously negating and preserving it. This work represents a continuation and development of the egalitarian vision of society which has existed long before marxism appeared, and of which marxism is but the most significant incarnation. Gorz is *following* this egalitarian tradition *after* marxism, and in this sense could be considered *post*-marxist. If marxism represents the egalitarian vision as applied to industrial society, then Gorz's project could be viewed as groping toward a post-marxist egalitarian vision of post-industrial society.

In his analysis of post-industrial society, Gorz adopts a Marcusean critique of the proletariat for failing to perform its designated role as revolutionary subject of history.

> The development of capitalism has produced a working class which, for the most part, is not capable of taking control of the means of production and whose directly conscious interests do not agree with a socialist rationality.[5]

This is a significant shift in position for Gorz. As we saw in Chapter 9, the thrust of his political project during the 1960s and most of the 1970s was to modify traditional marxism in such a way as to preserve the privileged role of the working class as agent of social change, while at the same time recognize and analyze its shifting composition and attitudes.

That is why he could say in 1964, "There is no crisis in the workers' movement, but there is a crisis in the theory of the workers' movement."[6] (Ironically, in 1980 he reversed his position and claimed: "Marxism is in crisis because there is a crisis of the workers' movement.")[7]

To solve this crisis Gorz presented his theory of working class alienation in modern society and his political strategy of revolutionary, structural reforms. Because of the radical role they played in May 1968 and the radical demand for *autogestion* which they advanced then, Gorz's conviction, that this stratum of mental, intellectual, and technical workers was indeed the vanguard element of the working class, was reinforced.

However, in the aftermath of May 1968 Gorz saw this group assert more traditional professional and interest-group type attitudes of superiority over the production workers. Instead of casting them in the role of vanguard of a broadened new working class, this trend distanced the mental workers from the manual workers and reinforced their previous image as a distinct group with conscious interests different from those of the production workers.[8] While there were still radical elements within these strata, it became untenable for Gorz to consider them in any significant analytical sense as part of the working class.

In the early 1970s the failure of working class experiments with workers' power in France and Italy led Gorz to analyze the "modernized" production process of the newly emerging mutli-national corporations. The development of capitalist technology had changed the factory from an economic unit independently producing goods to merely one unit of production integrated with others hundreds of miles apart. Gorz concluded that such increased international division of labor and centralization of control above the plant level in the headquarters of the multi-national corporation had effectively undermined the possibility of workers' autonomy at the point of production. On the basis of this technological change Gorz concluded that workers' councils could *not* develop into independent centers of workers' autonomy and workers' power.[9]

Thus, neither new working class theory nor workers' council theory provided a basis for viewing the working class as revolutionary subject. Further, Gorz argued that the homogenous working class of traditional marxism is a myth generated by an abstract logic of historical necessity which has no foundation in social reality. "It is not the existence of a revolutionary proletariat which justifies Marx's theory. It is, on the contrary, his theory which permits him to predict the growth of a revolutionary proletariat."[10] Because it was totally dispossessed and dehumanized, Marx posited the proletariat as a universal class born of civil society yet denied entrance into it. He predicted that the realization of the proletariat as subject of history would bring about the dissolution of all classes.

Gorz argues that historical reality has not conformed to Marx's prediction. Instead of becoming the subject of history, the proletariat has been shaped by a technology which has "functioned solely in accord with the logic and needs of capitalism."[11] Gorz argues that the proletariat, thus shaped by capitalism, its technology of domination and its hierarchical division of labor,

> ...is constitutionally incapable of becoming the holder of power. If its representatives seize the apparatus of domination put in place by Capital they will reproduce the same type of domination and become in their day a *bourgeoisie de fonction*.[12]

Having thus abandoned the working class, the burning question for Gorz becomes, who is capable of realizing the utopian communist society he envisions? Who will become the subject of history and agent of social change? His answer: "the non-class of post-industrial proletarians." It is "all those people who no longer identify with their job and tend to consider it marginal to the meaning of their lives."[13] In post-industrial society this includes both manual workers and mental (or white collar) workers. This non-class has emerged as a consequence of two inter-related processes: 1) the de-qualification of production skills resulting from the intensi-fied specialization of the division of labor; and 2) the de-intellectualization of jobs resulting from the post-industrial technological revolution (computer technology, etc.). In much of modern production individuals perform tasks (whether manual or mental) which are not experienced as productive by themselves, nor as a basis for working class (or any other class) consciousness. Because of this they have little or no commitment to productivist values. Nor do they get a sense of their own power from their labor since the production process is so fragmented or the product is so intangible (e.g., "information" or "organization").

For such a group, work is totally alienating and meaning-less. Individuals in this group derive their self-identities not from their work but from their non-work experience. Accord-ingly, liberation for them would involve not their appro-priation of control over their work life but the expansion of their non-work life to its maximum potential. Because they seek to escape from labor, to refuse work in favor of auto-nomous activity, they embody a libertarian principle with revolutionary implications:

> The rule of liberty...may be instituted only by the founding act of liberty which...takes itself for the highest end in each individual. Alone the non-class of non-workers is capable of this founding act; for they alone incorporate at the same time beyond productivism the rejection of the ethic of accumula-tion and the dissolution of all classes.[14]

Thus, Gorz sees the expansion of the sphere of individual autonomy and the limitation of the sphere of necessity (both economic and political) as the primary goal of revolution in post-industrial society. This can be achieved by sharply limiting socially necessary labor time (via automation) and providing free access to "convivial tools" (à la Illych) to make and produce things of aesthetic value or personal use. Economic values would be subordinated to non-economic values and the ultimate goal of Marx's thought would be achieved: *the extinction of political economy as such.* Thus Gorz retains a utopian vision of communism "as the extinction of political economy and the measure of wealth not in terms...of exchange values but the possibility of the self-determination of happiness."[15]

While Gorz is able to provide us with a revolutionary (though not completely credible) subject to bring about his utopian vision, he does not provide a blueprint or strategy by which this revolutionary subject can achieve a new society. On this crucial point he remains openly uncertain and pessimistic himself.

> The crisis of the industrial system announces no new world. No overcoming salvation is written here. The present does not reveal the future...For the society which is decomposing under our eyes is not pregnant with another.[16]

As depressing as such an observation may be, it serves to free the individual from the logic of historical necessity: "The silence of history restores individuals to themselves. Returned to their subjectivity, it is up to them to speak in their own behalf.[17]

Where does this leave us? In a very real sense, it appears that in "returning to his subjectivity" Gorz has returned to the "vintage" existentialism of the early Sartre and his own youth.[18] If that is the case, it is an existentialism which has been greatly enriched by the experience of the new left, ecology, and the women's movement. Are we then back at the beginning? Are we back where this study began with the confrontation between existentialism and marxism?

> The beginning of wisdom is in the discovery that there exist contradictions of permanent tension with which it is necessary to live and that it is above all not necessary to seek to resolve...[19]

Notes

1. Gorz, *Ecology as Politics* (Boston, 1980), p. 11.

2. *Ibid.*, p. 11. In fact, the anarchist critic, Murray Bookchin, argues that Gorz is a dyed-in-the-wool marxist intent upon co-opting the issues of the ecological crisis—without really understanding them—in order to promote marxism. Bookchin's scathing polemic can be found in his review of Gorz's *Ecology as Politics* in *Telos* (Winter 1980-81), 45, pp. 177-190.

3. *Ibid.*, pp. 21-27.

4. *Ibid.*, p. 27.

5. Gorz, *Adieux au prolétariat: Au delà du socialisme* (Paris, 1980), p. 15.

6. Gorz, *Strategy for Labor* (Boston, 1967), p. 20.

7. Gorz, *Adieux...*, p. 13.

8. See Gorz, "Technology, technicians, and class struggle," in *The Division of Labor*, pp. 159-189. In a private letter to me (dated 2 April 1981) Gorz clarified his position as follows: "To my knowledge, I've never presented a theory of 'the new working class' (I limited myself to define new needs and aspirations as a result of new conditions of work and changed cultural environment). I don't remember considering the mental and technical workers a vanguard after 1968. On the contrary, that's when I started (by publishing various Italian translations in the TM, to begin with) to analyze the objective role of domination over workers which technical personnel hold."

9. Gorz, *Adieux...*, pp. 57-70.

10. *Ibid.*, p. 17.

11. *Ibid.*, p. 14.

12. *Ibid.*, p. 87.

13. Letter from Gorz, *op. cit.*

14. *Ibid.*, pp. 102-103. Letter from Gorz, *op. cit.*, "In my view as in Marx's, the extinction of political economy (i.e., mainly of the amount of labor as measure of wealth and of exchange value as measure of value) is not a utopian vision but a consequence of the abolition of labor by automatons. The abolition of labor and the collapse of economic logic are presently ongoing processes. Economists and politicians make great efforts to hide them and don't quite measure the consequences and stakes of the present technological revolution."

15. *Ibid.*, p. 124.

16. *Ibid.*, pp. 105-106.

17. *Ibid.*, p. 105.

18. Dick Howard noted this tendency as early as 1971. Since then it has increased dramatically. See Howard, *op. cit.*, p. 413.

19. Gorz, *Adieux...*, p. 169.

Selected Bibliography

Althusser, Louis. *For Marx*, trans. B. Brewster (New York, 1970).

———— *Lenin and Philosophy and Other Essays*, trans. B. Brewster (New York 1971).

Althusser, Louis and Balibar, Etienne. *Reading Capital*, trans. by B. Brewster (London, 1970).

Ardagh, John. *The New French Revolution* (New York, 1969).

Aron, Raymond. *History and the Dialectic of Violence*, trans. B. Cooper (New York, 1976).

———— *Marxism and the Existentialists* (New York 1969).

Aronson, Ronald. *Jean-Paul Sartre: Philosophy in the World* (London, 1980).

Axelos, Kostas. *Marx, penseur de la technique* (Paris, 1961).

Baudrillard, Jean. *The Mirror of Production*, trans. M. Poster (St. Louis, 1975).

Beauvoir, Simone de. *All Said and Done*, trans. P. O'Brian (New York, 1975).

———— *Force of Circumstance*, trans. R. Howard (New York, 1964).

———— *Memoirs of a Dutiful Daughter*, trans. J. Kirkup (New York, 1959).

———— *The Prime of Life*, trans. P. Green (London, 1963).

———— *The Second Sex*, trans. by H. M. Parshley (New York, 1974).

Belleville, Pierre. *Une Nouvelle classe ouvrière* (Paris, 1963).

Binstock, Allan. "Socialism or Barbarism," M.A. Thesis (Madison, 1971).

Boggs, Carl and Plotke, David. *The Politics of Eurocommunism: Socialism in Transition* (Boston, 1980).

Bourdet, Yvon. *Communisme et marxisme* (Paris, 1963).

Burnier, Michel-Antoine. *Choice of Action*, trans. B. Murchland (New York, 1969).

Callinicos, Alex. *Althusser's Marxism* (London, 1976).

Camus, Albert. *The Rebel*, trans. A. Bower (New York, 1956).

Castoriadis, Cornelius. *L'Expérience du mouvement ouvrier* (Paris, 1974) 2 Vols.

———— *L'Institution Imaginaire de la société* (Paris, 1975).

———— *La Société bureaucratique* (Paris, 1973) 2 Vols.

Caute, David. *Communism and the French Intellectuals* (New York, 1964).

Chatelet, François. *Logos et praxis* (Paris, 1962).

Cohn-Bendit, Daniel. *The French Student Revolt*, trans. B. Brewster (New York, 1968.)

———— *Obsolete Communism: The Left-Wing Alternative*, trans. A. Pomerans (New York, 1968).

Contat, Michel and Rybalka, M. *Les Ecrits de Sartre* (Paris, 1970).

Debord, Guy. *Society of the Spectacle*, trans. Red and Black (Boston, 1970).

Desan, Wilfred. *The Marxism of Jean-Paul Sartre* (New York, 1965).

Foucault, Michel. *The Archeology of Knowledge and the Discourse on Language*, trans. A. Smith (New York, 1972).

———— *The Order of Things* (New York, 1973).

Fejto, François. *The French Communist Party and the Crisis of International Communism* (Cambridge, 1967).

Fougeyrollas, Pierre. *Le Marxisme en question* (Paris, 1959).

Fromm, Erich. *Marx's Concept of Man* (New York 1961).

Gauaudy, Roger. *Literature of the Graveyard*, trans. J. Bernstein (New York, 1948).

———— et al. *Mésaventures de l'anti-marxisme* (Paris, 1956).

Glucksmann, André. *The Master Thinkers*, trans. by B. Pearce (New York, 1980).

Gombin, Richard. *The Origins of Modern Leftism*, trans. M. Perl (Baltimore, 1975).

Gorz, André. *Ecology as Politics*, trans. P. Vigderman and J. Cloud (Boston, 1980).

————*Socialism and Revolution*, trans. M. Nicolaus and V. Ortiz (New York, 1973).

————*Strategy for Labor*, trans. M. Nicolaus and V. Ortiz (New York, 1967).

Hegel, Georg F. W. *The Phenomenology of Mind*, trans. J. B. Baillie (New York, 1967).

———— *Texts and Commentary*, trans. W. Kaufman (New York, 1966).

Howard, Dick. *The Marxian Legacy* (New York, 1977).

Hughes, H. Stuart. *The Obstructed Path* (New York, 1968).

Hyppolite, Jean. *Studies on Marx and Hegel*, trans. J. O'Neill (New York, 1969).

Jameson, Frederic. *Marxism and Form* (Princeton, 1971).

Jeanson, Francis. *Sartre dans sa vie* (Paris, 1974).

Johnson, Richard. *The French Communist Party Versus the Students* (New Haven, 1972).

Kanapa, Jean. *L'Existentialisme n'est pas un humanisme* (Paris, 1947).

Kojève, Alexandre. *Introduction to the Reading of Hegel*, trans. J. Nichols (New York, 1969).

Labedz, Leo, ed. *Revisionism: Essays on the History of Marxist Ideas* (New York, 1962).

Laing, R. D. and Cooper, David. *Reason and Violence: A Decade of Sartre's Philosophy* (New York, 1964).

Lebesque, Morvan. *Portrait of Camus*, trans. T. Sharman (New York, 1971).

Lefebvre, Henri. *Au-delà du structuralisme* (Paris, 1971).

———— *Everyday Life in the Modern World*, trans. S. Rabinovitch (New York, 1971).

———— *L'Existentialisme* (Paris, 1946).

———— *The Explosion*, trans. A. Ehrenfeld (New York, 1969).

———— *Introduction à la modernité* (Paris, 1962).

———— *Le Matérialisme dialectique* (Paris, 1939).

———— *Problèmes actuels du marxisme* (Paris, 1957).

———— *The Sociology of Marx*, trans. N. Gutermann (New York, 1969).

———— *La Somme et le reste* (Paris, 1959).

Lefort, Claude. *Eléments d'une critique de la bureaucratie* (Geneva, 1971).

Lévi-Strauss, Claude. *The Savage Mind*, trans. G. Weidenfeld (New York, 1966).

———— *Tristes Tropiques*, trans. J. Russell (New York, 1965).

Lévy, Bernard-Henri. *Barbarism with a Human Face*, trans. by G. Holoch (New York, 1979).

Lichtheim, George. *Collected Essays* (New York, 1973).

———— *From Marx to Hegel* (New York, 1974).

———— *Marxism in Modern France* (New York, 1966).

Lukacs, Georg. *History and Class Consciousness*, trans. R. Livingstone (London, 1971).

Madsen, Axel. *Hearts and Minds: The Common Journey of Simone de Beauvoir and Jean-Paul Sartre* (New York, 1977).

Mallet, Serge. *La Nouvelle classe ouvrière* (Paris, 1963).

Marks, Elaine and Courtivron, Isabelle de (eds.). *New French Feminisms* (Amherst, 1980).

Marx and Engels, *Selected Works*, 2 Vols. (New York, 1964).

Merleau-Ponty, Maurice. *Adventures of the Dialectic*, trans. J. Bien (Evanston, 1973).

———— *Humanism and Terror*, trans. J. O'Neill (Boston, 1969).

———— *Sense and Non-Sense*, trans. H. & P. Dreyfus (Evanston, 1964).

———— *Signs*, trans. R. McCleary (Evanston, 1964).

Morin, Edgar. *Autocritique* (Paris, 1959).

———— *Lefort, Castoriadis, Mai, 1968: La Brèche* (Paris, 1968).

Nizan, Paul. *The Watchdogs*, trans. P. Fittingoff (New York, 1971).

Novack, George. *Marxism Versus Existentialism* (New York, 1966).

Odajnyk, Walter. *Marxism and Existentialism* (New York, 1965).

Posner, Charles, ed. *Reflection on the Revolution in France: 1968* (Baltimore, 1970).

Poulantzas, Nicos. *Classes in Contemporary Capitalism*, trans. by D. Fernback (London, 1975).

————— *Political Power and Social Classes*, trans. by T. O'Hagan (London, 1973).

————— *State, Power, Socialism* (New York, 1978).

Rabil, Albert. *Merleau-Ponty: Existentialist of the Social World* (New York, 1967).

Redfern, W. F. *Paul Nizan* (Princeton, 1972).

Sartre, Jean-Paul. *Being and Nothingness*, trans. H. Barnes (New York, 1966).

————— *Between Existentialism and Marxism*, trans. J. Matthews London, 1974).

————— *The Communists and Peace*, trans. M. Fletcher and P. Beak (New York, 1968).

————— *Critique de la raison dialectique* (Paris, 1960).

————— *Critique of Dialectical Reason: Theory of Practical Ensembles*, trans. by A. Sheridan-Smith (London, 1976).

————— *The Ghost of Stalin*, trans. M. Fletcher (New York, 1968).

————— *L'Idiote de la famille* (Paris, 1971).

————— *Situations*, Vols. I-IX (Paris, 1947-1972).

Schnapp and Vidal-Naquet. *The French Student Uprising*, trans. M. Jolas (Boston, 1971).

Singer, Daniel. *Prelude to Revolution* (New York, 1970).

Soubise, Louis. *Le Marxisme après Marx* (Paris, 1967).

Tiersky, Ronald. *French Communism 1920-1972* (New York, 1974).

Werth, Alexander. *France: 1940-1955* (New York, 1956).